Human Resource Management

(With Cases)

Human Resource Management

(With Cases)

Ajit Kumar Ghosh
Reader in MBA (HR) Programme
Department of Commerce
University of Burdwan

Manas Publications
New Delhi-110 002 (INDIA)

MANAS PUBLICATIONS
(Publishers, Distributors, Importers & Exporters)
4858, Prahlad Street,
24, Ansari Road, Darya Ganj,
New Delhi - 110 002 (INDIA)
Ph.: (O)23260783, 23265523
Fax: 011-23272766
E-mail: manaspublications@vsnl.com
www.manaspublications.com

First published, 2006

ISBN 81-7049-279-3
Rs. 495/-

Typeset by
Manas Publications

Printed in India by
Salasar Imaging Systems, Delhi
and Published by Mrs Suman Lata for
Manas Publications, 4858, Prahlad Street,
24, Ansari Road, Darya Ganj,
New Delhi - 110 002 (INDIA)

Preface

Human resource management is a new concept that has evolved from the earlier concept 'personnel management'. It considers people as the resource/assets that contribute best to the achievement of organizational goals. It subscribes to the notion that people are different from other non-human resources (which are inanimate, non-living, passive and become effective/useable through the people) and they need empowerment, involvement, satiation of psychological needs and a congenial culture/climate to manifest their worth, efficacy, commitment to their work, and the organization. So it is basically a strategic approach to procurement, motivation, and development of human resources and also conduct of relationship between the two parties (i.e., employer and employees) in an organization.

There has been a drastic change in the industrial activities after the introduction of new economic policy in 1990-91 in our country that put much emphasis on the concept of Liberalization, Privatization, and Globalization (LPG). This has made the companies much more competitive than they had been prior to nineties. Each organization seeks to obtain competitive advantage through the creation of reservoir of dynamic, committed workforce, who can be able to produce quality goods and services at a comparatively lesser cost and sell them at a reasonable price with customers' fullest satisfaction and delightment. In this situation organization generates strength, develops competences and efficacy to survive, grow and to confront challenges against the market players. Under such changing industrial environment organization demands human resources that have competences, positive values, beliefs, and attitude to accept assignments as a challenge and prove their worth, effectiveness through delivery of goods and services.

Hence, there is no denying the fact that human resources play a pivotal role to the growth and development of the organization. Organization can fulfil its mission, objectives, goals if it has satisfied, contented, dynamic, loyal, and committed world-class workforce. And this can be possible through strategic management, development and utilization of workforce. That means activities like procurement, compensation, development of workers, and also development of relationship between workers and management be made in a strategic way.

This book is designed to introduce the reader to the conceptual aspects of human resource management. It comprises eleven chapters. Chapter 1 provides introductory perspectives of human resource management that gives understanding and indepth knowledge on the subject of HRM and its evolutive aspects. This is followed by the chapter 2 on Human Resource Planning that discusses, inter alia, how to effectively assess human resource requirement of an organization. The chapter 3 provides knowledge on strategic recruitment and selection of human resources in organizations.

The chapters 4 and 5 present compensation perspectives. Employees give labour, and in exchange for their labour/ service they want compensation (that is money and non-monetary benefits). These chapters give ideas about designs of compensation plan including welfare, social security and fringe benefits provided to the employees in the organization.

The chapter 6 and 7 move towards development aspect of employees. The mechanisms enhancing competencies of employees including executives are discussed thoroughly in these two chapters. The chapter 8 focuses on performance appraisal systems that describes activities involved in appraisal, approaches to performance appraisal. It gives clear understanding on the probable limitation / shortcoming cropped up in the process of evaluating performance of subordinates. It also examines the potential perspectives of employees with emphasis on requirement for an effective potential appraisal system.

The chapter 9 discusses how to improve the level of morale of employees to create a contented and dynamic workforce. Worker's involvement through participation in quality circle and decision-making activity facilitates achievement of organizational goals.

No organization can grow, develop, and obtain the competitive advantage if industrial relations climate is unhealthy, and unconducive. The detailed analysis in the area of IRs is made in the chapter 10.

The chapter 11 focuses on the most important area of human resource management promoting healthy industrial relations by mitigating industrial conflicts / disputes. People feel happy and contented if organization settles disputes immediately in an amicable and systematic manner and takes necessary measures to prevent disputes. So origin of industrial disputes, disputes settlement and prevention machineries, role of tripartite bodies are discussed in this chapter.

There has been a great need for an introductory text in human resource management. Looking into this aspect and particularly to fill needs of the students, practitioners in business and industry, research scholars the text is designed. This book can be of great use for the students of MBA, M.Com., MHRM, MBA (HR), BBA and also the students prosecuting studies in technical and professional education programme. It can be used effectively as the main textbook as it covers the topics prescribed in the above course curricula.

The book has been written in a clear and concise style. Throughout there is analysis and reflection on both theoretical and practical issues cropped up in this field of activities. At the end of each chapter at least one 'Real Case' has been given. And all these cases are drawn from the real life situations the author has faced / managed, in the event of his performance / discharging responsibilities as functional head of the personnel department (now HRM department) in service industry and manufacturing industry for about 27 years. These case studies are used to enrich knowledge/ understanding of the reader on the subject as also to develop a thought process to find out the connection between the relevant body of knowledge (theoretical issues) and its application (practices).

The preface would remain incomplete without a public word of thanks to some personalities who helped make the book possible. First, I express my heartiest gratitude to my respected teacher, Prof. Amit Kumar Mallik, the Vice-Chancellor of Burdwan University for the constant assistance, guidance, and support extended to me to prepare this text.

I am grateful to Prof. P. Das, my respected teacher, former professor, Department of Commerce, Burdwan University who provided outstanding support and suggestion for the preparation of this book. His feedback provided insight in adding, deleting, and refining chapters of the book.

I express my gratitude to Mr. A. K. Khandelwal the Chairman and Managing Director of Bank of Baroda for his support and guidance extended to me to prepare this book.

It is needless to mention that it would not have been possible to make this book if the students of MBA (HR) and M.Com. would not have insisted me on writing such book. So thanks are also due to the students.

I express my thanks to my colleagues in the department of commerce, Burdwan University and research scholars carrying out Ph.D. work under my guidance, for their cooperation, encouragement and invaluable assistance.

A large amount of appreciation goes to my wife Dr. Bhabani Ghosh, my Son Dr. Nilmadhab Ghosh and my daughter Dr. Ananya Ghosh for their patience, support and encouragement.

Finally, I express my thanks to the publishers, Manas Publications for their untiring efforts in bringing out this volume.

Ajit Kumar Ghosh

Contents

1

Introduction to Human Resource Management

Meaning

Human Resource Management (HRM) is a recent terminology used in place of the term 'Personnel Management' / 'Personnel Administration' at the organizational level. Today people at work/employees in the organization, are treated as 'Resource' comprising of components like knowledge, skill, ability, attitude, aptititude, values, beliefs etc. In narrow sense, Human Resource Management means managing human resources in the organization to achieve individual goals, group goals and organizational goals. So human resource management encompasses those activities which procure, develop, motivate, and retain the human resources to achieve organizational goals. Michael Armstrong (1999) has expressed that HRM 'is concerned with the employment, development and reward of people in organizations and the conduct of relationships between management and the workforce'. According to him, human resource management is a strategic and coherent approach to the management of an organization's valued assets, *i.e.,* people who individually and collectively contribute to the achievement of its goals. HRM is that part of the management process which is concerned with the management of people at work in the organisation so that they contribute their best to the organization. So human resource management is a strategic approach to the management of people working in an organization for achievement of its goals. J. Storey (1995) has defined human resource management as a 'distinctive approach to employment management which seeks to obtain competitive advantage through the strategic deployment of a highly committed and skilled workforce, using an array of cultural, structural and personnel techniques.'

HRM is, therefore, viewed as a management process consisting of four functional activities—acquisitions, motivation, development, and maintenance. An outline of such activities as given below may help to have better understanding on the subject.

Acquisition

HR planning

Recruitment

Selection

Placement

Induction and Orientation

Motivation/Compensation

Job analysis

Job description, enlargement, enrichment, evaluation

Wages salaries, allowances, incentive, bonus

Health, Safety

Rewards

Welfare and social security measures

Employee benefits

Development

Employee training and development

Executive development

Career planning and development

OD

Performance appraisal

Potential appraisal

Counselling

Maintenance

HR information, record, research, accounting

Industrial relations

Trade unionism

Employee involvement, participation, empowerment

QC

Communication

HRM has following characteristics:

1. HRM is a people oriented approach. One of the major activities of HRM is to discover and develop people potential so that they can contribute their best to achieve goals—individual goals, group goals and organizational goals.
2. HRM is not an one time activity. It is a continuous process that takes care of people's need, requirement, expectation, desire on continuous basis.
3. HRM focuses on immediate solution of problem so that people feel satisfied in the matter of handling grievances.
4. HRM is not a 'fire fighting' activity, it is a 'fire prevention' activity. HR management must predict beforehand the probable problems that may crop up and design suitable method and device so that problems do not occur or get solved.
5. HRM makes the people committed, contented, and happy through formulation, implementation of effective HR policies, programmes, application of employee cum task oriented management approach, practices.

6. HRM improves the quality of life of employees through satiation of their economic needs and also psychological needs.
7. HRM focuses on 'customers delightment' and contentment by delivering quality products / services at lowest possible price to ensure continuity, growth and development of the organization and to create its image of reputation in the competitive market.
8. HRM is dynamic activity. It designs its action plan on the basis of business strategy, demand, corporate vision, policies and objectives.
9. HRM develops a link between line and staff people in the organization through integration of their activities in order to establish mutual understanding, confidence and faith amongst them.
10. Dynamic work force can exist in an organisation where corporate policies, vision, philosophy, approach are dynamic in nature. HRM helps to make the organization dynamic and also makes the people dynamic through training, counselling, performance management, career planning, motivation, OD etc.
11. HRM is not staff function only, it is the responsibility of all line managers to implement HR policies, programmes etc. for effective and efficient management and development of people working under them.
12. HRM is an interdisciplinary activity. Disciplines like law, sociology, psychology, anthropology, economics, political science, information technology, etc. contribute most to designing and formulating HR policies, plan, programmes, etc. HR specialists, therefore, need clear idea, concept, acquaintance on such disciplines for effective functioning /discharging of their role.
13. HRM as a system / functional activity exists in an organization. Existence of any organization without people cannot be thought of. So where there is people, there is HRM.

14. HRM as a process helps the organization in getting people, preparing / developing people, motivating people and retaining people so that organization can function effectively.
15. HRM focuses on corporate culture developed through values, benefits, mission, objectives and creates congenial and conducive milieu through adoptation of measures like communication, performance appraisal, counselling, training, career planning etc.
16. HRM includes all categories of people viz., workers, supervisors, middle management, senior management and top management people in the organization. It is concerned with managing and developing people at work.

Scope of Human Resource Management

The scope of HRM is vast. HRM is not limited to the activities concerning employment and retention of people. It has a wide area the coverage of which starts from forecasting and vision exercise, for HR demands of the organization till exit of the personnel including activities during intervening process. The scope of HRM has recently increased due to sudden technological advancement, increase of knowledge workers, changes in perception of employees about management activities, change in employee expectation, needs , requirement, work environment, organizational culture, changes in business stategy due to government's policy on LPG and the need for taking all measures to make the people at work dynamic to face the competition. So, in the changing economic scenario the scope of HRM extends vastly as every organization needs dynamic workforce to produce quality goods and to deliver the same to delight the customers.

The scope of HRM includes the following activities :

- Human Resource Planning
- Recruitment
- Selection

- Placement
- Induction and orientation
- Wage and salary administration
- Job analysis
- Job description
- Job evaluation
- Bonus
- Incentive
- Canteen, creches, rest rooms
- Housing
- Transport
- Education
- Employee stock option plan
- Lay off, retrenchment compensation
- Safety measures
- Health programme
- Medical benefits
- Workmen's compensation
- Pension, provident fund, gratuity
- Performance appraisal
- Potential appraisal
- Career planning/development
- Executive management development
- Employee counselling
- Quality of work life
- Quality circles
- OD

- Awareness development
- Self renewal
- Trade unions
- Collective bargaining
- Grievance procedure
- Disciplinary procedures, disputes settlement
- Code of discipline
- Communication
- Organizational climate, culture
- Team spirit
- Leadership
- Job satisfaction, morale
- Empowerment, involvement, participation
- Personnel record keeping
- Research
- HRIS
- HR accounting
- HR audit

The scope of human resource management is shown in Figure 1.1.

Objectives of Human Resource Management

HRM is not separate from the management functions. It is a part and parcel of the management process of the organization. Hence, principal objective of HRM is to achieve organizational goals through managing and developing human resources. For achieving organizational goals HRM sets its own objectives which include the following :

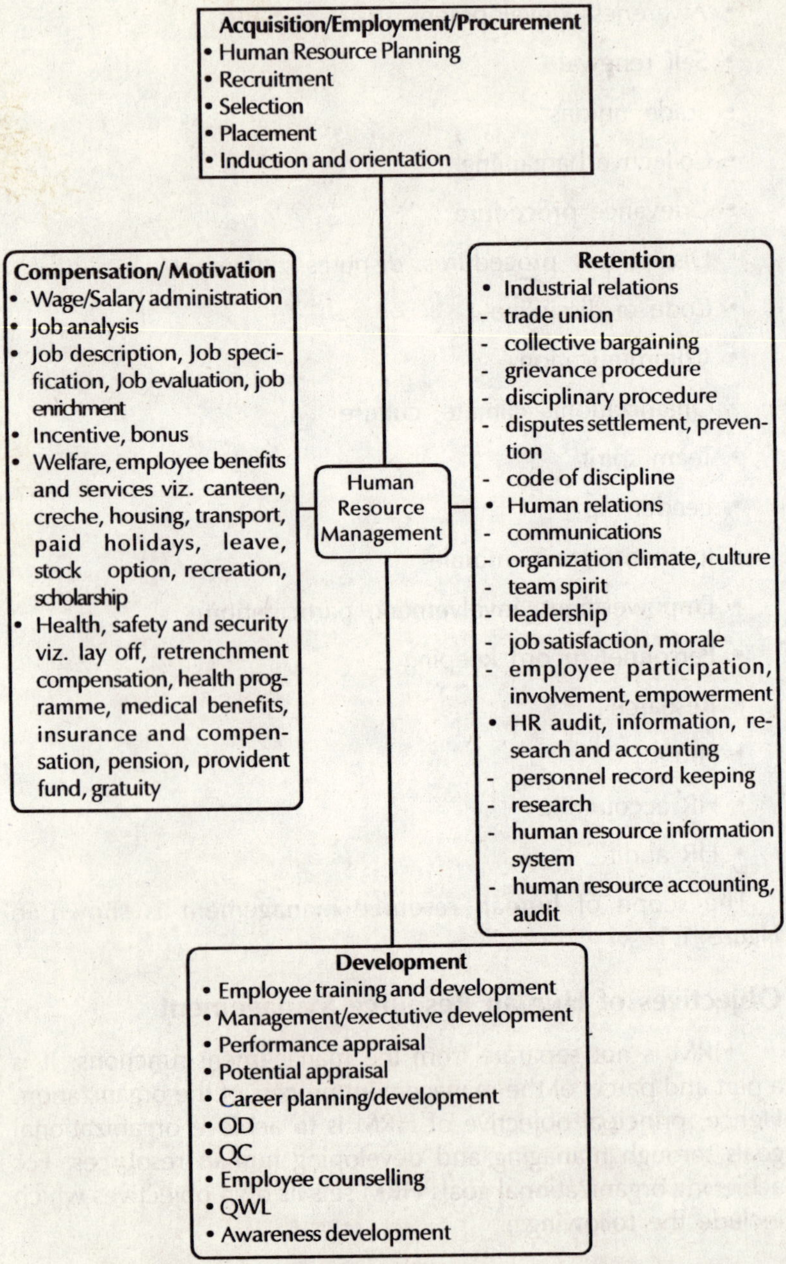

Figure 1.1 : Scope of Human Resource Management

1. *Providing right people to the organization in terms of needs*

   HRM, through Human Resource Planning technique, identifies requirement of personnel for different departments/sections and supplies the right number and kind of people selected carefully by the experts, to the indenters of the organization.

2. *Ensuring quality products/service*

   Because of LPG, there has been aggressive competition amongst companies in the market resulting in creation of such situation, that makes available of quality goods and services at reasonably cheaper rate. It is possible for the organization to produce quality product or provide excellent customer service only when people at work are dynamic and committed to work and organization. HRM makes the people dynamic and committed through its HR policies programmes, practices etc.

3. *Creating a new workers' community to face the challenges*

   Organizations pass through stiff competition which needs workers' community with a totally changed mind-sets to confront any sort of challenges. HRM acts as a change agent and develops mind-sets of the workers appropriately so that they can face challenges and deliver goods and services to the customers as per their requirement.

4. *Helping organization to meet up social obligations*

   Organization, as a part of society, has ethical obligation to contribute in the process of ameliorating conditions of the societal members so that they can have necessary infrastructure and support to live on. HRM helps the organization to formulate policies and design programmes to provide support, assistance and welfare facilities to the people in the society.

5. *Improving quality of work life to achieve individual and group goal*

   HRM policies are designed with an aim to improve quality of working life of the employees so as to develop a sense of belongingness, increase satisfaction in work, enhance empowerment, responsibility, and in the process employees feel that the climate existing in the organization inspires them to achieve their individual goals as also group goals.

6. *Ensuring equity, justice to create conducive climate of the organization*

   HRM policies are framed to provide compensation benefits, incentives, fringe benefits, after making thorough job description, job analysis, job evaluation, analysis of incentive perspectives etc. and also to settle disputes as per grievance procedure, collective bargaining agreement, awards, laws, practices etc. Workers are treated fairly and justly, are not deprived of their legitimate and due benefits, get promotion, transfer according to promotion / transfer policy and also after review of performance through performance appraisal system. All these measures ensure equity and justice in respect of the concerned issues and create confidence amongst employees, resulting in prevalence of conducive and congenial climate in the organization.

7. *Helping organization to retain its best lot of workforce*

   HRM through its compensation package, security and welfare programme, manifestation of dynamic approach and action of the top management towards treatment of employees and settlement of disputes, grievances, creation of an environment of *'weness',* 'togetherness', 'everybody wins' and a culture of flexibility stimulates the employees not to switch over the organization. The services of the best lot of the people are therefore available to help organization to run its activities effectively and efficiently.

8. *Ensuring establishment of a state of mutuality in organization*

   HRM helps bringing working people to come closer to the supervisors / management, involve in the work activity, apply creative and innovative ideas, thoughts and give suggestions to superiors for better way of operation and functioning of the organization's activities. Under such a system, employees get opportunities to interact frequently with the superiors and develop a state of mutuality — mutual understanding, mutual faith, mutual confidence, mutual respect, mutual influence and mutual responsibility between them; and in this process, a healthy human relationship is established to achieve organizational goal.

9. *Developing talent / potential skill, abilities of employees to make them achievers, performers and deliverers*

   HRM makes the organization, a learning organization, where systematic and continuous training programmes are conducted to develop, talent / potential skill, abilities of the employees so that, they can show their worth as achievers, performers and deliverers.

10. *Creating a balance situation in respect of needs of different stake holders*

    HRM policies and programmes look to the interests of stake-holders-employees, employers, suppliers, customers and societal members and control the needs, expectations and demands of the stake holders in terms of overall perspectives so that no maladjustment state is created.

11. *Developing psychological strength of the employees to change organization climate*

    People can develop their psychological base to work as best performers if their psychological needs (social need, esteem need and need for self-actualization), in terms of Maslow's hierarchy of needs, are satiated through company's policies, philosophy, management approach, and style of functioning. HRM has a role to develop psychological strength of the people.

12. *Making the people aware of their rights, duties and responsibilities through communication process*

    HRM initiates open communication channel to make the people transparent in their activities, rights as well as also their responsibilities so that, they can perform their assigned task effectively and efficiently.

13. *Placing human value as assets to the organization*

    HRM treats the employees as resource / assets and accepts its value as the one which can not be compared with any other resource. The HRM perception about the people at work as resource / assets, encourages the wholeworkers' community to work in a team, group to achieve team / group goals.

14. *Utilizing the workforce effectively and efficiently to reduce wastage and increase savings*

    HRM through its mechanisms redeploys the exact number and quality of people and in the process organization reduces wastages and increases savings.

Importance of Human Resource Management

Human resource is the most essential resource in the organization. It is indispensable from the formation stage of the organization (that is from the stage the planning activities start to form an organization for undertaking a venture / project) and its dominance as an important part of the activities continues till the organization survives. Organization cannot run, cannot operate its activities, cannot function its executive and non-executive work without human resource. Human resource, thus, plays a pivotal role in the organizational setting. HRM that deals with acquisition, motivation, development and maintenance/ retention of human resources is, therefore, very much important in the organization for its existence, growth and development. According to Winstanley and Stuart-Smith (1996), HRM is an activity that looks to 'people-interest' in the organization, and is based on the *four principles* :

(i) respect for the individual

(ii) mutual respect

(iii) procedural fairness

(iv) transparency.

Importance of HRM in the organizational context can be judged from the following :

1. HRM helps the organization to know details of HR profile, excess / shortage of personnel, category / skill wise requirement, quality, strengths and weaknesses of people. All these create a support-base data bank to guide the organization to take decision on vital issues.
2. HRM provides / supplies people as per indents (i.e. type, grade, skill, specialization of people, time of supply etc.) placed by the departments, and thus helps the departments in smooth running of the operational activities in order to produce the quality goods at reasonable cost as targeted.
3. HRM creates congenial and conducive atmosphere where people can develop mutual understanding, mutual trust, and confidence, which are prerequisites for work in a team / group.
4. Effective human resource management reduces employee absenteeism and increases productivity. So, it helps to achieve individual, organizational and social goals.
5. HRM helps the organization to change strategic activities to suit changing environment by way of creating a committed, dynamic workforce through OD intervention, awareness development mechanisms and other measures.
6. HRM develops knowledge, skill, abilities, aptitude of employees and moulds / changes their attitudes, values, beliefs to make a reservoir of contented, happy and

competent workers' community in order to deliver the goods and services to the delightment of customers.

7. HRM introduces **employees performance review system (EPRS)** to evaluate the present performance and protential of the employees for higher responsibilities wherein, Key Performance Areas (KPAs) are decided jointly by the subordinate and the superior. System of self-appraisal, counselling for better performance, evaluation by stakeholders make the EPRS more rational, just and accurate in its assesment process. Employees express satisfaction over performance appraisal system. They feel that the career development exercise mostly based on performance ratings and potential ratings makes wise judgement over the issues for promotion / advancement to higher posts.
8. HRM promotes the quality of working life of the employees through introduction / implementation of policies, procedures for satisfaction of physiological and psychological needs of the employees.
9. HRM helps the organization to fulfil the needs of the society by way of initiating measures for upliftment and wellbeing of the employees.
10. HRM provides the quality management by way of making an organization as a learning organization where people can learn and experiment innovative ideas, working as change agent to introduce quality oriented company milieu, involving people to promote team work for quality production and services and introducing a culture of partnership, cooperation and participation in the organizational activities.
11. HRM attracts the best quality people to join the organization and retains the achievers, performers by offering excellent pay packages, perquisites, challenging jobs,higher responsibilities, effective career planning and development.

Evolution / Origin and Development of HRM

Before we discuss the evolution of HRM concept, we feel it is pertinent to know the evolution of HR concept. HR concept has emerged from the following:

1. ***Slave Concept:*** Labour was treated as a commodity. Employer Labour did not think to give labour a human treatement. A situation of no fair wage, no healthy working condition, no fixed time was present. Workers worked as bonded labour.

2. ***Master-servant Concept:*** Workers were no more than servants. A climate of ill treatment, exploitation, unhygenic working environment, meagre wages, absence of paid holidays, rules, laws governing working conditions was in existence. Hire and fire approach was abruptly used.

3. ***Welfare Concept:*** Management showed their willingness to improve the wellbeing of workers by way of providing some health benefits, rest room, safety measures, shelter rooms, subsidised food. They were under impression that, productivity could be increased if, some welfare measures were taken.

4. ***Paternalistic Concept:*** Management tended to manifest 'father like' attitude like 'do the job I tell you to do as I look to your problems'. Management thought of getting desired results if father-son relationship was established The concept expressed more of a critical parent than a nourshing parent.

5. ***Philanthropic Cencept:*** This concept is based on the philosophy that the workers are human beings. They like to satisfy social and psychological needs. This concept emerges from the research carried out by *Elton Mayo* and his associates. Group interaction, teambuilding, a climate of 'we-feeling' are some of the outcomes of this concept.

6. ***Human Resource Concept:*** Workers are regarded as the most valuable assets of an organization and the

success of the organization depends on the development of HR. Workers can be satisfied if their psychological needs. (viz. social need, esteem need and self-actualization need) are fulfilled. Contented and committed workers help the organization to grow, to develop and to achieve.

HRM as a part of management functional process has got its origin recently. But, HRM was used as a system in the organization administration in 400 B.C. as revealed from Kautilya's Arthashastra. Then, for better and effective administration, a system was developed to hire, motivate people and retain the skilled people. Promotion at that time was based on performance and potential score of the people at work. Existence of HRM system is also evident from the Babylonian Code of Hammurabi in 1800 B.C. Though during those days emphasis was given for dealing with personnel problems, no initiative shift to management perception as to treating employees as resource / assets was found.

Today's HRM has originated / evolved from health and happiness concept, *i.e.,* major function of management to provide help, assistance and guide to the employees for maintaining health and making them happy. The strategy of evolution of HRM is discussed herein below.

1. *Health and Happiness (prior to 1931)*

In the early part of twenteith century and prior to that, no department was in existence in the organizational setting, to look into the aspect relating to employee requirement, handling grievances, motivation and employee development. Some companies created health and happiness department with officers / executives who were identified as non-performers / non-achievers. Rank and file in the organization, especially non-officers, did not expect much from the newly formed portfolio, as main task assigned to this department was to ensure performance of some ritual activities like arranging picnic, giving farewel to the retirees, making celebration of some occasions, looking to personal problems, providing some health benefits etc.

2. *Welfare (1931-1946)*

The Royal Commission of Labour submitted its report in 1931. The Commission recommended for appointment of labour officers in an organization to deal with recruitment of labour, in order to stop corrupt practices in industry, particularly in the area of selection and also to look into welfare aspects of the workers. The need to provide welfare facilities was also felt during Second World War, as workers' support and cooperation was exigently required, to increase production and to keep production activities smooth, to meet up necessities during war. Enactment of Trade Unions Act, encouraged workers to be united and form unions to represent their grievances to the employers for redressal. Most organizations started appointing welfare officers / labour officers to look to the workers' grievances particularly, the welfare aspects like drinking water, canteens, creches, restroom, working conditions etc. and a separate welfare department was set up.

3. *Personnel Administration (1947-1959)*

During this phase, many changes were observed. The vital labour laws which ensured providing welfare, social security, health and safety measures to workers were enacted. Some of such laws which prompted companies to open new departments under the nomenclature 'Personnel Administration Department' for dealing with personnel matter, welfare, health and safety problems, industrial disputes etc. are undermentioned :

(i) The Industrial Disputes Act 1947

(ii) The Factories Act 1948

(iii) The Dock Workers (Regulation of Employment) Act 1948

(iv) The Employees' State Insurance Act 1948

(v) The Plantations Act 1951

(vi) The Indian Mines Act 1952

(vii) The Employees Provident Fund and Miscellaneous Provisions Act 1952

(viii) The Employment Exchange (Compulsory Notification of Vacancies) Act 1959.

The Factories Act 1948 made it compulsory to appoint welfare officers in industrial establishement, where 500 or more workers were employed. Factories and industrial establishments started appointing Personnel Officers, Administrative officers, Labour officers, Welfare Officers. Such officers were given authority, power, status in the companies for smooth and effective discharge of their functions. They were also assigned responsibility to look into recruitment , basic training and record maintenance of the organization. Importance of personnel administration in industrial establishments was noticed. Executives, personnel professionals set up institutes—National Institute of Labour Management (NILM) at Mumbai and Indian Institute of Personnel Management (IIPM) at Kolkata in 1950s to exchange ideas, practices and innovations in personnel field amongst themselves in meetings, workshops, seminars of the institutes, so that they could discharge their assigned task effectively and efficiently.

4. *Personnel Management (1960-1983)*

This period showed state of unity and solidarity amongst workers. Five central trade unions (INTUC, AITUC, HMS, UTUC, CITU) emerged in the industrial settings with different charter of demands. Workers manifested their conscious activity to extend schemes for their growth, development, training. Formulation of rational policies, procedures for recruitment, selection, promotion, welfare benefits, compensation, incentives, grievance redressal was given much emphasis, in order to keep the workforce happy and satisfied. National Commission on Labour submitted its report in 1969, wherein, it stressed the need for ameliorating the conditions of workers through providing welfare, social security measures, ensuring equity, justice in compensation benefits, promotion.

To satiate psychological needs of the employees (viz. challenging job, increased responsibility, recognition, status, advancement etc.) some organizations introduced performance appraisal system to identify and promote achievers and potential people, participative management to involve workers in decision making process; job analysis, job description and job evaluation to give just and rational compensation to workers. The job role of personnel executives was enhanced during this period with the enactment of some laws viz. The Maternity Benefits Act. 1961, the Apprentices Act 1961, The Payment of Bonus Act 1965, The Contract Labour (Regulation and Abolition) Act 1970 and Payment of Gratuity Act 1972. However, the main function of personnel executives was to act as custodians of personnel policies implementation and to ensure that statutory requirements are complied with.

All the three main areas of personnel function (that is labour welfare, industrial relations and personnel administration) inspired the industrial establishments to give much more authority, recognition, support, power to the personnel professionals. In 1980, the two professional bodies-NILM and IIPM were merged to form National Institute of Personnel Management (NIPM) with its head quarter in Kolkata for better performance and functioning by personnel executive / officers in an organization.

5. *Human Resource Management (1984 onward)*

A new approach-HRM approach has emerged due to change in the product market environment arising out of stiff competition amongst indigeneous and multinational / transnational companies and also change in the organizational climate for growth and development. It is a change / development driven by product market condition which demands quality service and product at the reasonably lowest price. To achieve organizational objectives workpeople are considered as resource / assets and are given much more importance to contribute as world class workforce. The whole system of acquisition, motivation, development and retention of human resources is redesigned in line with corporate demands to face challenges and confrontation against competitors in the market. Apart from utilizing advanced technology in day to day operational activities, latest quality management concepts, performance and potential appraisal, career palnning and development, competency development programme are introduced.

From the preceding discussion it is observed that HRM concept has evolved along the years from the health and happiness activities in the organizations and HR concept has emerged from slave concept. The evolution of HR concept and HRM concept are shown in Figure 1.2 and Figure 1.3 respectively.

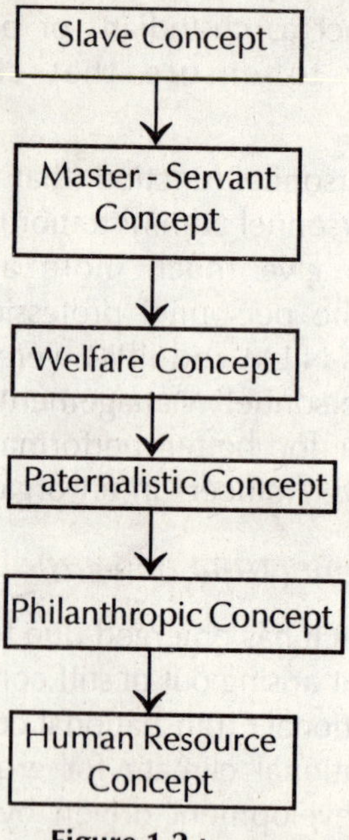

Figure 1.2 :
Evolution of HR Concept

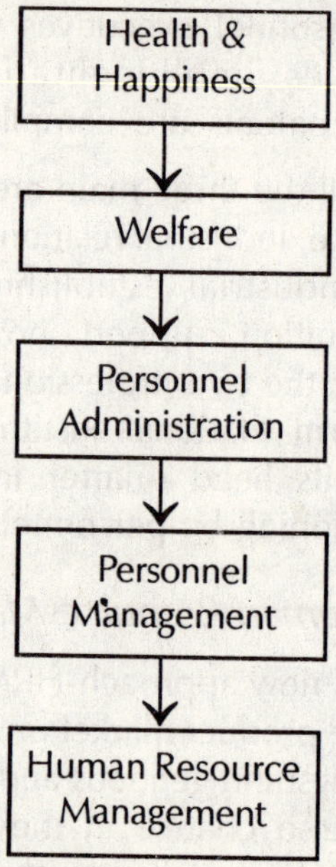

Figure 1.3 :
Evolution of HRM Concept

Origin / Development of HRM Concept

There has been a lot of confusion over the use of the nomenclatures 'Personnel Management' and 'Human Resource Management' in the mid-1980s when HRM has first emerged in the organizational setting as a clearly defined concept. Some companies retitled their Personnel Departments as Human Resource Departments and changed the designation of the personnel executives from Personnel Manager to Human Resource Manager. Some Universities, Management Institutes changed their curriculum and started offering courses in Human Resource Management. To have a clear concept on the subject 'HRM' it is imperative to discuss origin / development of HRM. The following researchers are pioneers / developers in the field of HRM.

1. *Fombrum etal (C. J. Fombrum, N.M.Tichy and M.A. Devanna, 1984)*

One of the first explicit statements of the HRM concept was made by them who asserted that, HR system and an organization structure should be managed in a way that is congruent with organizational strategy. Boxall (1992) named this concept as 'matching model'.

2. *Beer et al (M. Beer, B. Spector, P.R. Lawrenee and D. Quinn Mills. 1984)*

They were other founding fathers of HRM. They felt that today, organizations are facing tremendous competition and to confront such situations a broader, more comprehensive and more strategic perspective with regard to the organization's human resources is demanded. That means, situation creates a need for a longer term perspective in managing people and consideration of people as potential assets rather than merely a variable cost.

This concept was christened by Boxall (1992) as the Harvard framework.

3. *Walton R.E. (1985)*

He developed the concept of mutuality-mutual goals, mutual influence, mutual respect, mutual rewards, mutual responsibility. He thought that policies of mutuality will make the people committed and this committed lot will yield both better economic performance and greater human development.

4. *David Guest (1987)*

He carried out research work on Harvard model and developed it further by defining four policy goals which can be used as testable propositions.

(i) Strategic integration:

(a) Integrating HRM issues into its strategic plans,

(b) Ensuring coherence of various aspects of HRM

(c) Providing for line managers to incorporate HRM perspective into their decsion making.

(ii) High commitment:

(a) Behavioural commitment to achieve goals

(b) Attitudinal commitment to manifest identification with the enterprise.

(iii) High quality:

Aspects of managerial behaviour that bear directly on the quality of goods and services provided including employees management and investment in high quality employees.

(iv) Flexibility:

Flexibility from different perspectives.

Besides aforementioned researchers, Karen Legge (1989) Chris Hendry and Andrew Pettigrew (1990), Keith Sission (1990) and John Storey (1993) have made detailed study on this subject.

Role of HR Manager

HR manager plays a pivotal role to achieve organizational objectives. It is human resource/work people who perform task and achieve company goals. So, human resource is a must in an organization. To get the right number and right kind of human resource at the right time of company need and to motivate, prepare and develop the human resource to perform task, the person in charge of such job, *i.e.* human resource manager is no less important in an organization than human resource at work.

HR manager is a guide, philosopher, friend, path-finder, path identifier, problem solver, competence maker of the human resource. Ulrich (1997) has developed a model of multiple roles for HR professionals who focus ranges from long-term strategic to short-term operational, and activities range from managing processes (HR tools and systems) to managing people. Whatever the role HR manager plays, it helps growth and development of the people at work and organization as well.

Role of HR manager in an organization is discussed in brief as under.

1. *Advisory Role*

One of the major roles of HR manager is, to advise the top management in the matter relating to management and development of human resource, in order to achieve organizational objects. Looking to the company's vision, mission and long range planning, HR executive advises the higher management to formulate appropriate HR policies, procedures which may create a perceptible change in the minds of the workers' to help the transformational process of dynamism.

2. *Pro-acting Role*

HR manager ascertains the probable areas of conflict and differences between workers and management, identifies the factors that may create problems in future, forecasts the extent, quantum of loss that may occur and the department may suffer loss and takes remedial measures beforehand by way of developing organizational culture, climate, introducing system, mechanism, and does not leave any room to crop up problems, grievances.

3. *Welfare Role*

HR executive looks to the welfare aspect of the employees viz. canteen, creche, rest-room, hospital, transportation, housing accommodation, school, etc. His one of the principal roles is to provide welfare facilities to the employees for their betterment and well-being.

4. *Developmental Role*

Development of workers for attaining company goals is made by the HR manager through improvement of knowledge, skill, abilities, aptitude, attitude, value, beliefs etc. A dynamic organization needs dynamic employees and transformation of employee's mind-set to the process of dynamism is possible only when all the potential areas for growth and development are reinforced. HR manager takes all possible measures for growth and development of employees through formulation of HR policies in the matter of training, career planning and development, counselling etc.

5. *Mediator's Role*

HR manager works as a link personality between trade unions and top management in order to eliminate the differences of opinions cropped up in process of settlement of disputes. He takes initiative to sort out problems through collective bargaining/ bipartite negotiation process.

6. *Social Upliftment Role*

Organization is part and parcel of the society. As a societal member it has ethical and moral obligation to contribute to the society for its growth and development by way of taking necessary measures like creating and improving infrastructure, spreading learning institutions, providing medical facilities, generating employment opportunities. HR executive plays a vital role to give a proper shape in the formulation of suitable HR policies for the people in the society.

7. *Counsellor's Role*

Because of illiteracy and ignorance workers can not take decision in their personal problems and they need advice to sort out such problems, viz. education of children, medical treatment, marital matter, family problems, etc. HR manager, as he comes close to the workers because of his nature of work, develops understanding between them and advises, guides the workers in right direction.

8. *Spokesperson Role*

HR executive works as a spokesperson of the company especially, in the matter of depicting organization health, condition, strength etc. to the employees while negotiating for settlement of industrial disputes. He also acts as a representative of the workers when they are non-unionized/unorganized and cannot represent their case properly to the top management. Under such circumstances HR manager places their grievances, problems, demand to the top management for settlement/redressal.

9. *Motivator's Role*

One of the functions of HR manager is to motivate the employees to achieve their own goals, as well as organizational goals HR manager performs such role by way of introducing reward schemes.

HR manager's role of establishing mutual understanding, mutual confidence and mutual trust helps to motivate the employees to excel in the level of their performance.

10. *Procurer's Role*

HR manager helps to procure the right number and right kind of people at the right time, to enable the company to run smoothly, effectively and efficiently and to achieve its goals. He facilitates formulation of a dynamic recruitment policy, designs and develops Test/Interview techniques, selection process, suiting individuals and organization requirement in order to find out the right persons for the required jobs. He makes a systematic, problem free procurement exercise when workers express happiness, satisfaction and a state of contentment.

11. *Change Agent Role*

In changing scenario, workers are required to change their attitudes, belief, perceptible state, values to meet organization needs, requirement, expectation. In the age of stiff competition organization can survive and develop only if the workers are adaptive to change requirement. It is the HR executive who through establishment of sound human relation convinces the workers about the necessity of changing attitude, values to accept change role, as reinforced by introduction of OD programme, TQM concept, quality circle etc.

12. *Maintenance Role*

HR manager plays a pivotal role to retain the dynamic, excellent, highly skilled workers by providing attractive compensation package, introducing reward management, career planning and development, welfare, fringe benefits and social security schemes. Suitable policies are formulated, programmes are designed, necessary measures are taken to implement schemes for growth and development of employees, with and through the active efforts of the HR manager.

13. *Disputes Prevention Role*

HR manager takes remedial measures-curative and prophylactic to redress and prevent grievances, disputes in order to bring harmony and peace in an organization through introducing, grievence handling machinery, collective bargaining process, rational approaches to discipline management, quality of working life, participative concept and the like. HR executive creates congenial and conducive climate in the company by eleminating differences between management and workers and developing understanding on the basis of mutuality.

14. *Executive Role*

HR manager plays an important role to execute the policies, programmes, decisions. Formulation and execution tasks are interwoven and equally important for achievement of organizational goals. HR manager acts as an executor of the policy decisions in the company, for smooth functioning and effectiveness of the organization.

15. *Decision Maker's Role*

HR manager is the supreme person to make decisions in respect of management and development of human resource. Organizational policies, programmes objectives concerning human resource are formulated by him.

16. *Coordinator's Role*

HR executive coordinates the task of developing, interpreting of HR programmes, policies which are put into operation by the line people, and develops a team spirit amongst them.

17. *Strategist Role*

HR manager helps to accomplish business strategy of the organization through introducing and implementing HR strategies.

18. *Monitoring Role*

HR manager acts as regulator/monitor to ensure, that HR policies, procedures, programmes, so formulated are monitored effectively to meet the objectives.

Qualities of HR Manager

The main function of HR manager is to manage and develop human resource for achievement of organizational goal. For this, he performs the activities of procurement, motivation, development and maintenance/retention of human resource besides other activities. For effective and smooth functioning of above activities he should have some qualities. The qualitative attributes generally relate to technical aspects of operation (*i.e.,* knowledge, skill etc. in the subject area) and managerial aspect, (*i.e.,* ability to plan, organize, direct, control of HR.) So the competencies of HR manager include

- technical/professional competencies
- managerial competencies
- change/moulding competencies
- business competencies

However, the degree and extent of qualities of HR manager varies from company to company considering nature, size, type and objective of the company.

The principal qualities of HR manager are discussed below.

1. *Knowledge in sociology, psychology and allied discipline*

Since HR manager deals with the human beings having different values, belief, attitudes, and hailing from different families, societies, he should have knowledge in sociology, psychology, anthropology, economics etc. for clear understanding of human behaviour and sorting out the issues.

2. *Knowledge in acquisition process*

He should have thorough knowledge in the technique of human resource planning, identification and exploring the potential area of human resource, selection process, test techniques etc. in order to procure right persons for the right jobs.

3. *Skill for evaluating performance*

He should have clear concept on the various methods of performance evaluation, counselling technique, career planning process, OD programmes, reward management, TA and ability for its application/implementation in the organization.

4. *Skill to design training programme*

He should have adequate skill to design and develop training programme, executive development programmes, to impart training, to identify training needs and to evaluate effectiveness of training.

5. *Knowledge on behavioural theories and application*

He should have knowledge on the latest behavioural theories, research work, application of theories in industries and its outcome.

6. *Knowledge on motivation techniques*

He should have a thorough idea on different motivation techniques, stroking methods, identification of need factors, leadership theories, application of the motivation technique, TQM, QWL and participative system of management.

7. *Ability to perform managerial and operative functions*

He should have ability to perform effectively the managerial activities like planning, organizing, directing and controlling and also, the operative functions of human resource management in acquisition, development, motivation and maintenance.

8. *Ability to analyse, to diagnose and to redress HR Issues*

He should be able to analyse and diagnose the HRM related issues for redressal and settlement, to develop system for effective functioning of the organizational activities.

9. *Skill to collect, store, monitor and maintain data/ information*

He should have the skill for systematic collection, storage, monitoring and maintenance of HR data/information for future use.

10. *Knowledge for conducting survey on job satisfaction, morale and behaviour*

He should have the knowledge for conducting survey on job satisfaction, morale, attitude and employee behaviour.

11. *Skill to evaluate HR policies and procedures*

He should have the skill to evaluate the effectiveness of existing HR policies, procedures, programmes, practices and develop the more appropriate ones.

12. *Ability to develop team spirit and cohesiveness*

He should have the ability to work with other departments and develop team/group cohesiveness.

13. *Amiable and sober temperament/disposition*

He should have initiating capability, sober temperament, amiable disposition, rational mind-set and adequate tact for amicable solution of issues.

14. *Communication skill*

He should have skill to communicate organization expectation, requirement, need, policies, programmes etc. to the employees as also to the top management about employees' desire, wants, aspirations, urge to satiate their needs. To develop interpersonal relations, understanding, confidence, mutual trust between HR manager and the employees communication skill is a necessity.

15. *Active listening*

He should be able to listen to employee issues patiently so as to make them feel that he is empathic, open minded, sympathetic to their problems.

16. *Sincere and honest efforts to settle issue*

He should be sincere and honest to sort out problems, to settle grievances, to dispose of issues refered to him by the employees.

17. *Positive approach and thought process*

He should have positive thinking on the performance, activities, behaviour of the employees and should treat them as human beings.

18. *Imaginative and creative*

He should be sociable, friendly, unbiased, adaptable to situations, free and frank, imaginative, creative, interested in learning and teaching.

19. *Ability to introduce attractive compensation package*

He should have the ability to introduce rational compensation package, welfare, social security and fringe benefits schemes, incentive schemes.

20. *Ability to introduce grievance procedure, collective bargaining*

He should have the ability to introduce grievance procedure, collective bargaining mechanism, and establishment of sound human relation.

Armstrong (2000) indicates that HR manager should have competences to –

- develop and implement integrated and coherent HR strategies
- adopt HR strategies to fit business and cultural imperatives
- facilitate team building.
- coach clients to deal with own problems, transfer skills
- provide cost effective services in each HR area
- promote total quality and continuous improvement in HR function
- promote awareness in own function

Functions of HR Manager

HR manager's functions basically relate to managing and developing human resources for achievement of organizational objectives. He, therefore, performs a lot of activities looking to organization needs, requirement, strategy and goal. The areas of activities of HR manager are managerial, functional and facilitative. The functions of HR managers include managerial functions (viz. planning, organizing, directing and controlling) and operative functions. (viz. acquisition, compensation, development, and maintenance)

The principal functions of HR manager are discussed below:

1. *Planning HR Programmes, Procedures etc.*

HR manager chalks out plan to formulate HR policies, programmes, procedures, rules etc. in connection with recruitment, selection, training, career planning, performance appraisal, potential appraisal, executive development etc. with a view to achieve organizational goals. Organization needs right people to man the departments and for such purpose forecasting of requirement of human resources-skill wise, jobwise is needed. It is the functional responsibility of the HR manager to ascertain skills and competencies needed for an organization and to design and develop human resource planning system, to ensure supply of necessary human power to the organization as and when needed.

2. *Coordinating HR activities*

HR manager ensures that HR policies, programmes are carried out by line functionaries by way of providing constant and effective effort and coordinating of the activities amongst concerned departments.

3. *Controlling HR Functions*

HR manager sees whether work is performed as per plan designed / approved. HR audit, attitudinal survey, workshop, seminar, participation mechanism help the HR executive to know the actual extent of work performance and to initiate measure in the functional control area.

4. *Working as job analyst*

HR manager collects and examines data, information to establish specific requirements for individual jobs in an organization. This operative function is carried out by him as job analyst through preparation of job description, job specification employee specification and job requirements.

5. *Designing and developing recruitment and selection method*

HR manager explores the potential areas where people are available for the purpose of recruitment and stimulates them for participation in the process. He also ensures that the best technique of selection is introduced to identify the right personnel.

6. *Placement of personnel*

After selecting the right personnel the whole process may go waste if proper placement is not made. It is the task of the HR executive to see that the people selected are placed at the right job.

7. *Induction and orientation of new personnel*

After placement employees need induction and orientation for enrichment / increase of knowledge, skills, ideas in respect of operation, compan'y philosophy, policies, regulations, rules, expectation, work environment, career-planning, development etc. and for introduction to the people with whom they will work. This function is carried out by HR manager.

8. *Preparing employees to perform present job*

Due to variation in the level of knowledge, competencies amongst employees, some employees cannot deliver goods and service as per requirement. HR manager ensures to provide training to those employees who lag behind the expected level of competencies, skill, knowledge, values, activities manifestation, to enable them to show their worth in the organization. He helps the line management/training executives to design and conduct tailor made programmes, workshop, interface conference etc.

9. *Preparing employees for performance of future job*

Today's organization is very much dynamic. Changes in the brand of products, quality go through a regular phase of activities which demand updation of knowledge, skills of the employees. HR manager looks to this area and imparts necessary input to employees through training, counselling, so that, they can accomplish future assignment.

10. *Evaluation of performance*

HR manager designs and develops employee performance review format (EPRF), to evaluate the present level of performance as also to explore potential areas for development. The Employee Performance Review System (EPRS,) gives the clear idea about the effectiveness of the employees and the potentialities for promotion as well.

11. *Planning for advancement in career*

HR executive, designs specific career path/career advancement scheme to satisfy psychological need of the employees, for going ahead in their career. It is the necessity for the employees who are committed, potential, dynamic to achieve individual goals vis-a-vis organizational goals.

12. *Designing career development programme*

HR executive designs various development programmes for placement of employees in different roles. It is done through the process of role analysis, job enrichment, job rotation, creation and re-creation of autonomous work groups etc.

13. *Designing and implementing OD and Executive Development Programme*

In the dynamic organizational system changes occur very fast resulting in creation of lot of problems that need immediate solution/disposal. To confront such problems/challanges, whole employee community requires passing through a change process which provides diagnosing and coping capabilities to work as proactor. HR manager designs and implements OD programme to develop knowledge, skill, competencies of the employees and to bring about a change in their mind-set to manifest activities for solutions.

HR manager also designs and conducts Executive Development Programme, to reinforce technical, human and conceptual skills of the line management so that they can redress employee grievances and develop understanding between each other.

14. *Developing and implementing compensation plans and employees benefits programme*

Employees aspire for better wages, incentive, fringe benefits, social security in exchange for labour they provide. They become committed, contented, performer when they satisfy their level of expectation in respect of compensation package and benefits. HR manager develops compensation plans and benefits programmes, and implement them in order to create happy working force in, organization.

15. *Advising management on all aspects of employer-employee relations*

HR manager advises higher management about the importance of developing mutual understanding, mutual faith, mutual confidence in order to establish sound human relations for achievement of individual, group and organizational goals. For such purpose, HR executive enhances morale of the employees, redresses grievances through grievance procedure, settles industrial disputes through collective bargaining process, introduces participative system like quality circles, workers' participation in management decision-making; developing communication and leadership skills, handling disciplinary cases through mutually agreed disciplinary procedures.

16. *Ensuring compliance with provisions of related labour laws*

HR Manager ensures that equal employment opportunity laws and other statutory obligations are complied with.

Differences between Human Resource Management (HRM) and Personnel Management (PM)

There has been a lot of confusion, misconception over the use of the terms 'HRM' and 'PM'. Some are of the view that both HRM and PM are the same; it is just like 'old wine in new bottle'. Some opine that HRM is used in place of PM in the same manner as 'corporate communication' is used in place of 'public relation', or 'water resources' is used in place of 'irrigation'.

Torrington and Hall (1991) commented that PM is 'workforce centred' that directs itself to employees while HRM is 'human resource centred' and concerns itself with the overall human resource needs of the organization.

Different authors, experts, business magnets have given their views, opinions differently narrating similarities, dis-similarities between the concepts of PM and HRM. The fact emerges that HRM is different from PM in respect of areas/activities, viz. strategic integration, transformational/change leadership generating commitment, total quality and cultural change, workplace learning that creates systemic adaptation and innovation, unitary concept concerning interests of the management and the employees, and in other areas. J. Storey (2002) has narrated the differentiating aspects in four basic areas viz. beliefs and assumptions, strategic areas, line management and key levers.

However, Human Resource Management and Personnel Management are not entirely different concepts. In some areas these have similarities specifically in the 'maintenance' area like employment, collective bargaining functions while in some other areas these show differences to each other. The differentiating areas are presented in Table 1.1

Table 1.1 : Differences between Personnel Management and Human Resource Management

Perspectives	Personnel Management (PM)	Human Resource Management (HRM)
1	2	3
1. Concept	PM deals with management of people at work.	HRM deals with management of prime components people at work viz. skill, knowledge, ability, aptitude, value, beliefs, talents, attitudes.

(Contd.)

1	2	3
2. Functional	The main functional area of activities of PM includes employment (manpower planning, recruitment selection, placement, induction/orientation) compensation, industrial relations,training.	The main functional area of activities of HRM is employment, motivation, development training and education.
3. Approach	*(i)* It is a fire-fighting approach *i.e.* to solve the matter as and when crops up. *(ii)* It is an operation-alive' approach *i.e.,* to keep the operation running. *(iii)* It is traditional way of functioning. There is no creativity, no newness in methods of functioning. *(iv)* It is controlling approach. Employee's behaviour, freedom to work are kept restricted/controlled.	*(i)* It is a fire-preventing approach *i.e.* to take measures so that problems do not occur. *(ii)* It is an 'operation-alive' approach as also 'operation diversifying' approach to suit the changing need of the organization. *(iii)* It is an experimenting appraoch. New techniques, theories are applied in the functioning process in order to find out the outcome. *(iv)* It is a self-controlled approach. For performance of work employees exercise self control, self-direction.
4. Strategy:	*(i)* It does not consider corporate business strategy while designing and implementing plan of action.	*(i)* It decides/formulates HR strategy in line with corporate business strategy.

(Contd.)

1	2	3
	(ii) Business strategy has little or no role to play in the process of its functioning.	*(ii)* Success of its functioning depends on how accurately and to what magnitude it considers corporate business strategy while formulating HR Strategy.
5. Emphasis:	It gives emphasis on stereotype activities *i.e.,* in maintenance area of activities.	It gives emphasis on development area of activities, *i.e.,* all round development of the people at work.
6. Training:	*(i)* It has limited scope for training. Employees receive training on some specfic designated courses. *(ii)* Training mechanism for potential develepement is not used in a systemmatic way. *(iii)* It considers training as 'expense./liablity' for the organization.	*(i)* It has a wider scope for training. Tailor-made training given, assessing training needs/requirement of the employees for performance of the job. *(ii)* After identification of potential areas development process starts. *(iii)* It considers training as good investment which yields results in near future.
7. Development	It has no systematic/continuous plan of activities for development of people's skill, competence/ies.	It has people orientation activites. It looks to the development of people at its entirety. It considers development at all levels, *i.e.* at individual level, dyadic level, group level and organizational level.

(Contd.)

1	2	3
8. Assumption about employees	*(i)* Employees have no human value under such function. They are considered to be maketable articles ready for sales/ purchase. *(ii)* It considers employees as having lower order needs and they remain happy on satiation of physiological needs. *(iii)* Application of McGregon Theory X with regard to assumption on behaviour/activities of employees is common.	*(i)* It considers employees as assets/resource. *(ii)* It considers employees as having all hierarchial needs and after satisfaction of lower order needs they move forward for higher order needs i.e., psycholoical needs like social needs, esteem needs and self-actualization needs. *(iii)* McGregon theory Y contributes much to shape mind set of the HR professional o preceive employees as human resources.
9. Role	It has fixed role which is static, rigid, and can not go beyond the boundary of activities.	It is flexible and works in a dynamic system which considers changing situational variables in the process of accomplishment of job.
10. Competency	It lacks competence to face challenges arising out of changing organizational environment	It has competence, skill to confront challenges as crop up due to situational changes.

(Contd.)

1	2	3
11. Application of behavi-oural theories	It has limited scope for application of behavioural theories and research outcome in the industrial setting.	It considers organization as learning organization where research results, behaviour theories are constantly used.
12. Deployment philosophy	The objective of emp-loyees deployment is to utilize their services for the betterment/ benefits of the organization.	Employee's services are utilized for the mutual benefit of the organizaton and the employees.
13. Decision making and implemen-tation	It is slow in decision making and implem-entation.	It is very fast in decision making and implemen-tation.

Books Recommended

1. Michael Armstrong : A Handbook of Human Resource Management Practice (Kogan Page Limited, London, 2000)
2. W.B. Werther and Keith Davis : Human Resource and Personnel Management (McGrawHill, New York, 1996)
3. G. Dessler: Personnel/HRM (Prentice Hall, New York, 1991)
4. P. Subba Rao : Essentials of Human Resource Management and Industrial Relations : Text, Cases and Games (Himalaya Publishing House, Delhi, 2000)
5. Leen C Megginson: Personnel and Human Resource Administration (Richard D. Irwin Inc. Humewood, Illinois, 1977)
6. Udai Parak and T. V. Rao: Designing and Managing Human Resource Systems (Oxford and IBH, New Delhi, 1981)

7. T. V. Rao et al. : Alternative Approaches and Strategies of Human Resource Development (Rawat Publications, Jaipur, 1988)

8. J. Storey : Managing Human Resources in the 21st Century (Infinity Books, New Delhi, 2000)

9. D. P. Torrington and L. Hall : Personnel Management : A New Approach (Prentice-Hall, Englewood Cliffs, N. 1991)

10. C. L. Fombrum, N.M. Tichy and M.A.Devanna : Strategic Human Resource Management (New York, Wiley, 1984)

11. P.F. Box all : Strategic HRM : a beginning, a new theoretical direction (Human Resource Management Journal 2(3), 61-79, 1992)

12. M.Beer, B.Spector, P.R.Lawrence and D.Quinn Mills : Reward systems in Managing Human Assets (The Free Press, New York, 1984)

13. R.E.Walton : Towards a strategy of eliciting employee commitment based on principles of mutuality, in HRM Trends and Challenges, ed. R.E.Walton and P.R.Lawrence (Harvard Business School Press, Boston, MA, 1985)

14. D.E.Guest : Human resource management and industrial relations (Journal of Management Studies, 14(5), 03-521, 1987)

15. D. Winstanley and K. Stuart-Smith : Policing performance: the ethics of performance management, Personnel Review (Summer, 66-84, 1996)

Questions

1. Define the term 'Human Resource Management'. What are its objectives?
2. What is HRM? Outline its scope.
3. Discuss the conceptual perspectives of HRM.

4. 'Various stages can be identified in the evolution of Personnel Management vis-a-vis Human Resource Management'.What are those stages? Discuss.
5. Are PM and HRM the same? Discuss.
6. What are the qualities of HR executive? Discuss
7. What is HRM? Outline its salient features.
8. Explain the roles played by HR practitioner in the organization.
9. Explain the origin and development of HRM.
10. Discuss the functions of HR Manager in the organization.
11. a. What do you know by the term 'human resource'?
    b. Discuss the operative functions of a Human Resource Manager of a medium size company.
12. Discuss the managerial and job related qualities of Human Resource Manager.

Case Study No. 1

Mr T. N. Shah has been working as Head of HRM Department of a multinational company engaged in manufacturing cotton goods in Ahmedabad. The company's HRM Department is manned by 3 executives including Mr. Shah. The total workforce of the company is about 4000. Some more workers are decided to be added to meet the HR requirement of a new department to be opened shortly. Considering work activities of the company as also the work load of the executives of the HRM Department, it is felt that the HRM Department is understaffed. In the Board Meeting it is decided that some dynamic HR executives be hired through company's procurement cell. Mr L. N. Chowdhury, General Manager (Operation) has been assigned the task of selecting the most competent and effective candidates from external sources of recruitment who can be capable enough to mould the mind-set of the employees as change agents. Since, Mr Chowdhury is a line executive, he needs the help and co-operation of Mr. Shah to guide him in identification of qualities that a prospective HR executives must possess.

In the above context, discuss the following :

(i) Does it come under the job role of HR manager (Mr T.N. Shah) to help the line management (Mr L. N. Chowdhury) in the area of selection of executives?

(ii) Can Mr Shah think that selection of officers is the prerogative of HR management not line management?

(iii) What should be the qualities of the prospective HR executives for selection in the executive cadre of the company's HRM Department

Case Study No. 2

After doing MBA (HR) from a reputed University Mr Ramesh Jain has joined a medium size factory in Mumbai as HR executive. On the first day of his joining he was introduced to the executives, staff and some workers of the factory. Mr Jain liked the environment, induction system of the company very much and he developed a high impression about the company.

The factory runs a single shift from 8 a.m. to 5 p.m. (with a break of one hour) daily, except Sunday being weekly holiday. The duty hours of Mr Jain start from 8 am to 6 pm including a rest pause for two hours. On the second day of Mr. Jain's reporting two workers came to Mr Jain at about 5-15 pm. and requested him to give some time to listen to their personal problems. They also requested him to give suggestion, advice to sort out their problems. Mr Jain turned down their request and cautioned them not to come to him in future with their personal problems.

In the above context discuss the following:

a. Do you think Mr. Jain has done the right thing?

b. What should be the important roles of Mr. Jain as HR executive in that company?

2

Human Resource Planning

Meaning of HRP

Every organization needs human resources to perform its activities. Without human resources no organization can think of continuing its operation. So, human resource is a must in an organization like other resources. But for effective running of organization and for achieving organizational objectives, it needs right number and right kind of people at the right time at the right place. That means, organization does not require excess or less number of people or below standard of people at the time when their use is needed. Thus, the necessity to assess human resource requirement by some process as arises. Human resource planning is such a process which ascertains/identifies the exact number and kind of people an organization needs at the time and place as per its requirement. Bulla and Scott (1994) have defined HRP as 'the process for ensuring that the human resource requirements. of an organization are identified and plans are made for satisfying those requirements'. Human resource planning deals with the activity relating to human resource requirement of an organization i.e. identification of human resources – number, skill and deployment of human resources. According to D.A. Decenzo and S.P. Robbins (1989), human resource planning is the process by which an organization ensures that it has the right number and kinds of people, at the right places, at the right time capable of effectively and efficiently completing those tasks that will help organization achieve its overall objectives.

HRP is an important part of business planning which tasks into account corporate vision, strategies and changing perspectives at the time of its formulation. It looks to strategic aspect of an organization and also the process of human resource acquisition, motivation, development, and maintenance, which is carried out in line with corporate strategic planning, business objectives. So, in broader sense

- HRP is an activity process relating to human resource requirement.
- It ascertains the number of people required.
- It identifies the skills people should possess.
- It plans for deployment of people at the right time and at the right places.
- It is a strategic planning formulated on the basis of business strategy of an organization.

Objectives of HRP

In the changing business scenario, organizations can achieve strategic goals if, they have right number of talented, committed workforce to produce quality goods and services as per requirements. HRP helps organizations by way of supplying information to them in advance to create a dynamic, committed, proacting, loyal workers'community through recruitment process, moulding and development techniques to achieve strategic goals of organizations.

The objectives of human resource planning are discussed herein below.

(i) Providing information to organization in respect of available source of quality personnel

Organization needs different kinds/grades of people to meet

the challenges arising out of the changing situation. HRP indentifies the sources of human resources skill-wise and informs the top management to utilize the sources as per needs of the organization.

(ii) Helping organization to know the demands for people for different sections / departments

HRP makes a detailed study as to the requirement of changes in operation, system, structure of organization, quality and production, introduction of new techniques, methods, machines etc. and makes organization aware of the demands of the departments / sections for people with different skills. This sort of information helps the top management to man the departments / sections properly for effective utilization of human resources.

(iii) Identifying ineffective, incompetent, useless employees

HRP data help the organization know its dead woods. The company can, therefore, downsize the workers' strength by way of removing ineffective, incompetent employees through VRS and the like, and in the process it can increase efficacy and financial health and can achieve organizational goals.

(iv) Helping organization to implement succession planning scheme

HRP supplies necessary data pertaining to vacancies, arising out of superannuation, business policy / strategy etc. and also talent reservoir to fill in those vacancies under succession planning scheme.

(v) Making training system effective

HRP provides data / information with regard to the people who are potential and need training as also the people who lack competencies for performance of present job / future job. This information helps the training department to keep the records up to date and to design and conduct training courses/ programmes as per requirement, need of the individuals and organization.

(vi) Helping to implement business policy/strategy of organization

HRP makes strategic planning taking into consideration of business policy / strategy of the organization. Since, HR is a most vital factor for effective implementation of corporate business policy / strategy, strategic HRP contributes a lot to the process of implementation.

(vii) Helping the organization to create a dynamic and worldclass workforce

HRP provides detailed information to the top management regarding employees' profiles like name and number of performers, non-performers, potential people, deficit area of the workpeople, nature of training required for increasing coping and proacting capabilities, internal labour market situations etc. On the basis of such information, organisation takes the help of change agents and experts to make changes in the behaviours and activities of the employees and to create a dynamic and world class workforce so that they can deliver the goods, services as per needs of the organization.

(viii) Helping organization to increase production, productivity, quality of goods and to provide customers' delightment through trained, perfect, skilled workforce

HRP provides data support to the organization to create effective, competent, trained, perfect, skilled workforce who can provide customers' delightment and can give higher production, better quality of goods and maximum productivity.

Besides the above, purposes of HRP are.

1. to make the best use of human resources
2. to develop healthy industrial relations and to create congenial and conducive atmosphere in organization
3. to improve quality of working life.
4. to forsee the impact of technology on work.

5. to balance the cost between utilization of plant and workforce.
6. to forsee HR turnover and taking measures to check turnover
7. to introduce expansion, diversification programme as per requirement

Importance of HRP

Human resource planning is a strategy for procurement, utilization, development and retention of human resources in organization. It gives the indication/information to the company in respect of:

(i) number and kind of people to be recruited
(ii) methods of recruitment, selection
(iii) surplus or deficit employees
(iv) utilization of employees
(v) training methods
(vi) moulding of employees' attitudes, values, perception
(vii) improving skill, knowledge, competencies of employees
(viii) compensation and benefit packages
(ix) career planning and development
(x) employee participation, involvement and empowerment
(xi) maintenance of industrial relations and the like

On the basis of the information supplied by HR planner company formulates policies, procedures and takes necessary measures to achieve its strategic goals.

So, it is a vital process of HRM. Though it is not the function of HRM, yet its importance cannot be exaggerated. The whole purpose of HRM largely depends on the data / informaton provided, by HRP. So, HRP is omnipresent in HRM system and it is difficult to achieve organizational strategic goal without HRP. Importance of HRP can be judged from the following deliberations.

(i) Creation of willing, committed, contented workforce

HRP identifies the people who need change in attitude, increase in skill, competence; aspire for growth and development, and want to accept higher responsibilities. Organization, on the basis of these information, can prepare action plan and create a willing, committed and contented workforce.

(ii) Reduction in training cost

Since HRP indicates who needs what training, it helps the organization save money by way of giving such training to those employees who actually need. So, tailor made training can be given.

(iii) Less defect or nil defective products

On the basis of the data supplied by HRP, organization gives training continuously to the identified workers in a planned and systematic manner to enhance their knowledge, skill, competence so that they can produce quality goods with nil defect or less defect.

(iv) Uninterrupted, change driven production process

In a dynamic changing scenario, uninterrupted, change driven production process, is a must for the organization to keep its supremacy / dominance over the competitors and this is possible if organization is fed with the data / information about the employees, who need training for change, growth and enrichment of knowledge.

This is HRP which supplies information to the top management for training, OD intervention, development to those who need changes.

(v) Effective utilization of human resources

HRP indicates the people who are less utilized / underutilized and also those people whose skill, competences remain in latent state. Such information / indication, helps the top management to utilize human resources effectively.

(vi) Prognosis of company's health / achievement probability

Human resource plays a pivotal role in the achievement processes of the company. It is rather a yardstick to measure company's health. Availability of dynamic, skill workforce indicates positive sign of company's health / achievement of goals and non-availability / less availabality of such workforce gives the reverse situation. HRP supplies the necessary data to organization by which it can prognosticate its health or probability level of target achievment.

(vii) Right sizing / downsizing employee strength

HRP supplies information / data as to the net human resources requirement, along with other information. This points out excess or shortage of workforce. In case of excess human resources arising out of various factors like change in production process, introduction of computers, sophisticated modern technology, machines, diversification of business, adoption of new strategy and others, right sizing / downsizing employees' strength becomes a necessity through reduction of human resources by introducing VR scheme, sabbatical programme, etc. Thus, vital decision / policy formulation on such important aspects is possible because of availability of data through HR planning.

(viii) Retention of talented, skilled human resources

Organization, designs and formulates policies and programmes in the matter of promotion, development, training etc. on the basis of the information available from HRP and this way it creates a talented, skilled reserve force and ensures supply to the departments / sections as per need, requirements.

(ix) Smooth and effective functioning of the organization

Organization cannot function effectively and smoothly with out HRP. So, company needs HRP

- for indentification of excess / surplus employees
- for finding out deadwoods, non-achievers, potential people, performers

- for compliance with statutory requirements relating to personnel
- for confronting to the situation arising out of liberalisation, globalization policies of the government
- for examining trade union demands for increase of workers' strength, regularization of badil/casual workers

(x) Helping to formulate / design corporate business planning

Human resource planning helps to formulate / design corporate business planning. Company's production schedules, sales programme, expansion programme, decision to stop activities in some departments / units etc. have direct impact on human resource requirement of the company. HRP is, therefore, needed to help the organizations prepare corporate business planning.

(xi) Helping to economize cost

Company can foresee the total cost towards wages / salary, frings benefits, incentive, recruitment etc. with the help of HRP, and can economise cost through different measures like increasing production, turnover, reducing replacement costs, legal costs etc.

Process of Human Resource Planning

HRP requires to pass through different stages/processes. There is no specific / hard and fast HRP process that every organization needs to follow while preparing manpower planning. But, some stages are definitely common to all organizations. HRP process/ stage variances occur due to influence of some factors like nature of product produced / services rendered, financial health of the organization, consumer's market, international relations, global conflicts, legislation etc. The possible stages of HRP shown in Figure 2.1 are discussed herein below.

(i) Analysing company's mission, objectives

This is a vital step of human resource planning. What the organization is thinking about its expansion, diversification, contraction / reduction of business, what strategic approach it intends to activate, what mission it holds for growth and development– all these are basic to the ascertainment of human resource requirement, as these factors influence HRP to a great extent.

When the company decides its mission, objectives, it takes into account some external environment (viz. country's economic policy, foreign policy, relationship with foreign countries, global economy, market conditions and potentials etc.) and also internal environment like company's culture, milieu etc. So, top management gives stress on PEST factors (that is assessment of political, economic, social and technological environment) and also response factors to look how the organization responds and the corporate magnets ensure through SWOT analysis (revelation of strengths, weaknesses, opportunities and threats to organization) that the mission, objectives have pragmatic relevance / approach to achievement.

(ii) Studying and analysing of corporate plan

After coming to know organizational strategic objective, mission of the company HR planer studies corporate plan and starts with analysing it into segmental plans like production plan, sales plan, technological plan, financial plan etc. This analysis helps the HR planner to make effective estimate of HR requirement for different departments, sections of an organization.

(iii) Forecasting HR requirement

In terms of corporate goals, planning process starts to find out the HR requirement at unit levels and accordingly programmes are formulated to ascertain present strength of human resources skill wise, job wise, experience wise. Job analysis is made to assess the scope of designing / redesigning the job. In this process workload study is undertaken to see whether, services of the existing human resources are best utilized. If, they are underutilized workload ascertainment is made a fresh. Forcasting is made looking to both qualitative and quantitative aspects of human resources. So, for preparation of HR requirement estimation (demand forecasting) careful study / examination of the following areas/aspects is required to be made.

- annual budget
- organizational plan including segmental plans
- in respect of different departments/sections

The detailed discussions on the above techniques are made separately in the subsequent pages.

- number of workers-direct, indirect (skill wise, experience wise)
- standard hours for production of a unit
- productivity
- introduction of technology
- product market development
- production methods

The following techniques are used to estimate demand for human resources in the organizations:

(i) Managerial judgement

(ii) Delphi technique

(iii) Work study work load method

(iv) Ratio analysis

(v) Scatter plot

(iv) Supply Forcasting

This process ascertains the sources-internal and external-to supply human resources as per requirement. For supply of skilled / experienced workforce from internal sources techniques like job rotation, intra region / inter region transfer, inter departmental transfer, promotion, constant training are initiated. The planner studies the cases of superannuation, absenteeism, sabbaticals, layoff, dismissal, resignation, death etc.while forecasting supply. If, internal supply strength is not adequate or it meets the demand for higher position, the company needs to hire at the lower level. The supply of human resources through internal and external sources is affected by several factors. Migratory situations, number of voluntary retirees, ex-servicemen, laid off, retrenched employees, local unemployed youths, influence external labour market. HR skill inventory, employee profile, succession planning chart, gives the position of internal source of human resources.

(v) *Finding out Shortage / Excess of Human Resources*

This process forecasts the balance of human resources that is, whether supply of human resources is more than the demand for human resources or vice versa. The supply and demand forecasting of human resources is considered both from qualitative and quantitative point of view, that means, skill wise/grade wise human resource requirement is decided.

(vi) *Preparing action plan to deal with surplus / shortage of human resources*

If surplus human resources are available, the planner requires to draw up a scheme to deal with the issue. It happens when some departments have excess staff / workers while other departments suffer due to understaff. In such a case, excess staff is redeployed through transfer (inter-departmental) process, but where such possibility is not present or only to some extent redeployment is possible, then problem of dealing with the remaining staff exists.

Hence, action plan is prepared to deal with the excess human resource in the following manner.

(a) Staff reduction activities

* Identification of surplus human resources for lay off, retrenchment.
* Introduction of voluntary retirement scheme (VRS)

with the offer of attractive gratuity package and other benefits so that the people at work specially surplus human resources accept VR.

(b) Granting of sabbatical leave for a specific period during which no salary/wages and other allowances can be given to sabbatical leave optees.

(c) Formulating programme for job sharing between two employees.

(d) Outplacement service.

Formulation of programme for providing service to the redundant employees through the career counselling, training, guidance, enrichment of knowledge to help them in getting employment.

(e) Formulating scheme for reduction of working hours and payment of wages as per reduced hours of work.

(f) Preparation of detailed procedure for banning fresh appointment in place of vacant posts arising out of retirement, resignation, dismissal, retrenchment, lay off, superannuation.

HR planner needs to prepare action plan to provide human resources where deficit is forecasted. In such eventuality, it is examined whether deficit of human resources of one department can be met up through supply from surplus departments, and if such possibility arises then suitable programme is prepared in respect of transfer, promotion, training, OD intervention and above all human resource development. However, if HR supply from internal sources is not possible in future then fresh appointment is needed. In such case, external source for supply of right kind of people is explored, suitable measure is chosen for the job in the organization. That means recruitment process is programmed, steps for selecting the candidates are identified. Such steps include.

- Process for collecting information about candidates
- Application of Test technique/s

- Use of experiential technique to find out the level/ extent of knowledge, competence the candidates possess.
- Application of behavioural techniques to measure technical skill, human skill, decision-making ability as also the perceptible areas / mind set about the prospective job, organization and their own expectation desire, need, willingness, intentions etc.

After selection process is completed measures are chosen for induction and orientation programmes. In case of deficit or shortage of human resources Michael Armstrong (2000) has suggested that action plan should be made in the following areas:

- An overall plan as required to deal with shortage arising if there are demographic pressures
- A human resource development plan
- A recruitment plan
- A retention plan
- A plan to achieve greater flexibility
- A productivity plan

(vii) Alteration / modification of corporate plan, strategic approach

After the action plan is implemented it becomes essential to review, examine, and control such plans.

Sometime, it happens that future supply of human resources from external sources falls short of demand as forecasted by planner. HR planner suggests the organization if such eventuality arises.

- to alter or modify the organizational plan for some period till the required manpower is available.
- to continue the activities in the affected department/s without taking cognizance of the forecasted man power requirement temporary.

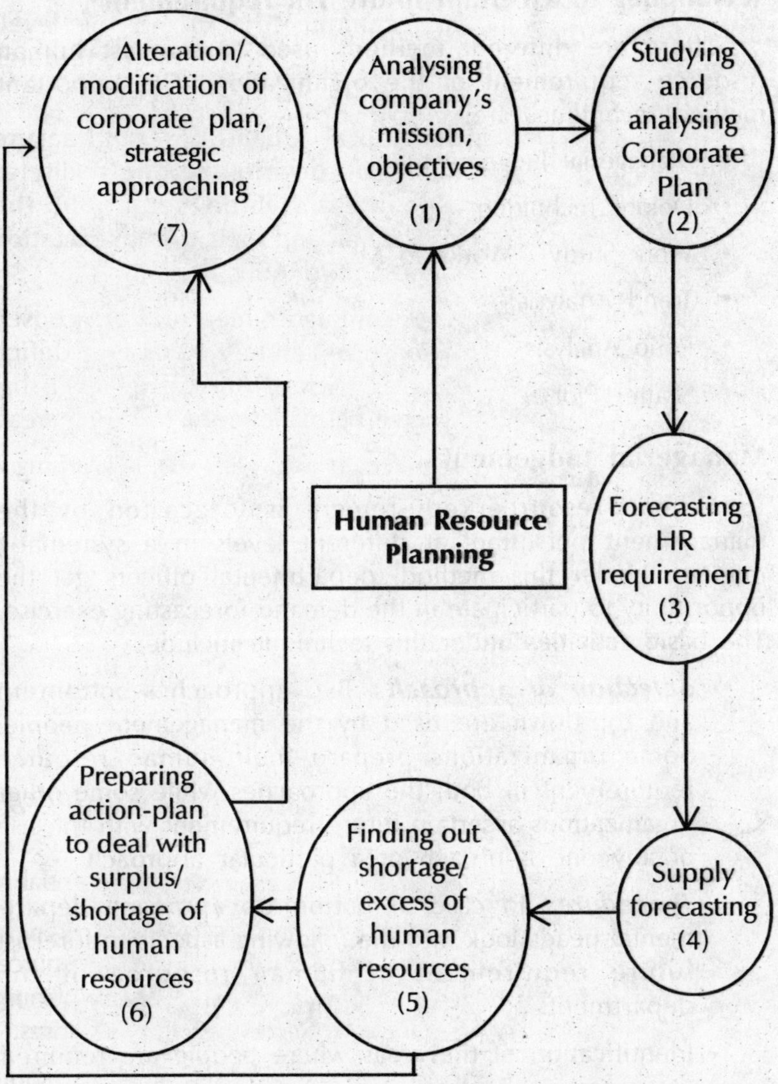

Fig.2.1 : Human Resource Planning Process

Techniques to ascertain future HR requirement

There are different methods used to forecast human resource requirement of the organization. The important methods/techniques are:

- Managerial Judgement
- Delphi Technique
- Work Study / Workload M
- Trend Analysis
- Ratio Analysis
- Scatter Plot

Managerial Judgement

Human resource requirement is forecasted by the management personnel at different levels in a systematic manner. Under this method, departmental officers get the opportunity to participate in the demand forecasting exercise. The basic activities under this technique include:

- ***Selection of approach :*** Two approaches-bottom-up and top-down are used by the management people. Some organizations prepare their human resource requirement in both the approaches while some other organizations ascertain future requirement with the use of any one approach or a particular approach
- ***Procedure :*** In case of bottom-up approach departmental heads look into the following aspects to forecast future requirement of human resource of the departments

1. Identification of the areas where people are required
2. Introduction of new technology
3. Expansion programme
4. Launching of a new product
5. Market penetration and discussion with the departmental officers.

After threadbare discussions and positive interactions departments prepare a note sheet containing departmental requisition for human resources and submit to the higher management. On receipt of requisitions for human resources from different departments, the higher management calls them for review and consideration.

In case of top-down approach top management prepares the departmental forecast of human resource requirement and sits with the concerned departmental heads for discussion and review.

Merits

This method has following merits.

(i) It is very easy and simple to use in the organization to forecast its future human resource requirement.

(ii) It is less expensive. For application of this method does not need huge money as preparation of demand sheet does not require involvement of outside experts.

(iii) Demand forecasting can be made at a short period of time.

(iv) Ina bottom-up approach departmental officers are involved in demand forecasting exercise. So they develop a sense of belongingness' and a feeling of 'we-ness'.

(v) It helps to promote the level of morale of the officers as this technique acts as a motivation mechanism.

(vi) It gives accurate forecasting especially in small and medium size companies.

Limitation

(i) It may not give perfect forecasting where organizational activities are very complex.

(ii) It may not yield results in bigger organizations that use latest technology, methods and devices.

(iii) It may not be suitable in those organizations where human resource information system works excellently.

Work Study / Work Load Method

This method can be used to forecast human resource requirement of an organization. By measuring work and standards this method can make demand forecasting. The steps involved in the process of forecasting are –

- *Measurement of work*

  The work to be performed in the year i.e. planned output for the year needs to be measured. In case of manufacturing company the production budget is prepared.

- *Measurement of standard hours*

  Time needed to complete a job (or to produce a unit) has to be measured. As for example, 3 hours may be required by a person to produce a unit.

- *Determination of effective time*

  The time available for a person to perform the work in the relevant period has to be determined. While calculating the effective period weightage is given to factors like number of paid holidays, absenteeism, forecast levels of idle time.

- *Conversion of projected work into man-hours*

  The projected work is converted into man-hours to find out the total hours required to complete such work. That means, total man-hours required to perform the planned work / to produce the projected output, have to be ascertained.

- *Determination of human resource requirement through conversion of man-hours*

  The total number of human resources required by an organization to accomplish the planned work is determined through conversion (that means, man-hours are divided by the effective working hours of an operator).

Example :

- Projected output for the year : 25,000 units
- Standard hours per unit : 4 hours
- Projected hours required : 25000 x 4 = 1 ,00,000 hours.
- Effective hours available for the year per person (allowing absenteeism, normal overtime, holidays etc.) : 2000 hours.
- Number of direct workers required $\frac{1,00,000}{2000}$ = 50 workers

Number of indirect workers required for the year can be ascertained through ratio analysis/trend analysis.

Merits

1. This method is easy to use. It does not need training to ascertain human resources required for an organization.
2. It is much more effective in manufacturing organizations where work can be measured and standard can be set.
3. This method may yield accurate results if during the period no change in job methods is made. That means, organizations, use the same technology in the concerned period.
4. It is not expensive to use.

Limitations

1. It may not yield results in organizations where job methods are frequently changed.
2. It may not be an effective tool in service industry especially, where work measurement can not be made accurate
3. This method can not be used to ascertain the number of indirect workers required for an organization.

4. Efficacy of the method depends largely on, how efficiently and correctly time and motion study are used as faulty/ defective study affect the whole process of measurement.

Delphi Technique

It is an old concept to forecast human resource needs of the organization. The term 'Delphi' has come from Greek. It is a group process to arrive at a consensus result. Its usage is basically in the area of personnel need estimation. HR need forecasting is made from the view point of experts who are asked a series of questions in a planned way.

Method of Application

1. *Selection of coordinator*

   Coordinator is selected to initiate and coordinate the activities with the experts.

2. *Selection of experts*

   The persons who have profound knowledge and skill in the concerned area are chosen. The experts may be from inside/ outside the organization.

3. *Preparation and administering questionnaire.*

   The coordinator prepares questionnaire and invites opinions from the experts.

4. *Summarizing of opinions and preparing new set of questions.*

   The coordinator summarizes the responses of the experts, prepares a fresh questionnaire on the basis of opinions given by majority experts and gives to the experts for submission of their opinions.

5. *Repetition of the process till the consensus arrived at*

   The same process (viz. editing / summarizing of opinions, preparing new set of questions and circulating among experts) continues till experts' opinions agree.

6. Consensus forecasting

After repeating the process several times, the coordinator finds that the opinions agree. This agreement gives the HR need forecasting.

Merits

1. Since personnel need estimation is made on the basis of experts' opinions, this method gives accurate forecasting.
2. Data / experts' opinions can be collected from far off places. Distance / geographical location can not create hindrance to obtain experts' views.
3. It is not an expensive method. The whole exercise (right from designing questionnaire till reaching the consensus of opinions) may be conducted internally by the company's own people.

Demerits

1. It is a time consuming method. All the activities involved in this exercise need a lot of time to arrive at consensus estimation.
2. It needs a dynamic, competent coordinator who should have expertise to prepare questionnaire, summarize opinions, evaluate responses, set new questionnaire and to make consensus estimation. So, this method can not yield results if the coordinator does not have requisite qualities.
3. Interactions among experts are not possible. So, the experts can not exchange their views to assess personnel needs of the organization.
4. This method can not make proper estimation if experts are wrongly selected.

Trend Analysis

It is one of the methods used to forecast personnel needs of the organization. Under this method estimation of personnel requirement is made on the basis of the past employment trends of the company. This method involves the following activities:

- Computation of number of employees (section/department/sub-group wise) at the end of each of the last 5 to 10 years.
- Finding out the trend of employment level
- Estimation of future employee needs.

Merits

1. It is an easy method to calculate future needs.
2. It does not need expertise to use in organization.
3. This method is less expensive. No training cost is involved as executives do not need training for predicting personnel needs.
4. It can be used as effectively in small organizations as in those where frequent changes in work methods are not made.

Demerits

1. It ignores productivity while predicting future needs. Hence, change in productivity affects forecasting.
2. It may not yield results in the changing scenario. The situations like expansion, diversification, opening up of new markets etc. may make the technique ineffective.
3. It is difficult to use this method in those organizations where work methods are frequently changed.
4. Estimation based on historical employment trends may not be accurate.

Ratio Analysis

Ratio analysis is a method used to predict future personnel needs of the company. Prediction is based on the ratio of causal factor and number of people required. For determination of future staff needs this technique involves the following activities:

- finding out causal factor (like sales volume, production volume etc)
- Computation of ratio between causal factor and number of people required
- Determination of projected/planned figure (like sales volume)
- Ascertainment of future personnel needs by using ratio

The following example will help to have an idea about this method:

Sales volume in 2003-04 : 50,00,000 units

Number of Sales people in 2003-2004 : 10

Ratio between Sales people and sales volume : 10:50,00,000 i.e. 1: 5,00,000

Projected Sales in 2004-05 : 90,00,000 units

Number of Sales people required in 2004-2005 $\frac{1X90,00,000}{5,00,000} = 18$

Merits

1. It is very easy to calculate future personnel needs of an organization under this method.
2. No expertise is required to use this method. So, no extra cost is involved towards training of personnel who are deployed for such purpose.
3. It does not need much time to estimate future personnel requirement.
4. This method is effective in those organizations where frequent changes are not made in work methods, technologies, system etc.

Demerits

1. It is difficult to use in organizations that undergo a process of changes continuously.
2. It does not consider feasibility of maximum utilization of human resources and technologies.
3. Under this method, calculation is made on assumption that productivity level remains about the same. Such assumption is not justified and rational as productivity level can be increased through the use of various motivational mechanisms.

Scatter Plot Technique

A Scatter Plot is another approach to predict future personnel requirements of an organization. It makes forecast of future personnel needs provided the two variables-business activity and number of employees are interrelated. This technique includes the following activities:

- Collection of data on business activity and number of employees from similar different organizations of various sizes
- Computation of projected / planned business activity
- Determination of relationship between business activity/ performance and number of employees required with the use of a Scatter Plot.
- Number of employees is shown on the vertical axis and business activity / performance is shown on the horizontal axis. A straight line is drawn to reduce the distance between the line and each one of the plotted points. If the points fall along the straight line or in close proximity of the straight line, the two variables are related to each other
- Estimation of future personnel needs.

The following example will help to understand how this technique is used to predict staff needs of an organization.

Example : One banking company having a business of Rs. 800 crores (banking business includes deposits and advances)

Business figure (Rs. in crores)	Number of Clerical staff
600	750
700	800
800	900
900	950
1000	1100
1100	1150
1200	1200

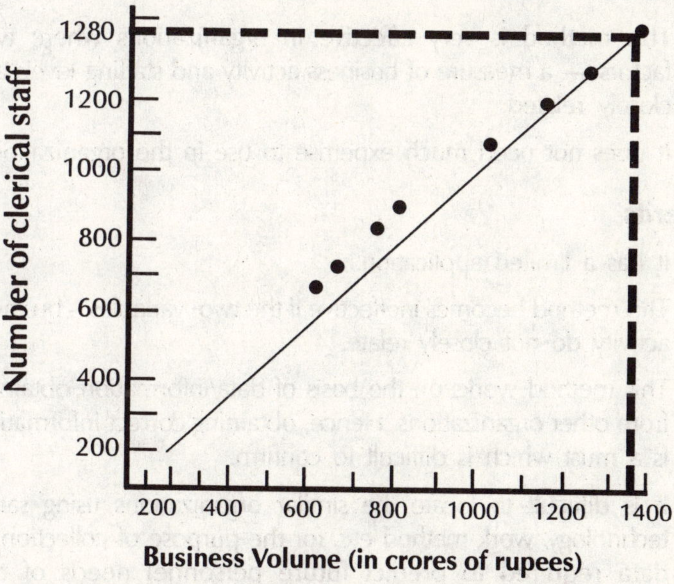

Figure 2.2 : Showing the Relationship Between Business Volume and Number of Clerical Staff

and 900 clerical personnel including special assistants, intends to increase its business to 1300 crores of rupees over the next three years. For determining the human resource requirements (particularly clerical personnel needs) for the projected volume of business, General Manager (HRM) gets the following business figures from different similar banks (using same technologies, having same proportion of bank branches in rural, semi urban, urban and metro areas) of various sizes.

So, for the volume of business (that means, for achieving targeted business of Rs 1300 crores) of Rs 1300 crores the General Manager (HRM) may need about 1280 clerical personnel for the bank as shown in Figure 2.2

Merits

1. It is very easy to predict personnel needs of the organization
2. Within a very short period the exercise for estimation of future staff needs can be completed.
3. This method is very effective in organizations where two factors — a measure of business activity and staffing levels are closely related.
4. It does not need much expertise to use in the organizations.

Demerits

1. It has a limited application.
2. This method becomes ineffective if the two variables – business activity do not closely relate.
3. This method works on the basis of data/information obtained from other organizations. Hence, obtaining correct information is a must which is difficult to confirm.
4. It is difficult to locate the similar organizations using same technology, work method etc. for the purpose of collection of data required to predict future personnel needs of the organization.
5. This technique can not be used if, business activity can not be measured.

Succession Planning

Succession planning means planning to make the people hold/possess the positions of the office in a systematic way. In other words, it is a process that makes projection or plan of the organization to occupy the higher positions by the subordinates/lower cadre people to run the business activities effectively and smoothly in accordance with the strategy already set. Generally, it refers to promotion / elevation of middle level management people to senior level management positions so that, aims of the organization to survive and grow are attained.

So, succession planning is an inventory report of the executives that helps the organization to select the executives occupy the higher positions. The help of succession planning or inventory report is required when the higher posts fall vacant due to death, resignation, discharge, dismissal, superannuation, promotion etc. or when a new post is created.

Peter Wallum (1993) indicated that succession planning includes the *following activities:*

(i) analysis of the demand for managers and professionals by company level, function and skill.

(ii) audit of existing executives and projection of likely future supply from internal and external sources.

(iii) planning of individual career paths based on objective estimates of future needs and drawing on reliable Performance appraisals and assessment of potential.

(iv) career counselling undertaken in the context of a realistic understanding of the future needs of the firm, as well as those of the individuals.

(v) accelerated promotions with development targeted against the future needs of the business.

(vi) performance related training and development to prepare individuals for future roles as well as current-responsibilities.

(vii) planned strategic recruitment not only to fill short term needs but also to provide people for development to meet future needs.

(viii) the actual process, activities by which jobs are filled. Process includes recruitment procedure, internal appointment procedure, methods of assessment, internal search mechanism and often, use of computer based information system.

Differences Between Human Resource Planning (HRP) and Manpower Planning (MP)

There has been a lot of confusion and ambiguity over the use of the terms 'Human Resource Planning, (HRP) and 'Manpower Planning' (MP). Some are of the view (e.g. Bennison and Casson 1984; Thomason 1988) that both HRP and MP are the same. K. Legge (1989) opines that HRP turns out to be the old wine of personnel management in new bottle. Thomson (1988) argues that there is no difference between HRP and MP. In the 1988 edition of **A Textbook of Human Resource Management** he writes:

Human resource planning (or manpower planning) may be defined as a process whereby courses of action are determined in advance and continually updated, with the aim of ensuring that:

a. the organization's demand for labour to meet its projected needs is as accurately predicted as the adoption of modern forecasting techniques allows and

b. the supply of labour to the enterprise is maintained by deliberate and systematic action to mobilize it in reasonable balance with these demands.

Some opine that HRP and MP are two different things. John Bramham (1989) argues that there is a big difference between human resource planning and manpower planning.

However, human resources planning and manpower planning are not entirely different. These have similarities in some areas while in some others areas these show differences to each other. The differentiating areas are discussed in Table 2.1

Books Recommended

1. David A. Decenzo and Stephen P. Robbins : Personnel / Human Resource Management (Prentice-Hall of India Private Ltd. New Delhi, 1989)

2. Gary Dessler : Human Resource Management. (Prentice - Hall, Inc. Upper Saddle River, New Jersey 07458, Eighth Edition, 2000)

Table 2.1 : Differences between Human Resource Planning (HRP) and Manpower Planning (MP)

Dimension	Human Resource Planning (HRP)	Manpower Planning (MP)
Concept	It is a planning/projection concerning core components of people (viz. skill, knowledge, ability, attitude, value, beliefs etc.)	It is a planning/projection concerning 'strength'/ 'power' of people
Process	Manager is concerned with motivating people-a process in which costs, numbers, control and systems interact	Manager is concerned with numerical aspect of forecasting, supply demand matching and control
Coverage	It has a wider coverage (both quantitative and qualitative aspects in the employment of people are considered)	It has a limited coverage. It looks into the quantitative aspect of employment
Emphasis	*(i)* Emphasis is given on culture management and individual growth and development *(ii)* Main focus is on the human and human aspects of people.	*(i)* Emphasis is given on the technical aspect of matching of supply and demand of manpower. *(ii)* Main focus is on the numerical elements of forecasting
Assumptions about people	*(i)* People are considered assets, resource *(ii)* People make the organization grow. Organizational goals are achieved through people	*(i)* People are considered costs. *(ii)* People are constraints, hurdles to the achievement of organizational goals.
Approach	It is a new approach concerned with broader issues	It is a traditional approach of manpower requirement.

3. Michael Armstrong : A Handbook of Human Resource Management Practice (Kogan Page Limited, London, 2000)
4. Bulla, D. N. and Scott, PM Manpower requirements forecasting : a case example in Human Resource Forecasting and Modelling, ed. D. Ward, T. P. Bechet and R. Tripp, (The Human Resource Planning Society, New York, 1994)
5. Casson, J : Re-evaluating Company Manpower planning in the light of Some Practical Experiences, (Institute of Manpower Studies, Brighton, 1984)
6. Rothwell, S : Human Resource Planning in Human Resource Management : A Critical Text (ed. J. Story, Routledge, London, 1995)
7. Quinn Mills, D : Planning with people in mind, (Harvard Business Review, November - December, 1983)
8. J. W. Walker: Human Resource Planning (McGrowHill, New York, 1980)
9. E. B. Geisler : Manpower Planning (AMA, New York, 1967)
10. M. Bennison and J. Casson : Manpower Planning Handbook (Brighton, IMS, 1984)
11. K. Legee : Human Resource Management: a critical analysis in New Perspectives in Human Resource Management, ed. (J. Story, Routledge, London, 1989)
12. G. Thomson: A textbook of human resource management (Institute of Personnel Management, London, 1988)
13. John Bramham : Human Resource Planning (Universities Press (India) Limited, 3-5-819, Hyderguda, Hyderabad, 1989)
14. P. Subba Rao : Personnel and Human Resource Management Text & Cases (Himalaya Publishing House. Mumbai, 2000)

Questions

1. 'It is said that HRP is the process for ensuring that the human resource requirements of an organization are identified and plans are made for satisfying those requirements.' - Explain
2. How does human resource planning contribute to the achievement of organizational goals? - Explain.
3. "Human resource planning is a strategy for procurement, utilization, development and retention of human resources in the organization." - Discuss.
4. What is human resource planning? Discuss the objectives of HRP.
5. As HR Manager of a medium size company what stages will you follow to assess manpower requirements of the company? Discuss.
6. What is succession planning? How does it help the top executive to achieve organizational goals?
7. "Human resource planning activities consist of some steps." Discuss in this context the different steps of HRP activities.
8. Write short notes on :

   (i) Demand Forecasting

   (ii) Succession Planning

   (iii) Importance of HRP

   (iv) Delphi technique

   (v) Managerial judgement
9. Discuss in brief different techniques used to ascertain human resource requirement of organizations.

Case Study

Mr. Ramen Banerjee has been working as Head of HRM Department of West Bengal Region of XYZ Bank Ltd. in Kolkata. On 2nd January, 2004 Mr. Banerjee has received a letter from the Chief Manager of India, Exchange Branch, requesting to provide adequate clerks, substaff and officers to run the branch smoothly and effectively so that customers' delightment can be attended and business targets can be achieved. The Chief Manager expressed that the work load of each employee is increased due to aggressive banking activities in the areas of deposits particularly Savings Bank Deposits, Advances. The Non-Performing Assets of the Branch which was 4.37 crores as of 31.12.2003, requires to be reduced to Rs. 1.10 crores by 31st December 2004. This has been decided by the General Manager of the Region through joint discussion in the Goal Setting Session.

Some additional information are available on the records of the Regional office as of 1st January 2004.

1. **Number of employees:**

   Officers - 30

   Clerks - 80

   Sub staff - 15

2. **Deposits :** 238 crores

   SB : Rs. 175.50 crores

   Current : Rs. 35.7 crores

   Term : Rs. 15.8 Crores

   Others : Rs. 11 Crores

3. **Advance** Rs. 62 Crores

4. **Retirement (Date of Superannuation)**

   30.9. 2004 : 2 clerks

   31.12.2004 : 3 officers including Chief Manager

   31.12.2004 : 2 peons

5. **Employees under disciplinary procedings :**

   Orders for proposed punishment issued on

   2.1.2004 : 2 clerks

   30.12.2004 : 1 officers

6. **Trend of Resignations :**

   In 1999 : 2 officers 1 clerk

   In 2000 : 1 officer 1 clerk

   In 2001 : 2 officers 2 clerks

   In 2002 : 1 officer 1 clerk

   In 2003 : 1 officer 1 clerk

7. **Targets :**

   As of 31.3.2004

   Deposit : Rs. 345 Crores Advances : Rs. 75 Crores

   SB : 250 Crores

   Current 50 Crores

   Term : 25 Crores

   Others 20 Crores

   As of 31.12.2004 : 20% increase in all areas (base period 31.3.2004)

8. **Under orders of transfer from**

   India Exchange Branch (Under Job Rotation Scheme):

   Officer : 2

   Clerk : 5

   Transfer agreed under compassionate grounds: (from India Exchange Branch)

   Clerk : 1

   Peon : 1

9. **Launching of new products / schemes w.e.f. 1.1.2004**

   (i) Credit card

   (ii) Super Savings

   (iii) House Building Loans

(iv) Instant car loans

(v) Deposit as you earn scheme

The branch would require one clerk and one officer to render services to customers in the areas mentioned in point number 9.

Mr. Banerjee has been advised by the General Manager of the Region to prepare human resource plan for India Exchange Branch and submit to him for perusal and consideration.

1. In which areas Mr. Banerjee should look into for preparing human resource planning?
2. What should be the steps for HRP?
3. Estimate human resource requirements of the Branch for the year 2004-2005.

3

Recruitment and Selection

After the completion of the HRP process, it may happen that the company may need to initiate exercise for obtaining personnel to meet up its requirement. The change in economic / business policies of the government which permit foreign business houses to carry on business activities along with indigenous organisations, makes the competition very much tough and stiff; and under such situation the organizations which produce and deliver the quality goods / services at relatively low market price, as per exact need / requirement of the customers earn, ability to compete, survive and grow. All this is possible if the right number and right kind of people are provided at the 'right' time, at the 'right' assignment. Hence, strategic recruitment and selection of human resources are of urgent necessity of the organizations. Discussions on recruitment and selection are made in this chapter.

Definition of Recruitment

Recruitment is defined as a process of searching out the prospective employees and stimulating them for offering candidatures for the job in the organization. So, it is an activity to find out the potential candidate for filling up the vacancies of the job and to encourage them to apply for those jobs. It is a connecting function between job seekers and job providers with necessary stimulation to the former. Dale Yoder (1958) defined recruitment as a process to discover the sources of manpower, to meet the requirement of the staffing schedule and to employ effective measures for attracting that manpower in adequate numbers to facilitate effective selection of an efficient work force. Recruitment system in any organization has following characteristics:

(i) Role analysis exercise, employee specification, and job analysis are carried out to find out demand for and supply of the human resources.

(ii) Human resource planning is designed / formulated in line with the corporate strategy, vision, objectives, before recruitment process starts.

(iii) Main thrust of recruitment exercise is on searching out exact / right number and type of people as per need/ demand of the jobs.

(iv) It is a 'linking activity' between prospective employees and management who needs employees.

(v) It has two-fold functions-identification of prospective candidate and motivating of such candidates.

(vi) Success of recruitment depends very much on how accurately and systematically earlier phase of activity accomplishes the task and reach the targeted requirement of personnel.

(vii) Slight mistake in identifying the right people may create a disastrous effect on achievement of organizational goals.

Objectives of recruitment

Organizations initiate recruitment process to fulfil the following objectives.

(i) To provide best available personnel

Organization needs people for different jobs as per human resource planning formulated / designed by planner. It is the recruitement process which digs out the sources of human resource supply and identifies the people looking to the needs, requirement of the organization and also qualitative attributes, potential areas, aptitudes, skill, knowledge, abilities the people possess.

(ii) To help to ensure uninterrupted running of the organization

In these days of stiff competition organization needs people with different types of skill, knowledge, abilities, values, attitudes, experience to meet up requirement of various departments, so that, the production and other activities remain unaffected and organization functions smoothly and effectively. Recruitment process helps the top management to ensure uninterrupted functioning of organizational activities by exploring/identifying the prospective employees.

(iii) To facilitate to introduce TQM in the organization

Self-quality awareness, consciousness and introduction of the concept of world class quality are the prerequisites of total quality management (TQM) and this is possible only when organization itself has world class people at its disposal. Recruitment system helps the organization to make a 'quality driven employee community' so that TQM is introduced in the organization.

(iv) To make a dynamic workforce to accept changes in the organization

In the changing environmental scenario, role of workers is pivotal to make changes in the organization. It is the workers' community that can make things happen as per need of the organization. This is possible when dynamic, committed workers form the workers' community of the organization. Recruitment process helps the organization to prepare the workers' community dynamic so that, they spontaneously / willingly accept changes in the organization.

(v) To help to achieve strategic human resource management

Strategic human resource management means, achievement of organizational objectives in a planned and systematic effort / direction through people. Corporate vision, mission, objectives are decided by the top management in the organization and thereafter, HRM strategy is formulated in line with corporate strategy. However, HRM strategy can be achieved if human resources of the organization realize its importance, and develop ability, skill, knowledge, attitudes, intention to achieve. Hence there is the necessity of recruitment system.

(vi) To get the required number and quality of employee at minimum cost to meet up human resource needs of the organization

One of the objectives of the recruitment process is to make cost-benefit analysis while identifying prospective employees, and to obtain quality employees and also required number of employees as estimated by the planner at the minimum cost. The idea is to look to all the perspectives e.g. cost, quality, time, demand specification at the time of identification of employees for satisfying human resource needs of the company.

(vii) To keep the unqualified applicants away from the entry to the organization.

(viii) To increase individual, group, and organizational effectiveness.

(ix) To maintain healthy industrial relations by way of changing composition of workers.

(x) To determine the effectiveness and usefulness of different recruitment methods and techniques in the organization.

Sources of Recruitment

The demand for human resources is met up either from the existing internal candidates or from external sources outside the organization or from both the sources. Hence, sources of recruitment include internal sources and external sources. Details of sources are discussed below.

Internal Sources of Recruitment

This source is company source. That means, internal candidates of the company are identified to fill up the required vacancies. Generally, demand for personnel is met up internally in the following ways.

- through apprentices as per Apprentices Act 1961
- casual / badli workers
- temporary workers
- deceased dependents on compassionate grounds under company's scheme for recruitment of deceased dependents
- through promotion under company's promotion policy
- retired, retrenched employees
- employee's close relative in case of his incapacitation to work due to accident while on duty or being invalid on medical grounds
- present permanent employees
- dependents of present employees

Benefits of Internal Sources of Recruitment

Benefits of recruitment from internal sources include the following.

(i) It increases the level of morale of the employees. Employees feel proud of being the members of the company.

(ii) Employees feel contented and happy with the job they perform.

(iii) It develops mutual understanding between employees and boss as they come close to each other. Employees

change their mind-set and develop positive image / impression about management and the company.

(iv) Employees find opportunity to go up through company ladder / career path to satiate their psychological needs and develop a sense of belongingness and a feeling of 'we-ness' and 'togetherness'.

(v) It ensures uninterrupted supply of quality human resources as per needs of the company.

(vi) It increases production and productivity as employees show their worth, effectivenes through their performance.

(vii) It helps to use dormant / latent areas of knowledge of employees and through promotional scope development of human resources is possible.

(viii) Cost of training, recruitment, induction is meagre as the employees are internal people who know the operation, job process, activities, boss, peers, working conditions etc.

(ix) It takes less time to select the candidates as short cut process is used for selection.

(x) It helps the selectors to select the right / fittest condidates as they are aware of the prospective employees' strength and weaknesses during the course of performing their function, except the candidates who are employees' relatives and are recruited under specific scheme.

(xi) It works as a motivation mechanism to make the employees sincere and committed.

(xiii) It gives more information about the candidates.

(xiii) The possibility of making error in selection of candidates is less.

(xiv) It helps to develop a healthy relations between trade unions and management.

Disadvantages of Internal Source of Recruitment

Recruitment from internal sources has following disadvantages

(i) Company has to choose / pickup the candidates / employees from limited / small number of employees, as a result right person may not be available as per need / requirement of the company.

(ii) Selectors may find difficulties in selecting the quality people as there is the possibility to influence them to select some people who may not have adequate experience, ability, skill for the post/s.

(iii) If the people are selected internally from the company, much more weightage is given on seniority than merit. So, the possibility of selecting old people with less merit is not ruled out.

(iv) The demand for innovative, creative, and dynamic people may remain unfulfilled as a result, the organization may not be able to produce quality goods. Company has to choose candidates / employees from limited / small number of employees / candidates as a result right person may not be available as per need / requirement of the company.

(v) It is difficult to make the people dynamic as the leader and his team members go through a same stereotype, traditional culture of activities.

(vi) Since employees / leaders are not taken from external sources where the people work in different culture, environment, climate as per changing needs of the company, it may not be easy to convince the workforce to accept changes in the organization.

(vii) Internal recruitment discourages experienced and skilled employees from outside the organization.

(viii) It deprives the outsiders to prove their excellence, worth and driving energy to achieve, to succeed, to win.

(ix) Internal candidates may not be able to deliver the goods and services as per demand, requirement of the customers.

External Sources of Recruitment

It is a fact that the organizations do not get the required number and quality of personnel internally all the time. It is, therefore, needed to get them externally i.e. outside the organization. External sources of recruitment mean the sources outside the organization that gives the indication of prospective employees / candidates as per requirement of the organization.

External Sources Include

- Employment exchange
- Professional agencies / placement consultants / search consultants
- Educational institutions
- Merger, acquisition / takeover
- Unsolicited applicants
- Temporary help services
- Leasing
- Independent contractors
- Family relations
- Trade unions

The details of the above external sources are discussed below.

Employment Exchange

This is a statutory body constituted by the Government to help the organizations in getting suitable candidates for employment as also to inform the registered candidates about the vacancies cropped up in the organizations. Companies can obtain list of candidates from employment exchange on sending request to them. In case of government offices and public sector units it is obligatory to notify vacancies to the respective employment exchanges before they are filled, as per Employment Exchange (Compulsory Notification of Vacancies) Act. 1959.

Professional agencies / search consultants / placement consultants.

These private placement firms keep records of job seekers, remain in constant touch with them and inform them about prospective employement. Organizations may take the services of such professional agencies for filling up the vacancies against fees charged by them. Some professional firms are mainly involved in finding out suitable executives, particularly in the middle management/senior management level and supply them to the business houses as and when requested. Such professional organizations are also called body shoppers or head hunters.

Educational Institutions

Today educational institutions are good providers of fresh candidates to the companies, particularly in the area of management, engineering, computer applications. The schools like IIMS, IITS and other universities, management institutes, engineering institutes arrange for campus recruitment of their final year students for different companies in the institutions, keep a good rapport, liaison with the business houses who as per requirement select the students for employment. As a, prerequisite or a step towards selection some companies arrange (as per request of the universities, institutes) for industrial training and live project work of the students at their organizations before campus recruitment takes place.

Merger, Acquistion and Takeover

It happens that some organizations take the services of some employees of other organizations who are declared surplus after the merger, acquisition and takeover process takes palce. Such organizations, contact other organizations which take over / acquire other companies for supply the list of personnel as per specification.

Unsolicited Applicants

Sometimes organizations receive applications for employment from various candidates. In such cases, companies keep records of those candidates in respect of qualification, age, experience, present status, area of interest, aptitude etc. and feed the information in the computer. Companies may use this sources for the purpose of selection as and when need arises.

Temporary Help Service

This is one of the external sources of recruitment. Company may need the services of some employees for a temporary period in some areas of activities. So, it may contact temporary help service agency who provides employees for temporary period. Sometime, retired officers / employees, ex-servicemen work with companies for a short period. Under such arrangement both the parties-company and individuals are benefitted. Company gets motivated, willing, experienced, senior, effective employees at minimum salary with no obligation to pay pension and retiral benefits. Individuals use employment place as a platform to have fun out of work, to pass on time, to avoid drudgery of retired life, and also to get compensation in exchange for service to meet up day to day needs.

Leasing

Company may contact leasing firm to provide employees to perform such functions which are temporary in nature. Company makes consolidated payment against the services of such employees and has no obligation to provide welfare, social security benefits, retiral benefits, increment etc.

Independent Contractors

This is like a outsourcing agency. The company contacts independent contractor to perform some specific function at the company premises or at the premises of the employees. If the work is done at the person's residence, he keeps informed to the management of the company over phone, fax, e-mail about the day to day progress of the job. Such arrangement is cheap as cost of work is much less than the cost occurred in the event of being performed by regular employee. Company has no financial obligation to pay provident fund, gratuity and other retiral benefits.

Family Relations

If the establishment is family owned firm, relatives are given preference for employment. Under such cases, the qualities like loyalty, trust, commitment get priority and these exist amongst new entrants.

Trade Unions

Some organizations may obtain lists of candidates from trade union leaders. Such organizations may develop understanding with union leaders in respect of recruitement of some candidates, to maintain peace and harmony in the organization.

Benefits of External Sources of Recuitment

Benefits of recruitment from external sources are mentioned herein below:

1. Management has a wider scope to select people from amongst large number of candidates. Hence, it is possible to get killed, right kind of people for the organization.
2. It is possible to make the people accept changes in the organization as their leaders/executives who are selected externally are dynamic and change personalities.
3. It helps to create a balance in employee composition which can bring a culture of mutuality, essential for growth and development of the organization.
4. Staff cost under external recruitment process is comparatively less than the staff cost under internal recruitment process particularly, when people are promoted on seniority basis. Generally, new candidates are given initial salary / minimum emoluments.

5. Selection of people is made on the basis of skill, ability, experience, competences people possess, as per requirement of job; and scope of influencing selectors is very remote.
6. Organization gets right kind of people, ensures delivery of quality goods and services to the customers.
7. External candidates are free from inbuilt preferences and prejudices.
8. Reservoir of quality, dynamic, committed human resource is created.

Disadvantages of External Sources of Recruitment

Recruitment from external sources has following disadvantages.

1. Existing employees get demotivated as they do not find scope of going ahead in their career.
2. Employees feel dissatisfied, unhappy as their psychological need, recognition, status, authority which come from position, higher assignment through promotion, remain unfulfilled.
3. It makes the existing employees disloyal, discontented as the employees develop a mind-set / impression about the management, that it is not people centred / concerned for people.
4. It reduces the level of morale of the employees, increases absenteeism and labour turnover rate.
5. It affects organizational growth and development as production is decreased, quality of product is deteriorated, accident rate is increased.
6. Cost of training, induction, recruitment of external candidates affects economic health and profit of the company.
7. This process is expensive and time consuming.
8. External candidates take much time to adjust with organizational environment, culture and to acquaint with the people of the organization.

9. It generates a feeling of insecurity amongst the existing employees.

Techniques of Recruitment

Apparently there is no difference between 'sources' of recruitment and 'techniques' of recruitment. It seems both the terms are same. Many organizations do not make any difference between 'sources' and 'techniques and use terms interchangeably.

But, these terms have different meanings. Sources of recruitment indicate available areas of prospective personnel, that is, the areas, localities, agencies, firms, institutions, persons, body of persons etc. from where prospective candidates/ personnel are available, where as techniques of recruitment involve means or mechanisms to communicate the prospective personnel about job, job description, employee specification, core empetences and expeiences and to motivate/ stimulate them in such a manner so that they offer their candidatures.

Now, we discuss major techniques of recruitment which are generally used by most of the companies. These include *(i) in case of external sources of recruitment :*

- Advertisement
- Walk-ins/consult-ins
- Employee referral/recommendations
- Scouting
- Internet/cyberspace

In case of internal sources of recruitment

- Promotion
- Transfer

Advertisement

It is one of the important techniques of recruitment. Many companies use advertisement as an effective tool to attract candidates, to generate interest on the job, to create desire and to stimulate them for immediate action. To make this technique useful and result-yielding organizations need to look to two areas of its activities :

(i) Selection of media

(ii) Construction / design of advertisement, usage of words, phrases etc.

Success of advertisement depends to a great extent on selection of media, that is, whether it should be newspaper, if so, which newspaper, or it should be TV, journal, professional journal, periodical and the like. So, selection of media needs to be carefully made as different nature of job indicates different media of advertisement.

Another area that needs emphasis is, construction of advertisement as it introduces prospective candidates to the organization and job, motivates and calls them for offering their candidatures.

Walk-Ins/Consult-Ins

This technique calls the candidates to have interface discussion with the company people who help them to know about company, job, company expectation, duties and responsibilities of prospective candidates. Company representative, generally HR / personnel executive, stimulates the candidates, creates inquisitive/interest in job and the company. This technique is of recent origin which is economical, short run process. Today's company uses this method for hiring junior/senior management people.

Employee Referral/Recommendation

Sometime organization hires people through employee reference / recommendation. For such purpose, organization communicates the present employees verbally, or through company house journal about availability of job. The concerned employees give the information to their own people and stimulate them to submit their candidatures.This technique works well and acts as very much effective to supply quality people. It is quite natural that present employees through whom candidates are available, always strive to give the best lot as they want to remain in the good book of the management. This process is also time saving as the present employees who show their effectiveness and loyalty, encourage the candidates, create interest and take prompt action to please boss.

Scouting

This process of stimulating prospective candidate is involved when organization collects the names of short listed candidates/ detailed list of candidates from the professional agency/ consultancy service. Under such system, company sends representative to the concerned professional agency to know details of candidates (their experience, qualification, desires, expectation, beliefs, values, attitudes etc.) to make them know about company, job, to encourage and stimulate them to offer their candidatures.

The success of this process depends on the skill, competency of the representative, reputation of the company and the professional agency.

Internet/Cyberspace

This recruitment technique is of recent origin. Companies can find out the resumes of competent, effective employees on the internet and contact them. Some companies use internet to recruit personnel in different ways. Some organization posts job descriptions on website. Some use the interest to search for temporary workers.

It has many advantages. Internet recruiting does not cost much. It is easily available. Companies can contact the candidates at no point of time.

Promotion

It is one of the techniques used in the organization to meet up the requirement of personnel in the positions above the grass root level internally but, the demands for people in the base level are taken care of through external recruitment process.

It is true that most of the people have desire to go up, to cross the company framed ladder, to satiate their psychological need for status, recognition, authority, challenging job, responsibility. In other words, they want elevation, advancement in their career. Promotion is such mechanism that, encourages/ stimulates the people to satisfy their need for advancement.

Departmental heads, supervisors or other line management of the departments make the people at work aware of the promotional scheme / policy and encourage them to participate in the promotion process.

Transfer

It is a process of employees movement from one section / department to another section / deaprtment of the organization. If the organization has more than one units, this movement may occur in different units. Under such process, employees skills, competencies are utilized in the department / section / units of the organization as per requirement, without any monetary incentives, benefits. Line mangement and also HR people stimulate the employees to accept transfer willingly and spontaneously.

Meaning of Selection

Selection activity is the most important activity as production, productivity, quality of products, attainment of organizational target depend on the the skill, competencies, aptitudes, and prosonality of the people who are hired through this process. This is the third activity after human resource planning and recruitment activity in the procurement process of the organization.

Selection is the process of choosing the suitable candidates who possess requisite qualifications and characteristics to fill jobs in an organization. Thomas H. Stone (1989) defines selection as the process of differentiating between applicants in order to identify (and hire) those with a greater likelihood of success in a job.

In the process of selecting candidates selector is likely to make two types of error — 'reject errors' and 'accept errors'. Reject errors are those errors which selector makes by rejecting candidates (that means making errors by not selecting candidates) who would later perform successfully on the job. Accept errors are those errors which selector makes by accepting the candidates who subsequently perform poorly on the job.

For selecting candidates the selector makes objective assessment of the candidates' experience, skill, competencies, qualification etc. in terms of job specification and then takes decision. It is not that all decisions the selector takes are correct. Obviously, are either correct or wrong. Correct decisions invariably relate to successful performance of the employees hired / selected. That means, the candidates who were thought to be successful in selection performance, later proved successful in their working with the organization. Wrong decisions relate to those decisions taken in selecting or rejecting the candidates, which were proved to be wrong as the selected candidates showed poor performance while the rejected candidates would have performed successfully.

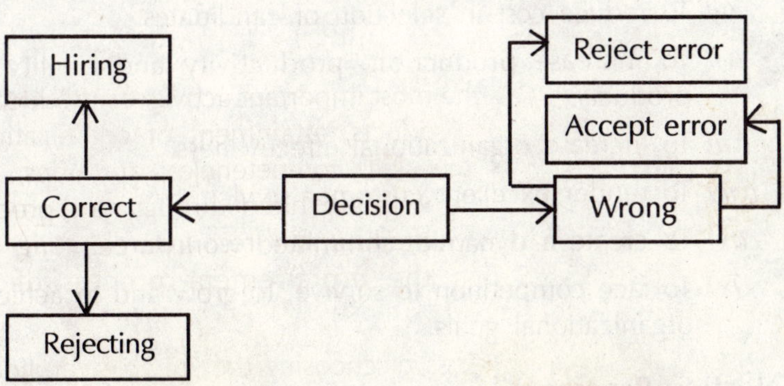

Figure 3.1 : Showing Diagrammatic Representation of Decision Making Activity

The Figure 3.1 shows diagrammatic representation of decision making activity.

Purposes of Selection

The purpose of selection is to choose the most suitable candidate in terms of job specification, from amongst the applicants who can be a performer, if appointed. So, matching of employee to the job is the activity of selector. This task of selector is very crucial and important as wrong selection may cost the organization unnecessary / wasteful expense toward hiring, induction and training . The aim of selector is to see that mismatch of candidate to job does not occur.

Now, purposes of selection are discussed in brief :

(i) To predict which job applicants would be successful if selected.

(ii) To provide information to the candidates about the company and the job so that candidates themselves can make self-select.

(iii) To find out the right between applicants and job of the organization.

(iv) To increase the level of morale of the employees through rational, unbiased and perfect selection.

(v) To reduce cost in selection of candidates.

(vi) To increase production, productivity and quality of products.

(vii) To increase organizational effectiveness.

(viii) To render excellent customer service.

(ix) To create a dynamic, committed work force.

(x) To face competition to survive, to grow and to achieve organizational goals.

Selection Process

Selection process goes through different steps/stages. Steps vary from organization to organization, even within the same organization steps in selection procedure are not the same. Steps differ from job to job also. Some jobs may not need written test, group discussion, while for other jobs these tests are essential.

The main objective of selection activity is to select the most suitable person in terms of job specification and for such purpose selector needs data, information about the employees, their attitudes, skill, competences, abitily to perform and so forth. Shaun Tyson and Alfred York (1982) stated that effectiveness in employee selection requires:

(i) Awareness of the essential nature of the task and its inherent problems.

(ii) Clear and comprehensive definitions of the criteria for effective performance by job analysis.

(iii) Understanding the implications of the concept of reliability and validity for employee selection.

(iv) Awareness of the range of possible selection methods, their potential values and predictive capabilities.

(v) Thorough training for selectors to make them aware of the inherent problems and to develop the necessary skills for effective practice, for example, training in interviewing skills.

(vi) A follow-up system to check how well the predictions made in the selection process have turned out in practice.

The selection task is difficult task with all its inherent and unavoidable limitations. Looking to nature of job, organizational structure, mission, strategy steps in employee selection are decided. The following are the usual steps in selection process:

1st step : Processing of Application Forms

2nd step : Selection Test

3rd step : Selection Interview

4th step : Verification of antecedence background

5th step : Medical Examination

6th step : Selection Decision

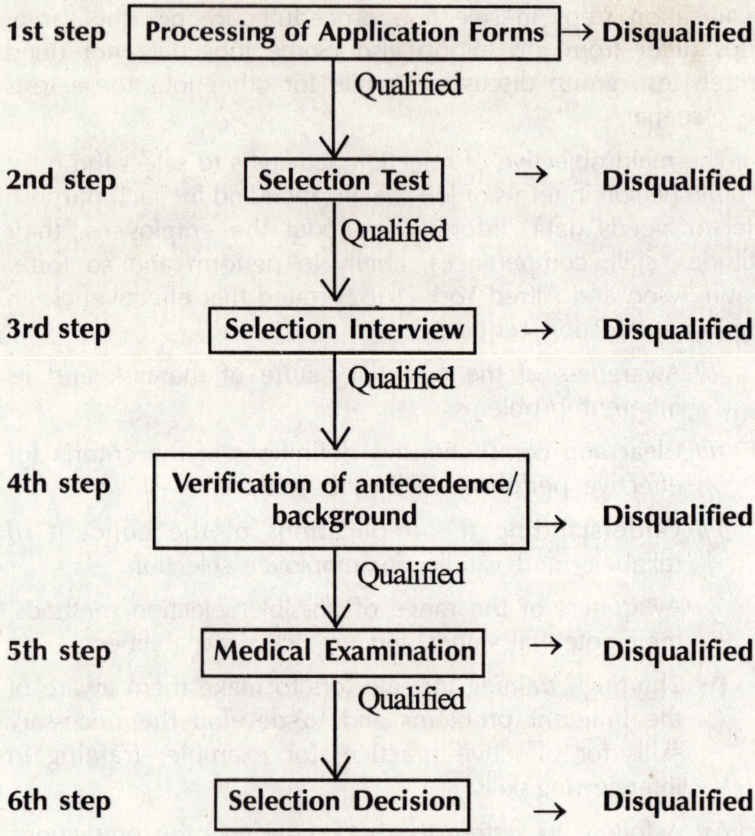

Figure 3.2 : Flow Chart of the Selection Process

Each step in selection process is important as decision taking factor is involved. Favourable positive decision of one step makes the activity of next step continue. That means, candidates must qualify / pass in each step to obtain job offer. The flow chart of the selection process is shown in Figure 3.2.

First Step : Processing of Application Forms

Information in respect of candidates (i.e. particulars of candidates in respect of age, qualification, experience, marital status etc.) are received as follows:

- Unsolicited applications (applications designed / structured by applicants themselves / curriculim vitae.)
- Application Forms

In most cases, required information are not available from unsolicited application. So, management designs application format (application blank / form) and obtain information from the applicant. However, most organizations do not use a particular application format for all the jobs. Such organizations prepare different sets of application, forms for different categories of jobs / professions. So, nature of information called for, varies from job to job. Generally, the information required to be furnished by the applicants is called on the following items :

(i) Personal and family information

(ii) Marital status

(iii) Physical data

(iv) Educational qualifications

(v) Work experience

(vi) Salary-present and expected

(vii) Extra-curricular activities

(viii) Details of previous employment

(ix) References

On receipt of application forms from the candidates management starts the exercise to screen / process the applications to find out whether candidates fulfil the criteria in terms of job specifications / advertisement. So, applications are liable to be rejected on job related reasons.

Second Step : Selection Test

After screening application forms next step is to predict amongst qualified candidates as to who will be successful on the job. So, the use of a test to assess job performance ability is a must.

Selection tests attempt to measure intelligence, personality traits and abilities of the candidates. Performance simulation tests including work sampling and assessment centres are used by the management in the organization to find out potential candidates to perform the jobs successfully.

Various tests are conducted by the organizations as selection tools. Some of the commonly used selection tools / tests are

- Aptitude Test
- Intelligence Test
- Personality Test
- Achievement Test

The use of Graphology, Poligraph and Honesty tests is also made by some organizations.

Third Step : Selection Interview

The Interview is considered to be an effective tool of the organizations to select personnel of all categories. W.D. Scott expressed that 'an interview is the purposeful exchange of ideas, the answering of questions and communicating between two or more persons. It is not conversation for the sake of conversing, a social relationship.' It is a process of collecting information from the candidates by the interviewer to find out suitability for job. It may be traditional interview i.e. single interviewer interviews the applicant or panel interview involving several individuals who interview an applicant at once.

Some interviewers prepare questions and expected responses before hand and accordingly they conduct interview exercises. In some cases, interviewers create an uncomfortable milieu in which interviewee is put to the test to find out his level of confidence, stress tolerance and coping capabilities.

It occurs that interview tool is not used properly, rationally to predict candidate's abilities, skill, competence, aptitudes, attitudes to match with jobs. The reliability and validity of interviews are found to be low because of the following reasons:

- Interviewer's lack of thorough knowledge, understanding of subjects tends him to make 'accept errors', 'reject errors' in selection decission.
- Interviewer's personality, human relation skill affect the interviewee.
- Interviewee's dress, manners, mode of expression, physical appearance influence judgement/decision of interviewer.
- The order in which applicants are interviewed often affects interviewer's judgement.
- Data/information of applicants received by the interviewer prior to interview creates an image / impression about applicants on the mind set of interviewer that influences evaluations.
- Negative information influences much to the interviewer.
- Interviewer may forget the quality of response made by the applicant within minutes after conclusion of the interview.
- Interviwer's likes and dislikes may affect interviewer's judgement.
- Interviewer sometimes favours the candidate who shares his attitude.

In order to make the interview effective and unbiased, the following measures may be adopted

(i) Interviewer should have thorough knowledge about job description so that, he can assess employee specification in terms of job description.

(ii) The interviewer should ensure congenial environment so that applicant feels comfortable. Interviewer may start talking in a very informal way on some common aspects.

(iii) There should be consistency in asking questions to the applicant. The interviewer should ensure to structure the interview schedule and to see that interview follows a set procedure.

(iv) The interviewer should have proper training with regard to conducting interview, norms, codes, jurisdictional area of asking questions etc.

(v) The interviewer should review the application form/ resume of the candidate and should jot down the weak, ambiguous areas for clarification in the interview discussion.

(vi) The Interviewer should record his observation in the course of interview discussion to help him to evaluate applicant's suitabilty at a later stage.

(vii) The interviewer should give much emphasis on observing, listening to the applicant rather than talking too much. This way interviewer obtains adequate information.

(viii) The evaluation form should be standardized.

(ix) The interviewer should make judgements on the basis of the factual information he obtains about candidate's attributes, skills, competences, experience in relation to the employee specification.

Fourth Step : Verification of Antecedence / Background

This step is required when an applicant's name appears on a list perepared for a particular job. One function of this step is to obtain information / report from the police authority with regard to applicant's antencedents and also his activities, character. This sort of information is required in case of employment in public sector banking organizations and some other organizations.

The another function is to verify the data / information from the person/s whose name is mentioned by the applicant in the application form as referees that the information provided by the applicant is true or otherwise. The other function is to obtain report from the referee/s in respect of character of the applicant.

References are required to obtain information to ascertain honesty, integrity, moral rectitude, character and track record of the applicant. Verification of applicant's antecedents and background may be made through :

- *Sending confidential letter by mail/courier service*
- Telephonic talk by senior executive
- Personal visit by responsible officer

References have some drawbacks. These are

(i) Applicant gives the names of such referees who can not give negative views. So the actual data / information can not be obtained.

(ii) Referees may be reluctant to express negative aspects of the applicant in writing.

(iii) As most of the referees are unwilling to make reports that may hinder somebody to obtain job, their opinions are not likely to result in accurate assessment.

(iv) The validity and reliability of references are rather poor (Hunter and Hunter, 1984)

(v) In most cases, reports from referees / Police authority are obtained much late than the time / date stipulated. However, some organizations offer jobs to the candidates conditionally subject to receipt of satisfactory reports from the police authorities and in the event of having received unsatisfactory reports the applicants are informed that they are liable for termination from services.

Fifth Step : Medical Examination

Since some jobs require certain physical characteristics, medical examination has some validity. If the applicant requires to take medical examination, organization should have reasoning behind this requirement that such activity is job related.

The main objective of medical examination is to see that the applicant is physically fit to perform the job assigned to him.

That means, the applicant should have physical fitness to perform the job without any injury or physical difficulty. So, to obtain appointment letter / job offer the applicant should have satisfactory medical examination report/medically fit report, that means applicant is medically suitable for the specific job.

Sixth Step : Selection Decision

This is the final step in the selection process. The activity under this step is very important as final decision is taken from the pool of candidates who pass tests, interview, reference verification and medical examination. Line manager in consultation with HR executive / manager ascertains the strengths and weaknesses of each candidate. Line manager also looks to economic implication, present and future demands of the job, matching of individual specification with job description and then takes selection decision.

The job offer is sent to the selected candidates through letter of appointement that contains, inter alia, the date by which appointee is required to report for duty. Unsuccessful candidates are also intimated about the decision of the management.

Assessment Centres

Assessment centres are events rather than physical places. A variety of assessment methods viz., interview, leaderless group discussion, management games, personality traits, individual presentation, objective tests and in-basket / in-tray exercises are used in assessment centres.

Assessment centres are generally used for executive selection, promotion and development purposes. Modi Xerox, Crompton Greaves and some other organizations are using such techniques successfully. Various performance simulation tests are administered to such centres. Its use is made largely for ascertaining potential of executives for their development and elevation. The activities / functioning of assessment centres are given below :

(i) Assessment centre's activity focuses on behavioural manifestation of the candidates.

(ii) Candidates'performance, potential inputs and competences are assessed by trained senior line executives and in some cases psychologist's help is taken to assess / ascertain strengths and weaknessess of candidate's mental state, ability, emotion and ego pattern.

(iii) Candidates are required to face a series of tests, interviews and group exercises. The whole process/ exercise generally takes 2 to 4 days.

(iv) Assessors, usually in pairs, observe and record the behaviour of candidate in individual and group situational problems. In a situation where clinical psychologist is engaged, summary of personality tests is recorded.

(v) Ratings of each candidate's performance in different tests, interviews, group exercises etc. are taken together and an overall rating is prepared.

(vi) Assessment centre attaches much importance / emphasis on the area of assessing stress tolerance, creativity, decision making, communication skill, assertiveness, planning and organization ability, coping capability, diagnostic skill, ability to develop culture of mutuality etc.

Shaun Tyson and Alfred York (2001) have suggested for application of some principles, to the establishment of assessment centres. They are :

1. Assessment centres need expert assistance to design.
2. Extensive research on exercises is required to establish centres' validity and reliability.
3. The observers / assessors must be properly trained and must have practised observation.

4. The administration of centre must be professional, with suitable accommodation available, and documentation well prepared in advance.
5. Candidates, whether successfully or not, should be given expert feedback on their performance, and reasons for selection or non-selection.
6. Confidentiality must be maintained with data.

Assessment centers have following advantages

(i) Assessment centre creates confidence amongst candidates and assessors.

(ii) Candidates' leadership, communication skills, problem solving skills, coping capability, reaction to stress, pressures can be seen through the use of such techniques.

(iii) Candidates get the opportunity to measure their capability through participation in the centre's test exercises, so that they can decide whether they are likely to fit or not.

(iv) Feedback provision of this tool helps the candidates to build on their strengths and tackle their weaknesses.

(v) Assessment centres have high reliability and validity as a selection tool.

(vi) The cost of mounting assessment centre for selection purpose is justified, as the test exercises ensure that wrong people are not selected or elevated.

Assessment centres have some disadvantages. They are:

(i) The selection tool is time consuming and costly to administer.

(ii) Assessors give much more importance on non performance related factors (viz. appearances, social skills, attitudes of candidates) than performance related factors.

(iii) It adversely affects the morale of the candidates who are not selected to participate in the exercise.

(iv) Employees feel morosed, a sense of uncongenial atmosphere and partisan attitudes of assessors when they are not promoted, selected for higher posts.

Evaluation of Selection Programme

The aim of selection programme is to select the right type of people with skill, competencies, values, personality as per job specification. This is possible to select the suitable people if recruitment / selection activities are designed, programmed and accomplished perfectly, judiciously, systematically and strategically. So, effective selection is the ultimate objective of the selection programme. That means selecting or hiring productive, competent effective people, who are capable of producing goods and services as per company stipulation/schedule.

It becomes essential to find out the effectiveness of selection programme as the company's survival, growth, development depends upon the quality of human resource it has. If the company could hire skilled, talented and competent people it is possible to produce quality goods and services to satisfy customers' needs and to achieve individual goals, team goals and organizational goals. Now, the question arises as to how the efficacy of the company's selection programme can be evaluated?

The answer is evaluation of programme through HR audit, interview and survey.

HR audit : It includes some of the important activities

- To see whether company has defined-policy in respect of recruitment, if so, whether recruitment is made as per policy, procedure.
- To examine the wage / salary programme, extent of welfare, social security benefits, fringe benefits, incentives and to make a study to find out from other similar industry in the locality whether any variation / difference in above areas is noticed.

- To see whether company has career planning and development scheme and, if so, whether the concerned persons are well aware of such scheme.
- To verify and check from the promotion policy to find out whether selection is made in conformity with the policy.
- To see whether there is any provision in the policy to give extra benefit to the extra ordinary talented candidates if so, whether this is complied with.
- To see whether application/use of some specific selection tool has been made.
- To verify the records whether interviewers are well trained and have sound knowledge, exposure, competence in the concerned area.
- To see whether all effective sources of recruitment have been utilized, if so, whether the company's position, job prospect, job description and specification have been rightly highlighted.
- To verify from records to find out the extent/number of 'accept errors' and 'reject errors' in selection decision.
- To verify and check up from records to ascertain absenteeism, production, productivity of the employees whose selection has been identified as 'accept error', and to make a comparative study with the average employee.
- To ascertain from exit records the number of employees resigned and the cause of resignation.
- To verify and check up from records to ascertain the cases relating to 'discharge', 'dismissal', 'termination' 'retrenchment' of employees of the company and to see whether such delinquent ex-employees are from those who have been selected wrongly.

Interview

Interview with
(i) the persons who have left the organization.
(ii) the persons who have been selected wrongly.

(iii) the persons who have been rejected wrongly.

(iv) the persons associated with consulting/ private agencies, campus recruitement in university / institutes. may give some idea regarding selection tools used, treatment made by selectors, procedures followed in conducting interview etc. Effectiveness of selection programme can be assessed to some extent through interview exercise.

Survey

Organization can make some assessment through survey method as to whether the workers in general are happy with the compensation package, promotion policy, participation scheme, recruitment programme, management style of functioning, company philosophy, supervision. All these aspects convey the signal of employees' acceptance to management policy, procedures.

If, the above measures are taken in a planned and systematic manner through well trained personnel, effectiveness of the selection programme can be assessed.

Books Recommended

1. Dale Yoder et al : Handbook of Personnel Mangement and Labour Relations (McGraw Hill Book Company, New York, 1958)
2. W.D.Scott : Personnel Management : Principles, practices and point of view (Tata McGraw Hill Publishing Co. Ltd. New Delhi, 6th Edn.)
3. Shaun Tyson and Alfred York : Essentials of HRM (Butter-worth - Heinemann Jordon Hill, Oxford 2001)
4. R. Wood and T. Payne : Competency - based Recruitment and Selection (Wiley, Chichester, 1998)

5. C. Woodruffe : Assessment Centres (Institute of Personnel Mangement, London, 1990)
6. J. Munro - Fraser : A Handbook of Employment Interviewing (Macdonald & Evans, London, 1954)
7. R. Edenborough : Using Psychometrics (Kogan Page London, 1994)
8. J. Toplis, V. Dulewicz and C. Fletcher : Psychological Testing (Institute of Personnel Management, London, 1991)
9. Milton M. Mandell: The Selection Process (D.B.Taraporewala Sons & Co. (P) Ltd., Mumbai, 1970)
10. George Strauss and Leonard R. Sayles : Personnel : The Human Problems of Management (Prentice Hall of India Pvt. Ltd., New Delhi, 1980)
11. G. Roberts : Recruitment and Selection : A Competency Approach (Institute of Personnel and Development, London, 1997)
12. Gary Dessler : Human Resource Management (Prentice-Hall, Inc. Upper Saddle River, New Jersey 07458, Eighth Edition, 2000)
13. J.E. Hunter and R. F. Hunter : Validity and utility of alternative predictors of job performance (Psychological Bulletin, 96(i), 1984)

Questions

1. Define the term 'recruitment'. Do you find any difference between recruitment and selection? Elaborate those differentiating areas.
2. 'Recruitment is a linking activity between job seekers and job providers with necessary stimulation to the former' - Do you agree? Justify.
3. 'One of the objectives of human resource management is to help strategic human resource management' — How will you justify this statement?

4. What do you know by recruitment? What are the sources of recruitment? Discuss the merits and demerits of external sources of recruitment.
5. Do you think internal sources of recruitment are much more advantageous than external sources of recruitment?- Discuss in support of your views.
6. What is selection? State the purposes of Selection.
7. What do you know by 'techniques of recruitment'? Is there any difference between techniques of recruitment and sources of recruitment? Discuss
8. (a) Discuss some important techniques of recruitment used by most of the organizations in India.

   (b) What are the parameters for selection of a specific technique of recruitment in an organization?
9. 'Selection process goes through different steps that vary from organization to organization, even in the same organization steps in selection procedure differ from job to job? Do you agree this statement? Discuss.
10. What is 'assessment centre'? How does it help the organization in the hiring process of executives?
11. 'To make the assessment centre activities effective some principles need to be applied in a planned and systematic manner' — Do you agree? What are those principles.
12. How will you evaluate the efficacy of the selection programme of a company?

Case Study No. 1

After doing MBA (HR) from a reputed University in West Benagal Mr Rakesh Mahapatra has joined a medium size Cotton Textile Mills in Ahmedabad as HR Executive. On the first day of his joining he was introduced to the executives, staff, some trade union members and workers of the factory. Mr Mahapatra liked the environment of the factory and induction programme arranged by the company. He enjoyed the day very much.

The factory runs a single shift from 8 am. to 5 pm with a rest pause for one hour. The duty hour of Mr Mahapatra starts from 7am to 12 noon and from 2pm to 6 pm. On the second day of joining of Mr Mahaptra two of the union leaders of the recognised union of the factory came to Mr Mahapatra at about 5-15 pm to discuss some Labour issues. They requested him to give them some time for such purpose. Mr Mahapatra turned down their request and cautioned them not to come to him in future without appointment.

In the above context discuss the following :

(i) Do you think Mr Mahapatra has done the right thing?

(ii) What could be the appropriate way to tackle such issue?

Case Study No 2

Mr A.K. Singh has been working as Chief of Human Resource Management Department of a large size Cotton Textile factory in Mumbai. The main activities of the factory include spinning, weaving, dyeing and printing of high quality cloth, bed covers etc.

The total strength of employees is as follows:

Workers	1700
Clerks	75
Executives :	
Jr Management :	80
Middle Management :	45
Sr Management :	25
Top Management :	7
Supervisors (non-executives)	35
Sweepers, watch and ward staff, peons, maintenance staff	38
Total	**2005**

The company has 30 casual / badli workers who are engaged to work in place of permanent workers during the period of their absence.

The company has earned reputation in the market. Some of its achievements include

(i) market share of the company in textile industry in India in 2003 is 45%

(ii) human resources of the company are certified as excellent (i.e. world class work force with high degree of commitment, acceptance to changing situations)

(iii) the company has obtained Outstanding Performance and Quality Award in 2001, 2002 & 2003.

(iv) the training institute of the company is ranked first (in respect of quality training imparted, number of courses offerd, transfer of learning to work, faculty competences etc.)

(v) this is the only company in textile field that uses assessment centre for selection and development of executives.

In the recent Board Meeting the following resolutions have been taken for implementation

(i) to recruit 20 workers and 40 junior executives.

(ii) to promote 10 middle management and 3 senior management executives.

(iii) to open one unit in the factory for expansion of printing activities.

The Executive Director Mr L.N. Kumar sends a note to Mr Singh directing him to submit his comments / views on points No. (i) & (ii) immediately to him so that acquisition/ promotion process can be completed within 2 months. Mr Singh is also asked to look into the following aspects while submitting his views:

(*a*) Selection process

(*b*) Type of Tests to be conducted

(*c*) Use of assessment centre

(*d*) Recruitment technique to be used

(*e*) Sources of recruitment

You are advised to submit your views / comments as Chief of Human Resource Management Department of the above factory.

4

Wages and Salary Administration

Compensation : Meaning

Employees give labour and in exchange for labour/service they want money and other benefits. Such money and other benefits are compensation. The term 'compensation' may be defined as the money paid for the job performed and the benefits/services provided to the employees. The compensation is given in the following form.

Compensation

Monetary/Direct	Non-Monetary/Indirect
i.e. wages or salary	welfare measure, social security, paid holidays, earned leave/ privilege leave, sick leave, etc.

Wage

The dictionary meaning of the term 'wage' is the pay of artisans or labourers receiving a fixed sum by hour, day, week or month, or for a certain amount of work. In a narrow sense 'wage' is the remuneration paid to blue-collar workers for their services, usually on hourly rate or daily rate.

Thus we find that

- wage is remuneration
- it is paid to workers, especially maintenance and production workers
- it is payment in exchange for service / labour
- it is paid generally on fixed hourly / daily rate

Wages may be expressed in terms of money called nominal wages, or in terms of purchasing power with reference to some base year called real wages.

In broad sense, 'wage' refers to economic compensation paid by the employer to his workers in exchange for their labour / service, under some contract. So, wage includes basic wage and also allowance like overtime pay, holiday pay etc.

Salary

Salary is a periodic, fixed payment for services, especially for official or professional services. It usually refers payment to weekly or monthly rated employees like clerical, technical, supervisory and managerial employees.

From the above it is observed

- Salary is economic compensation
- It is a periodic fixed payment
- It is paid to white-collar employees like office staff, technical staff, managerial staff, professional staff
- It is paid by employer in exchange for services rendered by above categories of employees

Thus, 'Salary' is defined as economic compensation paid by employer to his monthly / weekly rated white-collar employees for their services, under any contract / agreement.

Wage Structure

Every organization formulates different scales of pay and grades for its employees; and employees are paid in terms of scales/grades they are fixed (for example, seven Officers' Grade and Scales in banking industry, viz. JMG/S I,MMG/S II, MMG/S III, SMG/S IV, SMG/S V, TMG/S VI and TMG/S VII) Such pay scale with ranges of pay within a particular grade is wage structure. That means, wage structure is a wage/salary relationship within a particualr grade. Each pay grade has a range and that the ranges overlap. Organizations design wage structures in each grade for a particualr period of service tenure and when employees reach the top of their grade they cannot have increment in pay if they do not move to a higher grade.

Objectives of Compensation Planning

Organization designs compensation plan to achieve its goal. So, compensation needs to be attractive to make the people happy, contented and to create a committed, loyal workforce. As we know human resource can make anything happen, so achievement of organizational goal is possible, if employees intend to do so.

Employees can put in their best efforts for achievement of goals, when they find compensation plan of the organization is favourable for their growth and development. Necessity for designing a reasonable attractive compensation plan with clear objectives is felt. So, the main objective of compensation management programme is to pay adequate, rational salaries / wages to make the employees happy, satisfied and contented to run the organization smoothly and effectively. Pay is decided on the basis of work performance (both quality and quantity), responsibilities and compensation paid by competitors. That means, objective of compensation programme is to ensure that equity (i.e. internal equity, external equity and individual equity) in respect of payment of salaries / wages is maintained. Some important objectives are mentioned below:

1. Justice to the worthy job

A lot of scales, grades are prevalent in organizations. Employees work in different scale/grades. The objective of the compensation management is to ensure that justice is made on the job. That means, employees doing complicated, worthy jobs get higher pay and benefits than other employees in the organization.

2. Rationale monetary compensation to employees doing similar nature of job

Employees who perform jobs similar to jobs employees of other organization/s perform may not get equal pay. Effective compensation management ensures that employees doing similar nature of work get rationale pay.

3. Attracting dynamic workforce

One of the objectives of a good compensation management is to design compensation plan in such a way that dynamic, qualified, experienced and world class employees are attracted and join the organization.

4. Retention of competent, effective workers in the organization

If the employees get much better compensation package as compared to other organizations they may not leave such organization. So, compensation benefit scheme is prepared appropriately to retain effective, competent employees in the organization.

5. Creation of a reservior of committed, loyal workforce

Organization can confront challenges, can face competition and can develop if it has a committed, loyal and world class workforce. One of the objectives of an effective compensation system is, to give attractive pay and to provide excellent benefit and services to the employees, so that they become committed, loyal to the organization.

6. Smooth and effective functioning

Organisation's functioning is disturbed due to agitational programmes of employees. Issues of agitation are mainly monetary compensation and non-monetory compensation. So, for smooth and effective functioning of organizational activities an attractive compensation scheme is prepared.

7. Achieving competitive level of performance

For achieving competitive level of performance (that is level of work quality, productivity or performance) competitive pay structure needs to be formulated.

8. Complying with legal provisions

Various labour laws have been enacted to protect the interests of employees. So, the employers are required to comply with statutory provisions and they need to pay salaries and provide benefits to their employees not less than the standard/ ceiling prescribed.

9. Motivating employees

Compensation management programme is an effective motivator for optimum job performance. So, organizations design compensation programme to make the employees feel that they are adequately compensated.

10. Valuing employees

Organizations formulate compensation management programme to value employees on the basis of skill, competition and contribution.

11. Encouraging employee behaviour

Effective compensation management encourages employees to behave positively to make changes in the organizations that will contribute to the achievement of the organization's goals.

12. Promoting customer's delightment

Customer's satisfaction/delightment comes through delivery of quality services/goods by employees and this happens when employees feel that compensation is adequate and attractive.

13. Controlling Cost

For successful operation of an organization it needs to control employee costs. But, it does not mean to control cost by giving them less than standard fixed. Effective compensation management programme designs compensation scheme to ensure that, employee cost is controlled and employees are not deprived of fair and reasonable compensation.

14. Establishing healthy industrial relations

Effective compensation management makes collective bargaining successful that contributes to the development of mutual understanding, trust and confidence between management and employees. All this promotes healthy industrial relations in the organization.

Objectives of Wage & Salary Administration

Wage and salary administration is a part of human resource management function. It is a vital area of HR activities. A company which introduces well defined/administered wage and salary package (compensation package) can be able to procure, utilize and retain competent and effective human resources. Developmental activities become smooth in such company. So, it is essential for the company to have sound, effective and rational wage and salary administration.

The objectives of compensation and administration programme are :

- to ensure maintenance of equity in respect of payment of salary/wages in terms of equal pay for equal work.
- to establish a system of job analysis so that job description and job specification activities can be accurate and specific.

- to create a pool of talented, skilled and dynamic work force, so that they can deliver quality goods and services at reasonable cost.
- to make employees aware of wage and salary policies, procedures, practice, latest amendments (if any), so that they can make comparative study with other organizations to find out salient changes/variations if any.
- to ensure effective control over all activities concerning wage/salary, welfare, social security, fringe benefit, incentive, bonus etc.
- to introduce a system for complying with provisions of law, statutes and for proper implementation of agreements, settlement in respect of compensation of employees.
- to make evaluation of jobs so that there can not be any dissatisfaction amongst employees in respect of their wages / salaries and other benefits.
- to evaluate employee performance accurately for identification of performers and non-performers so, that steps can be taken to develop competencies for performance of present jobs and future jobs also.
- to develop mutual understanding, faith and confidence between employees and management through introducing fair and attractive compensation package.
- to ensure maintenance of internal equity, external equity and individual equity in respect of providing compensation to employees.
- to establish cordial and healthy industrial relations as most of issues which arise out of wage and salary areas are given weightage.
- to make the employees happy, contented and committed through satisfaction of their physiological needs so that functioning of organization becomes smooth and undisturbed.
- to develop a 'culture of reciprocality' among two parties

(employer and employees) to contribute to each other through introduction of attractive compensation package.

- to ensure organizational effectiveness by way of creating contented and committed workforce.

Steps involved in determination of Wage Rate

Determination of wage rate of employees is one of the basic activities of management. Good wage package creates a situation for attraction of outside/external candidates for any organizational job and also for retention of existing dynamic, competent employees in the organization. So, organization's survivality, growth and development depend to a great extent on quantum of wages employees recieve from the organization. Attractive compensation makes the people contented, happy, loyal, drives them to produce quality goods and service, facilitates to promote healthy industrial relations. Hence, fixing rational, justified and appropriate wage rate for employees is of great need today. For determining such wage rate organization needs to take steps like:

- collecting information from other companies in respect of wages paid by them to their employees (wage survey)
- evaluation of each job (ascertaininig worth of each job) of the organization.
- classifying similar jobs into pay grades (establishing pay grades)
- developing wage curve for assigning pay rates to each pay grade.
- developing pay-rate level (pay rate ranges) and adjusting pay rates.

Collecting Information

Organization collects information from other similar organizations in the locality for the purpose of refixing pay rate of employees

- through wage survey conducted by the organization itself

- through wage survey conducted by external agency/ consultancy firm
- from reports / survey published by Government agencies, private firms, employers' association, trade unions and from other secondary sources.

Organization uses wage survey data to determine rate of benchmark jobs, to decide feasibility of providing fringe benefits and to establish pay grades and pay rate ranges.

Data collected relate to

(i) wage rate of different categories of employees

(ii) welfare facilities, fringe benefits, social security measure

(iii) minimum wage, maximum wage and average wage

(iv) pay grades, pay rate range

(v) number of employees, employee compositions, classification etc.

Job Evaluation

It is systematic process of evaluation of one job as compared to other job in an organization. It determines the relative worth of each job. Organisation has a large number of jobs which are assigned to employees. These jobs are not same, some are important and some are less important. So, worth of jobs varies from each other in terms of efforts, skill, responsibility, working condition, problem solving etc. This ascertainment/assessment of job's relative worth is made through job evaluation.

Job evaluation activity includes

- creation of a conducive atmosphere to accept this mechanism to determine worth of one job as compared to other job.
- obtaining co-operation from all concerned viz, supervisors, union representatives, employees and human resource specialists.

- constituting job evaluation committee
- identification of benchmark jobs
- determining factors for comparison viz responsibility, skill etc.
- deciding method for evaluation of jobs (like ranking method, job classification/grading method, point method, factor comparison method)
- evaluating worth of each job with the use of any one method.

Classifying similar jobs into Pay Grades (Establishing Pay Grades)

For ascertaining relative worth of each job evaluation committee finds out jobs which are nearly similar to each other in respect of skill needed, responsibility shouldered, efforts required and the like. These jobs have similar job evaluation scores. The committee then classifies such jobs into pay grades on the basis of some norms stipulated for such purpose (e.g. pay grade may comprise of all jobs falling within two or three ranks in case of ranking method used).

Now, question arises with regard to the number of pay grades the organization should have. It generally depends on :

- employees' strength
- number of evaluated jobs
- organization's structure
- corporate policy
- decision in respect of number of points to be assigned for each grade.

However, it needs to ensure that moderate number of pay grades is established to cover most of jobs in pay grades.

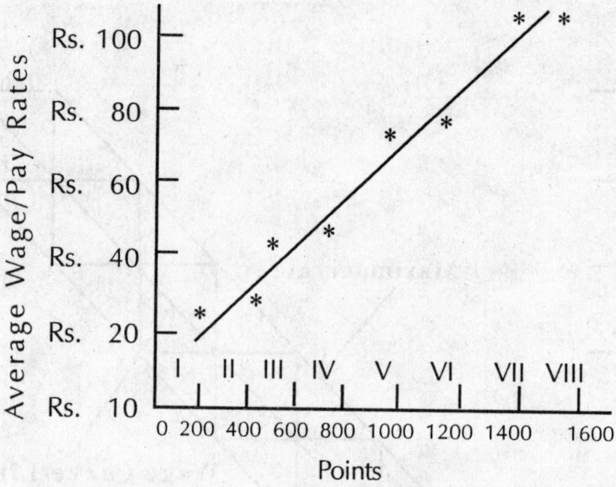

Figure 4.1 : Wage Curve Using Job Evaluation Points

Developing Wage Curve for assigning pay rates to each pay grade

After pay grades/ranges are prepared the evaluation committee takes step to price each grade. That means, pay rate for each grade is determined. For such purpose wage curve is developed.

The wage curve focuses the relationship between the value of the job and the current average wage/pay rate for grades/ jobs. *This is shown in Figure 4.1*

Pricing pay grades includes the following steps :

- ascertaining average wage/pay rate for each pay grade and showing the same on the vertical axis.
- showing pay grades, in terms of points along the horizontal axis
- plotting the wage rate for each pay grade
- fitting a 'wage line' through the points plotted
- pricing jobs.

Developing pay rate level/ranges and adjusting pay rates

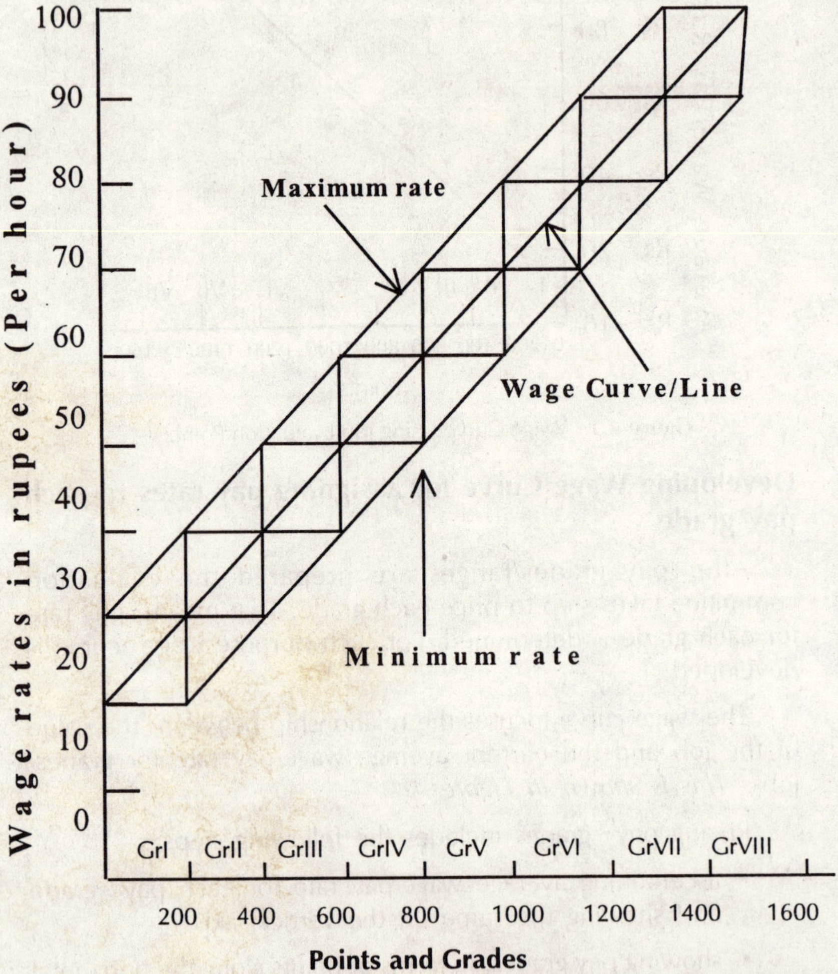

Figure 4.2: Pay Rate Ranges

Employees may not be happy if they remain at a particular pay rate and do not get yearly pay increase. They want increment in particualr scale. That means, they desire for pay range (pay scale). Companies also want to establish pay ranges as a measure to motivate and retain the competent employees and also to attract the quality employees by offering higher pay rate in a grade. So, necessity to develop pay rate level (pay rate ranges) is felt. For each grade a pay range is established. Movement of steps within a grade depends on number of years' service, performance rating and some other factors.

Pay rate level (pay ranges) is shown in Figure 4.2 which depicts minimum pay rate, maximum pay rate, target wage rate (i.e., wage line) and also a state of overlapping pay grade.

Wage line indicates target wage/salary rates. Company may pay wages/salary above or below the wage line or may pay targeted wage/salary rate along the wage line. So, employees may be overpaid, underpaid or may be paid rightly. In case of over payment and underpayment adjustment of payment is made by pay frreze and pay raise respectively.

Job Analysis

Meaning

Job analysis is the process of careful observation of a job and collecting, recording and analysis of all pertinent information to make the management enable to use the information effectively. So, job analysis relates to systematically study of job to provide data/information to the management to use for different purposes. It is the process of determining, by observation and study, and reporting pertinent information relating to the nature of a specific job (U.S. Department of Labour, Employment Service, Training and Reference Manual for Job Analysis, Washington, 1944, PI). It is a systematic study of information relating to the operations and responsibilites of a specific job.

Job analysis activities include the following

- observation of a job
- collection and recording of information particularly in the area of work performance, behaviour dimension, work schedule, incentive, personal qualitative attributes, job related knowledge, skill, performance standard in terms

of quality and quantity level for each job duty, material processed, products made, service rendered etc.

- analysis of information
- providing information to the higher management

Purpose of Job Analysis

Job analysis is a mechanism of analysing information of job that helps human resource specialists to perform basic activities effectively and smoothly. The whole process of HR functions starting from acquisition / hiring of people for the organization, till their exit from the organization involves a series of important information about job, and such information are available through job analysis. So, job analysis contributes to effective functioning of HRM activites.

Job analysis programme has various purposes. Some of the purposes are discussed herein below.

1. HR requirement

Job analysis helps to ascertain future needs of human resource through detailed and thorough analysis of job content. Such information facilitate human resource planning activities of HR planner. One of the purposes of job analysis is to make human resource planning meaningful and effective.

2. Training decision

Employees need training for development of their competencies. All employees may not require training of the same programme; some may need improvement of technical skill, some may require behavioural training, some may need to increase conceptual skill and the like. Hence, for nominating employees in the specific training programme management should have valid and reliable information. Job analysis provides necessary information to the management.

3. Performance review

Most organizations have developed a system to appraise

performance of employees for achievement of individual goals vis-a-vis organizational goals. The appraiser compares the subordinate's actual performance with the standard set for him/her. This standard is fixed through job analysis mechanism.

4. Identification of sources of recruitment

Organization needs to initiate recruitment exercise to search out and stimulate prospective employees for filling some posts. To make this exercise effective necessary information / data are needed. Job analysis provides information to the organization with regard to the sources from where potential candidates can be available.

5. Selection of candidates

Selection exercise becomes effective if right people are selected in terms of job requirement. So, selectors should have information with regard to job specification, job description to choose the perfect candidates and this information is available through job analysis.

6. Wage and Salary administration

Job analysis data help to determine the worth of each job. Job pricing depends on some factors like working conditions, level of education, skill, responsibility, efforts, safety and hazards. All these factors are assessed through job analysis. So job analysis helps to make wage and salary administration effective.

7. Coping with change situation

With the advancement of science and technology and also invention of new ideas, devices, methods, techniques a lot of changes take place in different areas of activities in an organization. For survival, growth and development organization needs to accept change and confront challenges arising out of changes. It can be possible for an organization to cope with change situation if it gets reliable and actual information on regular basis. Job analysis provides such information to an organization so that it can grow with changes.

8. Congenial and conducive work environment

Organization can take necessary measure to improve working condition, safety arrangement on the basis of the information provided through job analysis. So, job analysis helps to create a congenial and conducive work environment by way of pin pointing weak areas when rectification is required.

9. Creation of committed, contented and satisfied workforce through redressing grievances

Job analysis provides information with regard to the issues/ grievances of the employees which need immediate redressal for making them satisfied, happy and committed. On the basis of job information organization can take measure to solve employees' problems to create a satisfied, committed workforce.

10. Healthy industrial relations

One of the purposes of job analysis is to promote industrial relations situation of the organization. Job analysis provides information about the employees who are happy and who are unhappy. On the basis of job information organization can take suitable measure for improving industrial relations situation in the organization.

Steps Involved in Conducting Job Analysis

Job analysis involves indentification of all important information about a job. To perform such task

- it needs support of the top management
- it is necessary to make the people know the objectives, purposes of job analysis
- supervisors' support, assistance and help is required to job analyst
- it needs full cooperation of the concerned employees and also of their union to carry out job analysis programme

Then following steps as shown in Figure 4.3 are taken to conduct job analysis

1. Indicating the purpose of job analysis

First step is to indicate the purpose for which job analysis is required to be conducted. Identification of the purpose is necessary as selection of technique / method for collecting information becomes perfect if the purpose / use of job analysis is known beforehand.

2. Analysis of organization chart, workflow and job description to obtain background information

In this step job analyst needs to collect background information viz

- the importance of the relevant job in the organizational setting in relation with other job
- how the jobs are related with each other
- the contribution of the concerned job as also other jobs to the growth and development of the organization
- input and output flow of job
- existing job description to provide a starting point to prepare revised job description.

The above information is available from the organization chart and workflow.

3. Selection of representative positions for analysis

It is not possible for the job analyst to analyse all jobs in the organization. The representative positions (i.e. the jobs which are similar) are selected and analysed. This is done looking to the costs involved, time required and urgency for completion of the task.

4. Collection of data for job analysis

For the purpose of job analysis data are collected with the

use of appropriate techniques. Generally, collection is made on the following areas.

- job activities,
- skill, abilities, efforts needed
- qualities, traits required to perform the job
- working conditions
- employee behaviours
- responsibilities

5. *Verification of information collected for job analysis*

It is necessary to verify the information collected for job analsysis with the employee performing the job and also with the supervisor under whom employee works. Through verification process, the concerned employee can come to know whether the data collected by the job analyst are correct or not. The employee develops confidence on the job analysis mechanism when factual data are taken for analysis and accepts those data collected by job analyst.

6. *Creation of a Job Description*

This step involves creation of a job description. It is necessary as each employee wants to know what he is expected to do? How it is to be done? What standard is set? And what is his level of performance? From all these the employee can know the job description. The job description identifies and describes contents of a specific job, activities, accountablities and responsibilities of the job in a clear and concise way as well as important characteristics of the job.

7. *Developing a Job Specification*

After preparation of the job description the next step is to develop a job specification. It is importantly needed to prepare job specification as for effective accomplishment the job may demand for a particualr type of person. The job specification indicates requirement of various factors normally found in the job, like:

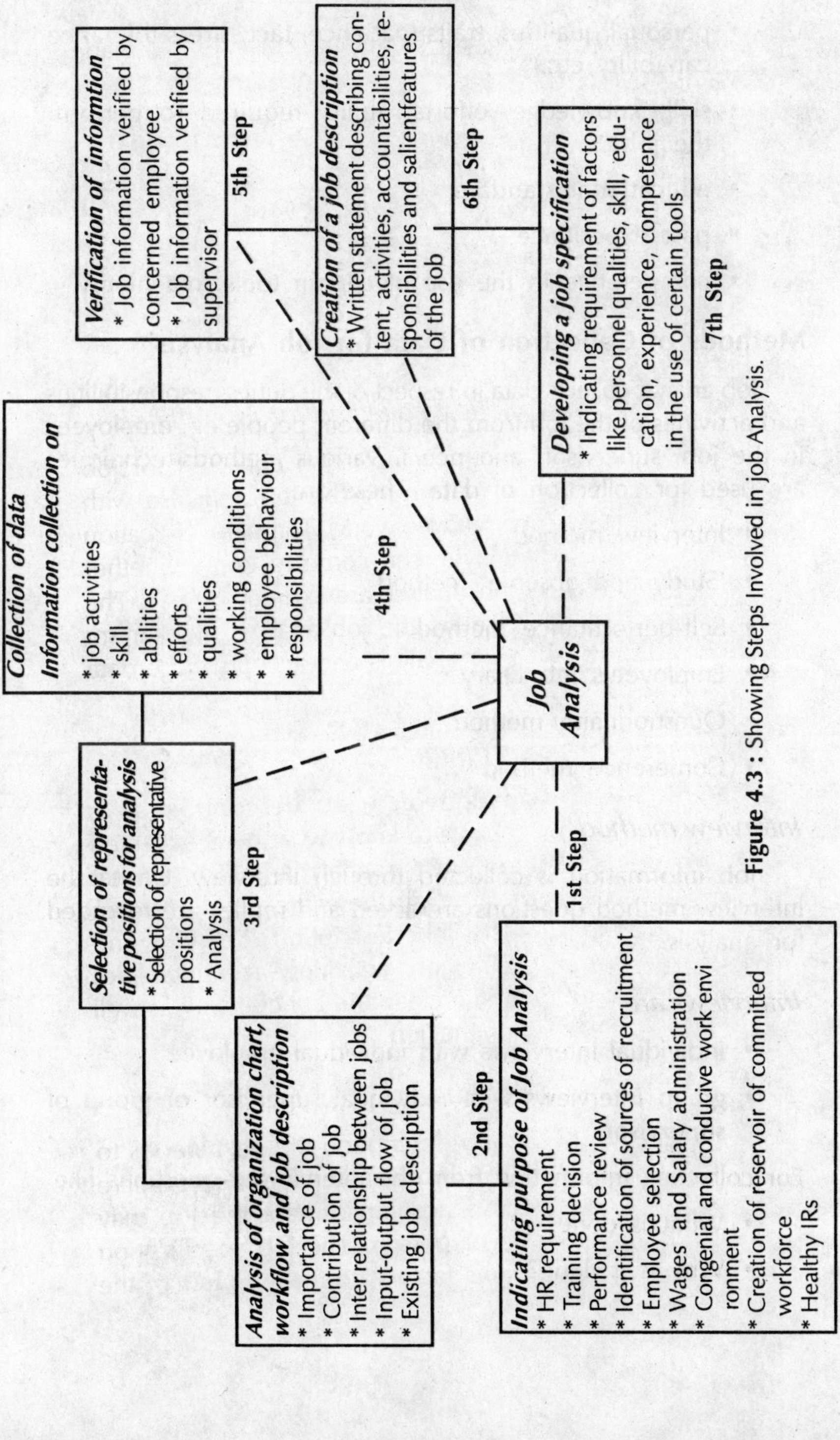

Figure 4.3 : Showing Steps Involved in Job Analysis.

- personal qualities, traits (patience, tact, stress tolerance capability etc.)
- skill, knowledge, efforts, ability required to perform the job
- educational standard
- past experience
- competence in the use of certain tools, machinery

Methods of Collection of Data for Job Analysis

Job analyst collects data in respect of the duties, responsibilities and activities of the job from the different people eg. employees in the job, supervisor, and peers. Various methods/techniques are used for collection of data. These are:

- Interview method
- 'Study and observe' method
- Self-performance method
- Employee's Job Diary
- Questionnaire method
- Conference method

Interview method

Job information is collected through interview. Under the interview method questions are asked and replies are recorded for analysis.

Interviews are

- individual interviews with individual employee
- group interviews with individual supervisor or group of supervisors

For collecting information from the interviewee questions like

- What is done?
- Why is it done?

- How is it done?
- When is it done?
- To what is it done?

are asked during interview. Questions are structured in such a way that the interviewee supplies all information about the job activities performed by him, as also characteristics of the job to the job analyst.

Interview method is very easy to use for collection of information. Generally, employees like to respond to questions made by those people who are very much interested to know their job activities, working conditions, hazards etc. Through well designed and effective interview job analyst may come to know some new area of activities / behaviour which may help him to arrive at some conclusion. Job analyst may get complete information at a short time from the employees, as they use this platform to elicit their difficulties, hardship etc. to others. Interview method is very much expensive. In large organizations it is difficult to use, to collect information. Employees may not give actual information / data to job analyst as they feel these data will be used for determining their pay rates and fringe benefits. Collecting information through interview method needs extra skill and ability of job analyst. Interview results are difficult to analyse.

Study and Observation Method

The another method of collecting information for job analysis is through study and observation of the job people do. This method involves:

- watching of the whole process of job activities and time taken to complete each process and also the entire process
- observance of situation, conditions under which an employee works
- study of responsibilities shouldered by the employee
- review of job performance of employee through films
- watching of the materials, tools used to perform job

This method is effective when jobs involve physical activities that are measurable. Job analyst gets thorough idea regarding the jobs employees perform. So job performance information becomes correct and accurate. This method yields reliable results as the data are collected through direct observation. Collection of data is very easy as it does not need extra skill, ability of the analyst.

This method is not free from limitations. It becomes unreliable and ineffective when jobs consist of unmeasurable mental activity (that means jobs need mental work, decision making, judgemental activity, planning, directing, controlling etc.) In some cases, job performance information may not be correct as constant watch of analyst over a job may create such situation where employees can not function freely and properly. It requires much time to complete the information collection exercise especially, in cases when employees occasionally need to perform some work.

Self-Performance Method

Under this method, job analyst engages himself to perform a job and records information. The approach of this method is like 'perform job and obtain information'. Job analyst through performance of job gets understanding of

- the whole process of activity i.e. job cycle
- time taken to complete some activity
- the hazards and difficulties faced to perform job
- the working environment, machines, tools used, supervision needed
- skill, ability, knowledge required to complete the job

This method is effective for job analysis when jobs are very simple and are easy to perform. But this method does not yield results if, the jobs are technical in nature and are difficult to perform without training. The scope of use of this method is limited.

Employee's Job Diary

Another technique to collect information on job is to use diary maintained by the employees to record their day to day activities in their work performacne. This method has the following characteristics:

(i) Each employee is given a diary to keep records of his daily activities

(ii) At the end of each work shift, the employee starts writing on the diary (a) all the activities he had undertaken that day (b) the time taken for completion of any process of activity (c) difficulties, problems if he had faced to perform his job.

(iii) Job diary needs to be maintained for a long period so that all activities are covered.

(iv) Information recorded by the employee in the diary are verified / checked by the concerned supervisor to ensure that factual data are taken.

This method is simple to use as it does not need extra skill, ability to record information. Since, employee himself writes diary it is possible that all job performance information are recorded.

Diary method is time consuming as it takes much time to collect information for job analysis. The employee may not remember the job activities at the end of workshift when he records in the diary. So, the data is based on assumption the employee holds.

Questionnaire Method

This is one of the methods used by organization to collect job information. Under this method job related questions are prepared and employees are asked to reply to the questions. This method is very much popular to gather information concerning job related duties and responsibilities of employees.

Questionnaires are of two types—structured questionnaire and open ended (unstructured) questionnaire. In case of structured questionnaire a long list of possible task items is designed and sent to employees with the request to indicate whether or not they perform the tasks as mentioned in the questionnaire and if so, how much time is taken to perform each task. Open ended (unstructured) questionnaire is very simple that asks the employees to describe something in respect of their job related duties, responsibilities etc. The question may be like 'state the major duties you perform'.

The specially designed questionnaires are sent to employees who submit them to supervisors after duly completed/filled out. Supervisors after verification, consultation with concerned employees, if need arises, give those questionnaires to the job analyst.

The questionnaire method is easy to use for collection of job information. Coverge of population under this method is wide. Questionnaires are sent to a large number of employees. So, it is a speedy and excellent way for gathering information at a shorter period of time. Costwise this method is cheap for collection of information.

The method is not free from limitations. Designing questionnaire (i.e. area coverage, type and number of questions to be asked for etc.) needs special skill. Employees may take it casually to fill out questionnaires and to return them. Generally, employees avoid to submit information in writing that may be due to their inability to express or due to their unwillingness to respond to the questions mentioned in the questionnaire. The preparation of questionnaire is also expensive and time consuming.

Conference Method

This is one of the methods of collecting information for job analysis. Under this method job analyst gathers information relating to job of employees through experienced and knowledgeable supervisors.

Conference method includes the following activities :

- Selection of areas, subject matter over which questions will be asked to supervisors
- Deciding on number of questions to be asked, design of questions whether open-ended or structured questions
- Structure of time for completion of interview with supervisor

This method yields results if supervisors are effective, competent, experienced and have a great depth of knowledge on subordinates' job. Collection of job information through this method is time consuming and expensive.

Job Evaluation : Meaning

Job evaluation is a systematic process that determines the relative worth of jobs within an organization. Various types of jobs are performed by employees in an organization. Some are different in respect of efforts, duties, skill, working conditions and reponsibilities to each other and some are similar belonging to same group or category. Some jobs are more important, some are less important in organizational activities in relation with other jobs. Most important job holders can obviously expect better pay structure and other fringe services, than the less important job holders. It is, therefore, necessary to establish a mechanism or a process to determine the relative worth of jobs, to develop a rational basis for the design and maintenance of an equitable pay structure, and also of a fringe service pattern in an organization. This mechanism / process is job evaluation. Job evaluation ascertains the worth or value of job, not the performance of people. The process does not look into the individual abilities or performance of the people at work.

Methods of Job Evaluation

There are many methods used to evaluate jobs. Out of them, the following four methods are frequently used:

- Ranking method
- Job Classification method
- Factor Comparison method
- Point method

Two of these methods (ranking and classification) are non quantitative while other two methods (factor comparison and point) are quantitative. But, all these methods need well written elaborate job description for evaluation of the jobs.

Ranking Method

This is the most simple method used for determining the relative worth of jobs in an organization. Job evaluation is made through comparison of one job with other job in an organization. The whole job, not the factors or components of the job, is compared. After comparison, ranking order is made from highest to lowest. Ranking method involves the following activities.

- Collection of information relating to all jobs within the organization
- Obtaining job descriptions data for each job
- Selection of rater (generally committee comprising of both management and employee representatives is assigned the job)
- Comparison of job (i.e. comparing of one job with other job) in terms of importance or difficulty
- Ranking of jobs
- Pricing of jobs (money values of non-key jobs are determined on the basis of monetary value of key jobs which is known)

Advantages

(i) This method is simple to understand

(ii) This is very much effective in case of small

organization where number of jobs is less and employees know the importance of each job.

(iii) It does not take much time to know the results of evaluation.

(iv) This method looks to the entirety of jobs while comparison is made. It, therefore, ensures that all significant areas are taken into consideration.

Disasdvantages

(i) It is difficult to use in big organization where number of jobs that need evaluation are many.

(ii) Raters / Committee members may not have thorough knowledge of all jobs of the organization. So, proper evaluation of jobs may not be possible.

(iii) It is difficult to compare jobs which have equal value/ worth

(iv) The method is subjective as no standard/yardstick is used to justify ranking. Ranking is made on the basis of perception committee members/raters hold a bout the jobs.

(v) It does not indicate the distance between jobs ranked.

(vi) In case of new jobs ranking method may not be effective.

Job Classification Method

Job classification method is a non-quantitative method for job evaluation. Under this method different jobs within an organization are ascertained and divided into various grades. The jobs requiring similar effort, knowledge, ability, responsibility are placed in same grade and evaluation is made after ranking of job grades.

Classification method involves the following activities :

- Listing of jobs operating in organization
- Establishing grades with distinct number on the basis of some criteria like responsibility, effort etc.

- Perparation of grades / classification description
- Ranking each position's job description against the classification/grade description
- Placing each job in appropriate classification
- Assigning money value to the key grades and other grades subsequently.

Advantages

(i) This method is very easy to understand. So, the evaluators may not need training to carry out job evaluation exercise. Employees also can understand without any difficulty.

(ii) It is easy and less expensive to introduce this mechanism for evaluation of jobs in organization.

(iii) This method is rational for making evaluation of jobs as grading is made taking into account of the vital factors like responsibilities, efforts, knowledge, skill, ability etc.

(iv) It looks to entirety of job, not some aspects of job.

(v) It is useful and effective in small organizations as number of jobs are few.

(vi) It is very easy to compare pay grade of one organization with that of other organization.

Disadvantages

(i) It is difficult and time consuming to prepare grade description.

(ii) It is subjective especially in the area of selection of number of different categories / grades and also of ranking of key jobs.

(iii) Placing of jobs into grades is not an easy task.

(iv) Grade descriptions which are inflexible in nature tend to be unconcerned with the situation arising out of

organization development and technological advancement.

(v) New jobs may not fit any existing grade.

Factor Comparison Method

Factor comparison method is a quantitative method used for evaluation of jobs in an organization. Each job consists of some factors. Under this method, key jobs are decided and all other jobs are compared to such key jobs based on factors that are present in all jobs.

Factor comparison method involves the following activities

- Selection of key jobs that are well known to everyone within the organization. Such key jobs that are found within the organization consist of representative characters.
- Identification of factors that are present to some degree in all jobs in organization. Generelly, factors like mental requirements, physical requirements, skill requirements, working conditions and responsibility are widely used.
- Describing / defining of factors so that the evaluators can have thorough knowledge about such factors.
- Evaluation of key jobs through ranking on a factor by factor basis. Ranking of key jobs is done
- Conversion of ranking into money rates. Existing wage rates for key jobs are taken to find out the worth of each factor in each key job as shown in Figure 4.5
- Evaluation of all other jobs in organization, through comparing each job to the key jobs on a factor by factor basis.

The factors of each job are examined to decide to which factors of key jobs they closely resemble, and money rates of those factors are taken for fixing the worth of such job. In Figure 4.4: key jobs of an organization are shown as A, B, C, D, E while factors are taken as mental requirements,

Key Jobs	Mental Requirements	Skill Requirements	Physical Requirements	Responsibility	Working Conditions	Total
A	5	5	2	5	2	19
B	4	2	5	4	1	16
C	3	4	3	2	3	15
D	2	1	4	3	4	14
E	1	3	1	1	5	11

(5 is top ranking)

Figure 4.4: Sample Key Job Rankings

Key Jobs	Mental Requirements	Skill Requirements	Physical Requirements	Responsibility	Working Conditions	Existing Total Hourly value (Rs.)
A	5	5	2	5	2	**19**
B	3.50	1.75	4.37	3.50	0.88	**14**
C	2.40	3.20	2.40	1.60	2.40	**12**
D	1.43	.71	2.86	2.14	2.86	**10**
E	.73	2.18	.73	.73	3.63	**8**

Figure 4.5: Money rates of key jobs

[***Note :*** Conversion of the ranking of factors into money values i.e. rupees is made assuming that the existing hourly wage rates for A, B, C, D, E key jobs are Rs.19, Rs.14, Rs.12, Rs.10, Rs.8 respectively.]

skill requirements, physical requirements, responsibility and working conditions. The key jobs are ranked on a factor by factor basis and the organization ranks each of such key jobs from top to bottom, for each of the factor.

In Figure 4.5: conversion of ranking into rupee value is shown using the present wage rate of each key job. The worth of each factor which is proportionate to the total wage rate of concerned key job is also shown.

The evaluation of other jobs is made by comparing each such job with the key jobs on factor by factor basis and also looking to such aspect of job that closely resembles to key jobs. After this money rates are determined.

Advantages

This method has the following advantages:

1. This method is easy to understand. Employees, union members, committee members can not find difficulties to comprehend modus operandi of the system.
2. No training is required to implement this system.
3. This is a justified method of evaluating different jobs in an organization as relative values are determined through comparing of other jobs with key jobs.
4. Standard jobs / bench mark jobs vary from organization to organization. Looking to different perspectives, organization requires to set key job for its own use. So, emphasis is given on the need and requirement of organization.
5. Since number of factors generally remains in the range of five to eight, possibility of overlapping or not considering any component is remote.

Disadvantages

This system has a number of disadvantages. They are:

1. Selection of key jobs is a difficult task that needs expertise, special skill and ability

2. This is a costly method to construct.
3. Use of same factors / criteria to assess all jobs in an organization may not be effective in situations when jobs vary within the organization.
4. Ranking of job factors is made on assumption / subjective assessment.

Point Method

The Point method is widely used to evaluate jobs in organizations. It is a quantitative technique of job evaluation. Under this method components / factors of jobs are ascertained and defined, degrees of each factor in jobs are decided, points are assigned for each degree of each factor, corresponding points of each factor are summed, jobs with similar point value are placed in similar pay grade / scale.

The point plan involves the following activities for job evaluation

- *Indentification of key jobs.*

  Benchmark jobs are identified for the purpose of job evaluation

- *Description of key jobs*

  Job description is made to let the committee members know that such sorts of work are actually performed.

- *Selection and description of factors*

Factors that are commonly present in jobs are selected (e.g. skill, responsibility, working conditions, physical activity etc.). Such factors are described to give the overall view / idea to the evaluators, in respect of factors and also the importance / influence of the respective factors for performance of jobs.

- *Ascertainment of number of degrees and description of degrees for each factor.*

  The number of degrees of each factor is ascertained to express exact amount or extent of factor existing in a job. So, total number of degrees varies from factor to factor. Details of degrees are described to make the evaluator easy to place factors in the appropriate degrees. An example of one factor-'skill' in respect of clerical employees of a management institute involving five degrees is shown in Table 4.6.

- *Assigning points to factors and degrees*

  Evaluators examine each job on a factor-by-factor basis and ascertain the degree that job fits into for each factor. Then factors and degrees are weighted or assigned points.

- *Preparing job evaluation manual*

  Job evaluation manual is prepared by the evaluation committee members. Such manual, which is also called 'point manual', contains factor and degree definitions, point values and job descriptions.

- *Rating jobs*

  Evaluators rate jobs with the help of point manual. First, they rate key jobs and after that they rate rest jobs. Job rating activities include:

  - determination of degree in respect of factors
  - finding out respective points assigned to degrees
  - adding points for all factors to ascertain total point value for each job.

Table 4.6 : Example of factor - 'Skill' under Point Method describing basic skill required for the clerks to perform the given job

Degree	Points	Description of characteristics
1	2	3
1st	10	Routine clerical job like filing, sorting, recording in registers, comparing, verifying letters, certificates / diploma
2nd	15	Use of sophisticated equipment, machine to cope with required speed of work, to perform job beyond routine work

1	2	3
3rd	20	Taking dictation, typing letters, reports etc,composing letters for surpervisor's signatures.
4th	25	Use of all types of machines, equipment including electronic typewriters for clerical work, clerical work mentioned in 3rd degree, making contact, arranging appointment with higher officials
5th	30	All clerical work including taking dictation, typing as described in the 4th degree as also ability to operate computers.

Advantages

This method has the following advantages

1. Point method is systematic and rationale to evaluate jobs in an organization
2. There is less or no chance for subjective judgement in evaluating jobs, as the factors and degrees are elaborately explained.
3. It does not require much expertise to use this method in organization for evaluating jobs.
4. This method gives accurate evaluation as points for factors / degrees are decided before job evaluation is made.
5. This method is acceptable to the employees and trade union members because it is difficult to manipulate evaluation.
6. Since, emphasis is given on 'point' factor not 'money' factor, this evaluation technique is unbiased and not influenced by any factor.
7. Each individual organization can use this method through selection of appropriate number of factors and degrees.

8. Rating scale prepared under point method for evaluation of jobs in an organization can be used for a long period.
9. Evaluation can be made for large number of jobs under this method.

Disadvantages

This method is not free from its limitation. It has following disadvantages :

1. Use of this method is much costly as, it needs substantial amount of money to conduct job evaluation exercise.
2. This method is very much time consuming. Selection of factors, determination of degrees and points, evaluation of jobs and completion of whole process need a lot of time.
3. It needs expertise to decide factors, degrees, point values.
4. Since, this point system is complex, employees, trade union leaders, supervisors find it difficult to understand the method.
5. It is difficult to change / modify any factor, degree or point value after a point plan is established.

Books Recommended

1. M. Armstrong and A. Baron : The Job Evaluation Handbook. (Institute of Personnel and Development, 1995)
2. M. Beer, B. Spector, P. Lawrence, D. Quinn Mills and R.Walton : Managing Human Assets (Free Press, New York,1984)
3. L. R. Gomez - Mejia and D. B. Balkin : Compensation, Organizational Strategy and Firm Performance (Cincinnati, South western Publishing, 1992)
4. M. Armstrong : Managing Reward Systems (Buckingham, Open University Press, 1993)

5. M. Quaid : Job Evaluation : The Myth of Equitable Assessment. (Toronto, University of Toronto Press, 1993)
6. D.W. Belcher : Wage and Salary Administration (Prentice Hall, New Jersey, 1962)
7. J.D.Dunn and F.M.Rachel : Wage and Salary Administration: Total Compensation Systems (Mc Graw - Hill, New York, 1971)
8. Richard Henderson : Compensation Management : Rewarding Performance (Upper Saddle River, NJ : Prentice Hall, 1994)
9. Gary Dessler : Human Resource Management (Prentice-Hall, Inc. Upper Saddle River, New Jersey, 2000)
10. Lawrence S. Aft : Wage and Salary Administration (Reston Publishing Company, Inc A Prentice-Hall Company, Reston, Virginia, 1985)
11. H.Chruden and A. Sherman : Managing Human Resources (Southwestern Publishing Company, Cincinnati, 1984)
12. J.Patton, C. Littlefield and S. Self : Job Evaluation (Richard D. Inwin, Homewood, Illinois, 1964)

Questions

1. What do you mean by 'Compensation'? What are the objectives of Compensation Planning?
2. What is 'wage'? Is there any difference between 'wage' and 'salary'?
3. 'A company which introduces well defined /administered wage and salary package can be able to procure, utilize and retain competent and effective human resource' - Do you agree? Discuss in support of your views.
4. Explain the steps involved in determination of wage rate.
5. What is job evaluation? Discuss job evaluation activities.

6. "Job analysis is the process of careful observation of a job and collecting, recording and analysis of all pertinent information to make the management enable to use the information effectively." - Discuss
7. What are the steps taken by Job Analyst to conduct job analysis?
8. "Various methods / techniques are used for collection of data / information"- What are those methods? Discuss.
9. What are the methods of job evaluation? Discuss the important methods used to evaluate jobs with its merits and demerits.
10. Discuss the main differentiating points between Ranking Method and Point Method.

Case Study

Mr. A.P. Verma has been working as Human Resource Executive in a Software company in Saltlake, Kolkata for the last 3 years. The company is not much old. It started its first business activities in 1998.

The company has 115 executives and 10 assistants in its permanent roll as on 31.01. 2004. All the executives have been recruited through Campus Recruitment technique from management / engineering institutes. Recently, the company has received a lot of complaints from the customers with regard to the quality of its product. To know the level of attitudes of the executives the company arranged to conduct attitude survey of the executives through a reputed private agency XYZ Consultants with the assistance of the factory's HR Audit, Information & Research Cell. The survey team collected information / data (i.e. response of executives) through Interview / Questionnaire method under 5 point scale. MR P.K. Master, Managing Director has received the Survey Report a few days back.

The analysis of the Report reveals that more than 80% of the executives expressed their unhappiness towards pay, promotion and job. It is also revealed from the company's records that turnover rate of executives is very much on the higher side.

Mr. Master called Mr. Verma and asked him to submit his plan of action to reduce the turnover rate of the competent executives.

In the above context discuss the following :

(*a*) What suggestions will you submit to MD as HR Executive of the company?

(*b*) When does the compensation package act as motivator?

(*c*) Do you think that if all the executives are promoted to the higher posts, turnover rate of executives will be zero?

5

Welfare Programme, Fringe Benefits

Meaning of Welfare

The dictionary meaning of 'welfare' is, the condition of faring well, prosperity or organized efforts by a community or organization to improve the social and economic condition of a group or class.

Generally, the term 'welfare' means, efforts made for well-being of individual/s. The well-being relates to physical, mental and emotional wellbeing of an individual or individuals. The efforts may be made by the State, non-government organizations, clubs, companies, community and the like. The recipient of benefits may be an individual or individuals or a group or a class. Labour welfare means efforts made by the employers, trade unions, non-governmental agencies, and governmental agencies for wellbeing of the employees. The Encyclopaedia of Social Sciences defines labour welfare as 'the voluntary efforts of the employers to establish, within the existing industrial system, working and sometimes, living and cultural conditions of the employees beyond what is required by law, the custom of the country and the conditions of the market (Encyclopaedia of Social Sciences Vol. XV, 1935,P395). The ILO at its Asian Regional Conference includes under labour welfare such services, facilities and amenities as may be established in or in the vicinity of undertakings to enable the persons employed in them to perform their work in healthy, congenial surroundings and provided with amenities conducive to good health and high morale (ILO, Asian Regional Conference Report, 1950, P3).

There is no precise definition of labour welfare. Different authors have defined 'labour welfare', in different ways. However, labour welfare means the facilities provided by the employers to their employees in terms of laws and through voluntary efforts or such facilities given by trade unions, governmental and non-governmental agencies for wellbeing and upliftment of their social and economic conditions.

Objectives of Labour Welfare

There is necessity to provide welfare measures to the employees for making them happy and contented. Workforce may remain with the organization when they find that, in addition to wages, company gives them fringe benefits to carry on their lives comfortably and conveniently. So, stable and loyal workers community is created in such situation.

The objectives of labour welfare are discussed below:

(i) To enhance the level of morale of employees.

(ii) To create a loyal, contented workforce inorganization.

(iii) To develop a better image of the company in the minds of the employees.

(iv) To enable the workers to live comfortably and happily.

(v) To develop efficiency of the workers.

(vi) To reduce influence of trade unions over the workers.

(vii) To expose philanthropic and benevolent activities of the company.

(viii) To make the workers know that the company takes care of them.

(ix) To develop positive attitude towards job, company and management.

(x) To reduce tax burden.

(xi) To develop a feeling of satisfaction of employees with the company.

(xii) To develop a sense of belonging to the company.

(xiii) To retain skilled and talented workers.

(xiv) To develop better human relation.

(xv) To prevent social evils like drinking, gambling through improvement of working conditions, cultural activities and social conditions.

Types of Welfare Programme

Two types of welfare programmes are introduced in the company for the betterment of the socio-economic conditions of the employees.

Types of welfare programme are

(i) Intra-mural welfare services

(ii) Extra-mural welfare services

Intra-mural welfare services

Intra-mural welfare services are those welfare activities which are provided within the factory. They are

- Canteen
- Creches
- Rest Shelters
- Washing and bathing facilities
- Uniform and protective clothings
- Drinking water
- Latrines and urinals
- Health and counseling services

Extra-mural welfare services

Extra-mural welfare services are those welfare activities which are provided outside the factory. They are

- Housing facilities
- Education facilities
- Recreation facilities including reading rooms, library, sports
- Holiday homes
- Leave travel concessions
- Transport facilities
- Co-operatives, consumers and credit societies

Welfare services may also be categorized into two ways viz. statutory and non-statutory.

Statutory welfare activities

Statutory welfare activities are those facilities and services, which are provided in terms of provisions of different acts. Such Acts are: The Factories Act, 1948, The Plantation Act, 1951, The Mines Act 1952, The Motor Transport Workers Act, 1961, The Merchant Shipping Act, 1958 Dock Worker's (Safety, Health and Welfare) Scheme, 1961, The Inter-State Migrant Workmen (Regulation of Employment and Conditions of Service) Act, 1979.

Non-statutory welfare activitie

Non-statutory welfare activities are those facilities and services, which are provided by the company voluntarily. For providing such welfare measure company is not responsible under law. Non-statutory welfare measures are like education of employee's children, fair price shop, loans for house building etc.

Approaches to Labour Welfare

Labour welfare concept has originated from the 'well-being' 'doing good' to people at work philosophy. Such feeling develops through a series of interactive processes over a period of time.

Today's welfare concept is not the same as it had been few decades ago. Technological advancement, changes in work practices, methods, devices, stiff competition, liberal thought pattern, paradigmal shift, change in strategic approach of business magnets and the like, lay much more importance on labour welfare activities. There are different other factors also that generate a feeling of providing welfare measures to the workers in the organization. So, approaches to labour welfare are many. However, the main approaches to labour welfare are:

- Protection approach
- Appeasement approach
- Humanitarian approach
- Traditional approach
- Human resource development approach
- Social service approach
- Human relations approach

Protection approach

This concept emanates from the paternalistic philosophy. The state government takes care of the employees and ensures that employers provide welfare measures for promoting social and economic conditions of their employees. The state enacts various labour laws concerning labour welfare, binds the employers to comply with the provisions for such laws, and protects the interests of the employees. The government also provides welfare benefits through creation of its fund.

Appeasement approach

Some employers think that workers may not create problems if some benefits in the area of welfare activities are provided. Such employers, to purchase peace and to keep running of business activities provide welfare facilities to their people at work.

Humanitarian approach

Workers are provided welfare benefits by the employers, non-government agencies, trade unions and philanthropists from humanitarian perspectives.

The concept is to promote the welfare of mankind. It is thought that employees as human beings need some welfare facilities for their growth and development.

Traditional approach

This approach indicates that some welfare benefits are required to be given to the employees as the customs, practices demand. Some employers think, that the scheme for providing customary allowances, facilities which have been introduced few decades ago, should not be discontinued. So, welfare measures are provided.

Human resource development approach

People are treated as human resource. Their skill, competencies are required to be developed; their attitudes, personality, aptitude need to be improved to produce quality goods and services to confront challenges, to achieve organizational goals. Labour welfare measures improve social, economic conditions of employees that facilitate development process of human resources.

Social service approach

Organization as a part of society can not deny social obligation. Some employers arrange for providing welfare measures like health benefit, education facilities, and water facilities to societal people, including employees of the organizations.

Human relations approach

Employers can run business activities effectively and smoothly, if healthy human relations between employee and management (boss and subordinates) are established. For developing human relations employers need to be happy and contented. Welfare measure can contribute to some extent to make the employees happy and satisfied.

Meaning of fringe benefits

The term 'fringe benefits' is not of recent origin. In the early phase of the industrial development of India, fringe benefits, which, consisted mainly of gratuitious payments were provided by the employers to their employees to meet contingencies like physical disability, sickness or insecurity on retirement. Coverage of fringe benefits has subsequently increased.

Now, let us know the meaning of the term 'fringe benefits'. Fringe benefits are simply those benefits which are given to the employees by the employers in addition to their salaries/wages. International Labour Organization (1956) in a study entitled 'International Comparisons of Real wages has defined fringe benefits. According to it, 'wages are often augmented by special cash benefits, by the provision of medical or other services, or by payments in kind that free part of the wage for expenditure on other goods and services. In addition, workers commonly receive such benefits as holidays with pay, low cost meals, low rent housing etc. Such additions to the wage proper are sometimes referred to as fringe benefits. The ILO also has indicated that 'benefits that have no relation to employment or wages should not be regarded as fringe benefits, even though they may constitute a significant part of the worker's total income. This seems fairly obvious in the case of public parks, sanitation services, police and fire protection, etc.

Fringe benefits are also described as 'sub-wages', 'social charges', 'wage supplements', 'welfare expenses', 'Trans pecuniary incentives', 'non-wage labour costs' or 'extra wages'.

Types of Fringe Benefits

Different types of fringe benefits are provided by the organizations. Nature of fringe benefits varies from organization to organization as the objectives, mission, strategy; vision and size of organizations vary.

However, following types of fringe benefits are provided to the employees by the employers:

1. *Fringe benefits paid for time not worked*

Under this heading fringe benefits include

- Casual leave with pay
- Earned/privilege leave with pay
- Sick/medical leave with pay
- Special leave with pay
- Paid holidays
- Paid travel period for attending meeting, training.
- Paid reporting/joining time

2. *Fringe benefits paid for profit and other bonus*

Fringe benefits under this heading are

- attendance bonus
- service bonus
- gratuitous payments
- profit sharing bonus
- waste elimination bonus

3. *Fringe benefits paid under statute or legal awards*

Benefits payable under this head can be classified under two groups viz,

(*i*) social security benefits and (*ii*) other obligatory benefits

Social security benefits include

- gratuity
- pension
- employer's contribution made to the employee's state insurance scheme

- employer's contribution made to the employee's provident fund

Other obligatory benefits include

- retrenchment compensation
- lay off compensation
- welfare cess payment under Coalmines Labour Welfare Fund Act.
- supply of protective clothing in the plantation industry

4. Fringe benefits under Voluntary Schemes

Fringe benefits provided by the companies under voluntary schemes are

- medical care
- educational scholarship to employee's children
- interest free festival loan
- compensation for injuries, accident, disablement
- payment of life insurance premium
- subsidy in house rent
- canteen facilities
- transportation/conveyance allowance
- washing allowance
- holiday homes
- cultural facilities
- assistance to co-operative societies
- house building loan and other loan at concessional rate
- miscellaneous payment

Employees Stock Option

Employees Stock Option (ESO) is a scheme to make the employees part owners of the company. The main objective of ESO is to motivate the quality people by way of giving part-ownership of the company, so that, they remain with the company. It is seen that specialists, skilled and talented employees do not remain in a company for a long period and they switch over the company when they get much more benefits, perks in other company.

So, the present company makes a scheme to allot some company's shares to such employees at a price below the market price. This scheme, is employees stock option scheme. Under this scheme eligible employees are empowered to purchase a certain amount of stock of the company in future at some concessional price. Employees stock option scheme, inter alia, lays down the eligibility criteria, price of share, number of shares to be allotted to eligible employees, advance amount to be sanctioned, installment amount to be recovered etc.

The objectives of ESO scheme are

- To create a reservoir of skilled, talented, competent performers of the company.
- To make the people at work happy, contented and committed
- To retain the outstanding employees within the company
- To establish sound human relation
- To create a congenial, conducive climate of mutuality through developing understanding, confidence and trust between employees and management.
- To reduce employee turnover
- To achieve individual goals, team goals and organizational goals.
- To increase production, productivity
- To promote healthy industrial relations

Industrial health and safety: Concept

A major part of employee's waking time is spent with the organization. He naturally expects that, his employer should make arrangement to create a congenial and conducive environment for working in a healthy way. He also expects that his employer should take necessary safety measures, so that his health is not affected due to industrial accident. If, the employee is happy with the measures taken by the management in respect of provision of health and safety he develops a positive impression about the company. This mind set drives him to increase productivity and to improve quality.

Now, the nomenclatures industrial 'health' and 'safety' need elaboration. Industrial health refers to:

(i) providing healthy working conditions to workers

(ii) maintaining and promoting physical, mental and social well-being of workers from unfavourable working conditions that may cause injury to his physical and mental state.

(iii) protection of workers from unfavourable working conditions that may cause injury to his physical and mental state.

Basically, industrial health relates to promotion and maintenance of physical, mental and social well-being of workers, protection of workers in their employment from risks resulting from factors adverse to health and prevention among workers of ill-health caused by the working conditions.

Safety refers to prevention of accidents arising out of unsafe work conditions, defective plant / shop layout, unsafe space for movement inside the plant/shop etc. Safety measures reduce the accident rate to a great extent, although, the objective is to take all measures to make zero rate of accident, but in reality it does not happen, as some accidents are caused due to misacts of workers.

Statutory provisions regarding health

The Factories Act, 1948 makes detailed provisions in respect of health and safety of workers. These provisions impose upon the occupier or manager certain obligations to protect workers from accidents, and to secure for them an employment conditions conducive to their health and safety. Sections 11 to 20 of the Act, deal with the provisions under which work is carried on in the factories.

1. Cleanliness (section 11)

Every factory should be kept clean and free from effluvia arising from any drain, privy or other nuisance. Accumulation of dirt and refuse should be removed daily, the floor of every work room should be cleaned at least once in every week by washing using disinfectant.

2. Disposal of wastes and effluents (section 12)

Effective arrangement should be made in every factory for the treatment of wastes and effluents, and also for their disposal.

3. Ventilation and temperature (section 13)

Effective and suitable provision should be made for securing and maintaining in every work-room adequate ventilation, by circulation of fresh air, comfortable level of temperature. The walls and roofs should be of such materials and so designed that the temperature should be kept as low as practicable. High temperature should be reduced by white-washing, spraying, insulating, screening outside walls, roofs, windows.

4. Dust and fumes (section 14)

Effective measures should be taken for prevention of inhalation or accumulation of dust and fumes in work-rooms. Exhaust appliances should be applied as near as possible to the point of origin of the dust, fume or other impurity.

5. Artificial humidification (section 15)

In respect of factories in which the humidity of the air is artificially increased, State government rules should be followed. Water used for this purpose shall be taken from public supply or other source of drinking water.

6. Overcrowding (section 16)

There should not be overcrowding in any room of the factory and each worker should have 500 cu ft of space.

7. Lighting (section 17)

Sufficient and suitable lighting, natural or artificial or both should be made available in the factory where workers are working or passing. Effective provision should be made for the prevention of glare, formation of shadow to cause eye strain or the risk of accident to any worker.

8. Drinking water (section 18)

Effective arrangement should be made to provide at suitable points, sufficient supply of wholesome drinking water. All such points should be legibly marked 'drinking water' in a language known by a majority of the workers. Every such point should be away from washing place, urinals, latrine, spittoons etc. Provision should be made away for cool drinking water during hot weather if more than 250 workers are employed.

9. Latrines and urinals (section 19)

Latrines and urinals should be provided separately for male and female workers. Latrines and urinals should be adequately lighted, ventilated and maintained in a clear and sanitary condition. Sweepers should be employed for keeping latrines and urinals clean.

10. Spittoons (section 20)

A sufficient number of spittoons should be provided at convenient places and maintained in a clean and hygienic condition.

Statutory provisions regarding Safety

The Factories Act deals with safety of factory workers. The concerned safety provisions are contained in sections 21 to 40 which are discussed below.

1. *Fencing of machinery (section 21)*

Every dangerous part of machinery should be securely fenced by safeguards of substantial construction.

2. *Work on or near machinery in motion (section 22)*

Examination of any part of machinery while in motion should be made only by a specially trained adult male worker wearing tight fitting clothing. Woman or young persons should not be allowed to clean, lubricate or adjust any part of machinery in motion, if it would expose them to risk of any injury from the moving part.

3. *Employment of young persons on dangerous machines (section 23)*

No young person be allowed to work on any machine unless (i) he has been fully instructed as to the danger arising in respect of the machine and also the precautions to be observed and (ii) he has received sufficient training to work on the machine or is under supervision of a knowledgeable and experienced person.

4. *Striking gear and devices for cutting off power (section 24)*

Suitable striking gear or other efficient mechanical appliance should be provided and used to move driving belt to and from fast pulleys. Driving belt, when not in use should not be allowed to rest or ride upon the shafting in motion. Suitable devices for cutting off power in emergencies from running machinery should be provided and maintained in every work-room. When a device, which can inadvertently shift from 'off' to 'on' position, is provided in a factory to cut off power, arrangements shall be made to lock the device in safe position, to prevent accidental starting of the transmission machinery or other machines to which the device is fitted.

5. Self-acting machines (section 25)

No traversing part of a self-acting machine in any factory and no material carried thereon be allowed to run on its outward or inward traverse within a distance of 18 inches from any fixed structure which is not part of the machine.

6. Casing of new machinery (section 26)

All machinery driven by power and installed after 1st April 1949, should be encased or otherwise effectively guarded to prevent danger to those working in the factory.

7. Prohibition of employment of women and children near cotton-openers (section 27)

No woman or child shall be employed in any part of a factory for pressing cotton in which a cotton opener is at work. But if, the feed-end of a cotton-opener is in a room separated from the delivery end by a partition extending to the roof or to a specified height, women and children may be employed on the side of the partition where the feed-end is situated.

8. Hoists and lifts (section 28)

In every factory hoists and lifts shall be of good mechanical construction, sound material and adequate strength and shall be sufficiently protected by enclosures fitted with gates. The maximum safe working load shall be plainly marked on every hoist or lift, and no load greater than such load shall be carried thereon.

9. Lifting machines, chains, ropes and tackles (section 29)

In every factory, lifting machines, chains, ropes and tackles shall be of good construction, sound materials, adequate strength, free from defects and properly maintained.

10. Revolving machinery (section 30)

In every room in a factory in which the process of grinding is carried on, a notice indicating the maximum safe working speed of the machine shall be kept near it.

11. Pressure plant (section 31)

If any part of the plant or machinery used in a manufacturing process is operated at a pressure above atmospheric pressure, effective measures shall be taken to ensure that the safe working pressure of such part is not exceeded.

12. Floors, stairs and means of access (sections 32)

Floors, steps, stairs, passages and gangways shall be of sound construction and properly maintained. They shall be kept free from obstructions and substances likely to cause person to slip and handrails shall be provided where necessary.

Safe means, access to place at which any person is required to work, shall be provided and maintained as far as possible.

13. Pits, sumps, openings in floors (section 33)

Pits, sumps, fixed vessels, tanks, openings in the ground or in the floor, shall be securely covered and fenced.

14. Excessive weights (section 34)

No person shall be employed in any factory to lift, carry or move such load so heavy as to cause him injury.

15. Precautions against dangerous fumes (section 36)

No person shall be permitted to enter any chamber, tank, pipe, or other confined space in which dangerous fumes are likely to be present to such an extent as to involve risk of. persons being overcome, thereby, unless it is provided with a manhole of adequate size or other effective means of egress.

16. Precaution regarding the use of portable electric light (36A)

No portable electric light or any other electric appliance of voltage exceeding 24 volts, shall be permitted for use inside any chamber, tank, vat, pit, pipe, flue or other confined space in a factory.

If, any inflammable gas, fume or dust is likely to be present in any chamber, tank, vat. pit, pipe, flue or other confined space, no lamp or light other than that of flame-proof construction shall be permitted to be used in the factory.

17. Precautions against explosive or inflammable dust, gas (section 37)

Where in any factory any manufacturing process produces dust, gas, fuel or vapour which is likely to explode on ignition, preventive measures shall be taken by effective enclosure of the plant or machinery, removal or prevention of the accummulation of dust, gas, fume or vapour, exclusion or effective enclosure of all possible sources of ignition.

18. Precautions in case of fire (section 38)

In every factory, the door affording exit from any room shall not be locked or fastened so that it can not be easily and immediately opened from the inside. The exit routes shall be marked in a language understood by majority of the workers. In case of fire, effective and clearly audible warning be made. Every room shall have a free passage-way to give access to means of escape. Effective measures shall be taken to ensure that the workers are familiar with the means of escape in case of fire and are adequately trained in the routine to be followed in such case.

19. Specifications of defective parts (section 39)

The Inspector may ask the occupier/manager of the factory to furnish drawings, specification etc. to determine whether the concerned building, ways, machinery or plant can be used with safety and also to carry out tests in the specified manner and inform him of the results.

20. Safety of buildings and machinery (section 40)

If, any building or machinery is dangerous to human life or safety, the Inspector may issue order in writing specifying the measures to be adopted and requiring them to be carried out before a specified date.

The Inspector may also prohibit the use of such building, machinery, until it has been properly repaired or altered.

21. Safety officers (section 40 A)

In every factory where 1000 or more workers are employed, a safety officer shall be appointed to formulate safety procedures, policy, to promote schemes to guarantee observance of legal requirement, to act as chairman/secretary of the safety committee, to organize safety education, training.

Need for Social Security

It is felt pertinent to define the term 'social security' before 'the need for social security' is discussed. Social security means the protection given by the society to its members. So, the measures provided by the society to its members for their protection at the time of need arising out of contingent situation are social security. Societal members may have problematic situation due to their accident, retirement, sickness etc. During this period they may need monetary assistance, support in other form to maintain them and their families. This sort of support is a measure of social security.

Social security is the security given to the members of the society against some odds so that they can combat and survive.

The need for social security arises from the following:

- Medical treatment is required when an employee falls sick. During the period of his ailment he remains absent from his work and he can not earn. So, for his own maintenance and maintenance of his family, as also for his medical treatment monetary support is required. Social security provides such support.
- Women employees when they are on the family ways can not attend duties for some time in pre-natal and post-natal period. They need help and support for their sustenance. Social security measures provide maternity benefits to such women.

- There is a possibility to meet with an accident when employees work on machines. The accident may cause injury making the employees partial disabled or total disabled. It may also cause death. Under such eventuality, compensation scheme under social security measures may save the employees/their families from ruining.
- Old age is a curse to most human beings as during such time they lose their ability to perform work and can not earn. But, such people can find pleasure and meaning to survive if they are given retirement/pension benefit under social security measures.
- Employees' job is not secured. They remain afraid of losing jobs any time. Present business scenario adds to their apprehension. Company retrenches employees when their services are not required. After retrenchment it becomes difficult for the employees to carry on if no monetary support is received. Social security helps the retrenched employees to restart their way of life.

The need for social security is also felt from the following:

(i) It enhances the level of morale of the employees.

(ii) It increases production and productivity as employees feel happy and contented.

(iii) A climate of mutuality is established. Mutual understanding, mutual faith and confidence amongst management and employees is developed.

(iv) It becomes easy to make the employees accept changes in the organization. OD techniques can be introduced to improve quality of goods and services so that organization can face the challenges.

(v) A sense of belongingness, 'we feeling', 'togetherness', amongst employees is developed which helps to achieve team goals and organizational goals.

(vi) Organization providing social security measures can attract skilled and experienced employees and also can retain the best lots.

(vii) Social security acts as a motivational mechanism. It inspires employees to give much more attention on their production and services than on other areas of activities like planning for future employment, tackling of contingent situations, sorting out medical issues etc.

(viii) Social security measures help to create a committed, loyal and positive workforce.

(ix) Social security makes' a change in the mind-set of employees. Employees' perception about company, company's philosophy, style of functioning, objectives, mission also changes. Thus a congenial, conducive industrial climate is established.

(x) Social security brings peace and harmony in industry.

Social Security in India

Social security is the protection given to the societal members against some apprehended odds. ILO includes following components under social security scheme.

- Medical care
- Sickness benefit
- Unemployment benefit
- Old age benefit
- Employment injury benefit
- Family benefit
- Maternity benefit
- Invalidity benefit
- Survivor's benefit

In India, importance of social security has been well accepted. Article 41 of the Constitution empowers State to provide security benefit to its members. The Article provides that "the state shall within the limits of its economic capacity and development, make effective provision for securing the right to work, to education and to public assistance, in cases of unemployment, old age, sickness and disablement and in other cases of undeserved want.

Two types of benefits are provided under Social Security Schemes.

(i) Social Insurance

(ii) Social Assistance

Social Insurance

The salient features of social insurance scheme are given below:

(a) A common fund is created from the contribution of employees, employers and the State.

(b) Employees' contribution is minimum so that they do not suffer any hardship for their contribution.

(c) Extent/quantum of benefits provided to employees depend on the contribution record of the beneficiary. The financial status/condition of the beneficiary is not given any weightage for providing benefits to him.

(d) The main objective of the creation of common fund is to provide benefits to the beneficiaries at the time of their partial loss or total loss of income, so that they can maintain minimum standard of living during this period.

(e) Benefits provided to the beneficiaries are in cash or in kind.

Social assistance

The main features of social assistance scheme are mentioned below:

(a) Benefits under this scheme are given to the people who are needy and are of small means.

(b) The benefits are provided by the State after ascertaining financial position of the person.

(c) Benefits like old age pension, maternity benefits provided to the persons falling under BPL (Below Poverty Line) are instances of social assistance.

(d) The main objective of providing such benefit is to give financial support to the people who are below poverty line, so that they can afford some expenses to meet up their sustenance, necessities.

In our country, different States have framed schemes to provide social assistance to the poorest of the poor, who do not have any means to meet up some expenses e.g. old age assistance scheme of Uttar Pradesh (scheme framed by Uttar Pradesh Government in 1957). Under such scheme, the people who are needy and have none to support them and are above the age of 70 years are given a monthly stipend to maintain their livelihood. National Social Assistance Programme (NSAP) has been undertaken by the Central Government to provide some benefits to the persons who are below poverty line. The benefits are maternity benefit, old age pension, support in case of death of breadwinner.

Social insurance benefits are provided to the employees as per the provision of the following Acts:

- The Workmen's Compensation Act, 1923
- The Employees' State Insurance Act, 1948
- The Employees' Provident Funds and Miscellaneous Provisions Act, 1952
- The Maternity Benefit Act, 1961
- The Payment of Gratuity Act, 1962
- The Industrial Disputes Act, 1947

The important provisions of the above Acts are discussed briefly as follows:

Social Insurance under various Acts

Workmen's Compensation Act, 1923

Coverage

1. This Act is applicable to workmen employed in factories, mines, plantations, transport establishments, construction works, railways, ships, circus and other hazardous occupations and employments specified in Schedule – II of the Act.
2. The coverage can be extended by the State Government by adding any hazardous occupation to the list of such occupations in Schedule – II.

Non-Applicability

This Act is not applicable to members of the armed forces, casual workers and workers covered by the ESI Act, 1948.

Administration

The Act is administered by the State Government that appoints Commissioner for Workmen's Compensation.

Benefits

1. Compensation is payable

(i) to a workman for all personal injuries caused to him by accident disabling him for more than 3days.

(ii) to dependents of a workman in case of death due to injury.

(iii) to a workman for any occupational disease contracted by him

2. Accident must arise out of and in the course of employment

3. Results of injury for which compensation is given are:

(i) Death

(ii) Permanent total disablement

(iii) Permanent partial disablement

(iv) Temporary disablement

4. *The amount of compensation to be paid depends on*
   - monthly wages of the workman
   - age of the workman
   - nature of injury caused by the accident.

Fund

Compensation is payable by the employer.

Employees' State Insurance Act, 1948

Coverage

1. This Act is applicable to all types of employees whether manual, supervisory or salaried employees whose wages excluding remuneration for overtime work do not exceed Rs. 3000 p.m. and who are employed in factories.
2. The coverage can be extended by the State Government with the approval of the Central Government.

Non-Applicability

This Act is not applicable to employees in seasonal factories run with power and employing 20 or more employees.

Administration

The Act is administered by the ESI Corporation set up by the Central Government. The Corporation consists of representatives of the Central Government, State Governments, employers, employees, Parliament and medical profession.

Benefits

As per the Act insured persons/dependants are entitled to six types of benefits as given below:

1. sickness benefits at the specified rate for the period of sickness.
2. Maternity benefit in case of
   - confinement
   - miscarriage
   - sickness arising out of pregnancy / confinement
   - pre-mature birth of a child or mis-carriage

   at the specified rate for all days on which insured woman does not work for remuneration during a period of 12 weeks of which not more than six shall preceed the expected date of confinement.
3. Disablement benefit to insured person for suffering from disablement as a result of an employment injury i.e. personal injury caused by accident or occupational disease arising out of and in the course of his employment.
4. Dependants' benefit in case of death of insured person as a result of an employment injury.

   Insured person's widow (during life or until remarriage), legitimate or adopted son upto age of 18 years and legitimate or adopted daughter upto 18 years of age or marriage whichever is earlier, are entitled to dependants' benefit at certain ratio.

5. Medical benefit

An insured person / a member of his family is entitled to receive medical benefit and this may be given

- in the form of outpatient treatment and attendance in a hospital or dispensary, clinic or other institutions
- by visits to the home of the insured person
- treatment as in-patient in a hospital or other institution

6. Funeral benefit

In case of death of insured person, the expenditure on his

funeral, known as funeral benefit is payable to the eldest surviving member of the family. Such benefit should be claimed within a period of 3 months of the death.

Funds

ESI Fund is set up with contributions received from employers and employees, donations, grants and gifts from Central Government, State government, local authorities or individuals.

Employess' Provident Fund and Miscellaneous Provisions Act, 1952

Coverage

The Act is applicable to

(i) every establishment which is a factory, engaged in any industry specified in schedule I, and in which twenty or more, persons, are employed.

(ii) any other establishment employing twenty or more persons or class of such establishment as notified in the official Gazette by the Central Government.

Non-Applicability

The Act is not applicable to

(i) co-operative societies employing less than fifty persons and working without the aid of power.

(ii) new establishments for 3 years from the date of commencement.

(iii) any class of establishments exempted by the Central Government by notification in the Official Gazette.

Administration

The Act is administered by a tripartite Central Board of Trustees consisting of representatives of employers, employees, Central Government and State Governments.

Benefit

The Act provides for 3 types of benefit-provident fund, pension and deposit linked insurance.

Under Provident Fund Scheme an employee

(i) can avail of non-refundable withdrawals

(ii) can obtain loans and advances for self marriage, marriage of dependants, for construction of house, sickness, higher education of his children, purchase of car, financing of life insurance policy etc.

(iii) gets the full balance at his credit inclusive of interest, after reaching superannuation age, leaving the company. On death of employee his nominees / heirs get the balance of provident fund.

Under the new Employees' Pension Scheme an employee gets

(i) superannuation pension after rendering 20 years' service on superannuation

(ii) short service pension after putting 10 or more years' service, but less than 20 years

(iii) retirement pension after rendering 20 years' or more

Besides, the scheme provides for disablement pension, orphan pension, widow pension and children pension.

Under the deposit linked insurance scheme, after the death of an employee, his legal heir / nominee gets an amount equivalent to the average balance lying to the credit of the employee in his provident fund during the preceding one year, subject to maximum of Rs.3500/-

Funds

The Employees' Provident Fund is made up of contribution by employees (8.33% of basic wages, DA, retaining allowance and cash value of food concessions) and employer (1.61%)

The Employees' Pension Fund is created with contribution of

employer (8.33% of the aggregate) and the Central Government (1.16% of the aggregate). The contribution of the Central Government and the employer is payable on the maximum amount of Rs. 5000/- if the pay of an employee exceeds Rs.5000/-p.m

The deposit linked insurance fund is created by the contribution of the employer (0.5% of the aggregate every month) and the Central Government (.25% of the aggregate every month).

Maternity Benefit Act, 1961

Coverage

The Act is applicable to women employees employed in factories, mines and other establishment as may be specified.

Non-applicability

The Act is not applicable to those women employees who are covered by the Employees' State Insurance Act, 1948.

Administration

The Act is administered

In case of coal mines :

by the Coal Mines Welfare Commissioner.

In case of factories:

by the Inspectorates of State Governments

In case of mines other than coalmines:

by the Director-General of Mines Safety.

Benefits

Maternity benefits are provided to a women employee if she has worked 160 days in twelve months, immediately preceding the date of her expected delivery.

Benefits are:

(*i*) Maternity leave:

(with average wage)

- upto 6 weeks including the day of delivery
- 6 weeks after delivery

(ii) Leave with wages

- in case of medical termination of pregnancy
- 6 weeks leave with wages
- in case of tubectomy operation
- 2 weeks leave with wages
- in case of illness arising out of medical termination of pregnancy or tubectomy operation
- one month's leave with wages

(iii) Medical bonus

if free prenatal and postnatal care is not provided)

- Rs.250 to the confined woman worker

Funds

All benefits are provided/paid by employer.

Payment of Gratuity Act, 1962

Coverage

The Act is applicable to every factory, mine, oilfield, plantation, port, railway company and to every shop or establishment in a State in which 10 or more employees are employed.

All employees employed in those establishment are entitled, for gratuity, irrespective of their wages.

Non-applicability

The act is not applicable to

- Apprentices
- Persons employed in managerial and administrative capacity.

- Persons who hold civil posts under the Central Government or a State Government.
- Persons who are subject to the Air Force Act 1950, the Army Act, 1950 or the Navy Act, 1957.

Benefits

Gratuity is payable :

- On superannuation or
- On retirement or resignation or
- On death or disablement due to accident or disease

Gratuity not payable :

- if the five years' continuous service is not rendered, but incase of death or disablement no minimum period of service is required.

Rate of gratuity

- 15 days' wages for every completed year of service or part there of in excess of six months, based on the rate of wage last drawn.
- maximum gratuity is 3.5 lakh

Funds

Gratuity is paid solely by the employer

Industrial Disputes Act, 1947

Coverage

The Act is applicable to all workmen employed in any industry to do any manual, unskilled, skilled, technical, operational, clerical or supervisory work.

Non-applicability

The Act is not applicable to such person

(i) who is subject to the Air Force Act 1950, the Army Act, 1950 or the Navy Act 1957

(ii) who is employed in the police service or as an officer or other employee of a prison

(iii) who is employed mainly in a managerial or administrative capacity

(iv) who, being employed in a supervisory capacity, draws wages exceeding Rs.1600 p.m. or exercises functions mainly of a managerial nature because of the nature of his duties or the powers vested in him.

Administration

The Act is administered by the judicial machinery of Labour Courts, Industrial Tribunals and National Tribunal.

Benefits

The Act provides following benefits:

Lay off compensation-

50% of the total of the basic wages and dearness allowance for the laid off period subject to maximum laid off period of 45 days.

Retrenchment Compensation

(i) one month's wages if no notice is issued

(ii) 15 days' average pay for every completed year of service or any part, thereof, in excess of six months.

Compensation in case of closing down of undertakings

(i) One month's wages if no notice is served

(ii) 15 days' average pay for every completed year of service or any part, thereof, in excess of six months.

Compensation in case of closing down on account of unavoidable circumstances beyond the control of employer

(i) One month's wages if no notice is served

(ii) 15 days' average pay for every completed year of service or any part thereof in excess of six months, subject to maximum of 3 months' average pay

Funds

All benefits are provided/paid by employer.

Books Recommended

1. International Labour Organization : International Comparison of Real Wage : A Study of Methods (issued by ILO, in Studies and Reports, New Series No. 45, Geneva, 1956)
2. A. Holt and H. Andrews : Principles of Health and Safety at Work (10SH Publishing, London, 1993)
3. R. Saunders : The Safety Audit (Pitman, London, 1992)
4. A. O. Martin: Welfare at Work (Batsford, London, 1967)
5. G. K. Suri (Ed.): Wage Incentive – Theory and Practice (Sri Ram Centre of Industrial Relations and Human Resources, New Delhi, 1973)
6. Dalton. E. Mcfarland : Personnel Management - Theory and Practice (Mcmillan, London, 1968)
7. K. N. Subramainum : Wages in India (Tata McGraw Hill New Delhi, 1979)
8. W. B. Werther and Keith Davis : Human Resources and Personnel Management (McGraw Hill, New York, 1996)
9. C. P. Thakur : Corporate Strategy on Fringe Benefits (Spectrum Publishing, Delhi 1985)
10. Michael Armstrong : A Handbook of Human Resource Management (Kogan Page Limited, London, 2000)

Questions

1. 'Welfare means efforts made for well-being of individuals' – Do you agree? Explain the concept of welfare, in this context.
2. State the objectives of labour welfare in the context of changing scenario in industrial activities in India.
3. Explain different types of welfare services provided by the Indian companies to their employees.
4. Discuss different approaches to labour welfare. Which of those approaches you feel influences Indian employers to formulate welfare policies for their employees? – Discuss.
5. What is fringe benefit? State different types of fringe benefit provided by the organizations to its employees.
6. What do you know by 'Employees Stock Option'? How does this scheme help the Company? – Discuss
7. What is 'industrial health'? Explain the statutory provisions in respect of health and safety of workers.
8. Define 'social security'. How will you justify the necessity of social security in Indian organizations?
9. How does 'social insurance' differ from 'social assistance'?
10. (a) 'Social insurance benefits are provided to employees as per provision of labour Acts' – State the relevant provisions of those Acts.

    (b) Discuss in brief the social insurance benefits provided to the employees in terms of provisions of Workmen's Compensation Act, 1923 and Employees' State Insurance Act, 1948.

Case Study

Mr. P. R. Mahajan is the Chief Manager (HRM) of XYZ Alloy Steel Pvt. Ltd. The factory is situated in Bhubaneswar and its first production activities started in the year 2000. The total number of employees including officers comes around 2500 of which 150 employees work with company's Head office in Cuttack. The factory is headed by Mr. P. R. Zamdani, Factory Manager who is assisted by Mr. A. P. Srivastav, Dy. Factory Manager, Mr. R. N. Mahapatra, Production Manager, Mr. L. N. Pati, Marketing Manager, Mr. S. P. Gupta Chief Engineer and Mr. P. R. Mahajan Chief Manager (HRM).

Dr Alok Chadha the Chairman and Managing Director of the company remains in the Head office 3 to 4 days a week and pays visit to factory at least one day in a week. He is a dynamic personality and believes in 'direct and open discussion' mechanism for sorting out individual problems. He is accessible to rank and file of the people at work of the company. Even, the employees in the lowest rung of the factory personnel can talk to him about their personal problems.

The company's financial position for the last Three years shows a promising state of health that can confront any challenges in the market. The market share of the company is about 45%. The net profits of the company for 2001, 2002 and 2003 are Rs. 100 cr. 150 cr. and 300 crors respectively. In 2003, the company is awarded 'Best Performance Prize' by the Ministry.

During the factory visit of CMD in the month of May 2004 some union members of the factory met him and requested to give favourable consideration of the following issues:

1. Transport facilities: The company does not provide quarter facilities to its employees. Majority employees stay at different localities and pay a considerable amount towards shared taxi / auto rickshaw fare for attending factory duties. To give some monetary relief to the employees introduction of a suitable scheme to provide transport services is requested.

2. Scholarship to employees' children : The company does not have any scheme to encourage the children of the employees who are doing outstanding performance in their studies. It happens some employees' children are

compelled to discontinue studies due to paucity of fund. An appropriate scholarship scheme may facilitate continuation of their studies. The total number of employees' children who are attending schools/colleges for different courses/studies is about 750.

3. Canteen allowance: In Bhubaneswar factory around 2350 employees including officers are working. Most of the employees particularly officers, supervisors, senior workers bring tiffin/lunch packets from home and nearby restaurants. The company has its own subsidised canteen but the quality of food and other items is not upto desired standard. The canteen is run by an outside contractor and to look into the canteen activities a canteen committee is constituted. Non-getting/non-supply of good food from canteen is a regular phenomenon which is expressed by all employees of the factory irrespective of cadres, grade and scale of employees. The food stuff which is supplied by the factory canteen is available at a lesser price in local hotels, restaurants. Factory employees desire that a scheme for providing canteen allowance to them instead of existing subsidised canteen service be introduced.

The CMD calls Mr. Mahajan in presence of Mr Mahapatra and advises him the following:

1. To make a detailed study of the issues concerning transport facility and submit a scheme with recommendation.
2. a. To let him know the feasibility perspectives of introducing a scheme for providing scholarship to employees' children.
   b. To submit a detailed scheme for giving such facilities.
   c. To give his views in a detailed note, with supportive arguments with regard to the necessity of introducing such scheme.
3. a. To submit a report in respect of canteen facilities provided to the employees

b. To let him know whether the company can grant canteen allowance to the employees in lieu of subsidised canteen facilities.

c. To draw up a scheme of canteen allowance and submit the same to him for examination and consideration.

4. To let him know the consequences/negative effect the company may face in a situation when requests in respect of above three issues are turned down.

5. To submit a detailed scheme of fringe benefits as the company wants to provide more benefits to its employees to promote morale and develop healthy industrial relations in the factory.

What should be the replies to all queries of the CMD if you are appointed Chief Manager (HRM) in place of Mr P. R. Mahajan? Discuss all the above questions.

6

Employee Training

Meaning of Training

Training is an important activity of HRM after the acquisition activity. It is natural that the people who join the organization have varying degree of knowledge, skill, ability, aptitude, attitude, value, belief and personality trait. Because of non-possession/ non-acquisition of optimum level of core components, people can not deliver goods and services as per requirements, needs and demands of customers. That means, people can not perform due to dearth/short of basic components and obviously can not achieve goals. Hence, organization should have some mechanism, to increase knowledge, skill, competences of people in a planned and systematic manner, so that they can improve performance. Such mechanism is training.

Training is a systematic and planned activity to improve current job performance. Raymond A. Noe, John R. Hollenbeck, Barry Gerhart and Patrick M. Wright (1997) defined training as 'a planned effort to facilitate the learning of job related knowledge, skills and behaviour by employees'. Training also prepares people for growth and development. Thus, training is an activity that makes the people perform their present job and also prepares for advancement.

The following are some important points concerning training

- Training is a planned and systematic activity
- Training improves people's knowledge, core competencies, aptitude and moulds their attitude, beliefs, values, personality.
- Training helps to achieve individual goals, group goals and oganizational goals.
- Training creates a congenial and conducive climate of the organization to accept changes by the people.
- Training prepares people to perform present job and develops them to perform higher job.
- Training facilitates learning.

Objectives of Training

Training is a process of enhancing skill, knowledge, competencies of employees so that they can perform present jobs. The basic objective of training is to help organization to achieve its goals by adding value to the employees. O. Jeft Harris (1976) has expressed that, 'training of any kind should have as its objective the redirection or improvement of, behaviour, so that the performance of the trainee becomes more useful and productive for himself and for the organization of which he is a part. Training normally concentrates on the improvement of, either operative skills (the basic skills related to the successful completion of a task), interpersonal skills (how to relate satisfactorily to others), decision making skills (how to arrive at the most satisfactory causes of action), or a combination of these'.

Training policy of the company is formulated looking to its vision, mission, and also employees' strength, operational activities, technological advancement and so on. The particualr objectives of training are discussed below:

1. Developing employee competencies

A systematic, planned training programme helps the employees to improve their knowledge, skill abilities. Employees through participation in training programme, workshop, can enrich their knowledge, can interact with the trainer to share views, to remove wrongful, rigid perception, can strengthen their weaker areas.

2. Effective job performance by new entrants

Training makes the new entrants effective by imparting skill, knowledge, moulding attitudes, beliefs, mindset, acquainting with policies, norms, rules, adjusting to the new environment, culture of the organization.

3. Helping to grow

Training helps the employees to grow with the organization as the necessary input requiring for job performance in changing scenario, is provided to the trainees.

4. Customers delightment

Training makes the people aware of rendering customer satisfaction and delightment, so that they can take necessary measure to deliver quality goods and services at reasonable cost.

5. Acceptance of change

Organization needs to introduce new methods, techniques, device, latest technology to cope with the situation arising out of stiff competition in the market. This is possible if the employees are aware of recent changing phenomena and accept changes. Training moulds the mind-set of the people appropriately to accept changes in the organization.

6. Preparing reservoir of talented, committed and loyal workforce

Training makes the people knowledgeable, skilled, competent, provides opportunity to utilize latent/potential areas of the people, makes the people know about rules, regulations, philosophy, policies of the organization. Thus, a reservoir of talented, committed and loyal workforce is created to ensure smooth supply of personnel to the departments as and when required.

7. Reduction of absenteeism, employee turnover rate and increase of production, productivity

Tailor made programmes are designed with the objectives of making the people know about the evil effect of absenteeism, necessity of increasing production and productivity, different schemes of the organization for providing welfare benefit, social security to reduce employee turnover rate.

8. Developing proacting capabilities

Training improves knowledges, skill, competencies of the people to indentify / predict the probable issues / problems to be confronted in near future, and to develop proacting capabilities to face the challenges.

9. Making the people dynamic

Dynamism is needed to activate amongst the employees, so that they can realize the necessity of dynamic activities for survival, growth and development of the employee community and the organization as well. Training is such a mechanism that makes the people dynamic.

10. Uninterrupted industrial / business activity

Training prepares the people to perform the job of higher responsibility through development of skill, knowledge, abilities and other areas of qualitative traits. So, organizational activities are not affected in a situation when higher posts crop up vacant due to retirement, death, resignation, dismissal, discharge etc.

Importance of Training

Organizational activities are performed through the people at work in organization and it is possible to function, if the people possess required skill, knowledge, abilities, attitude to perform. But, it is evident from the experience, reseach work that the degree/level of core competence, attitude differ from employee to employee. Hence, the employees who lack skill, ability, knowledge need reinforcement, strengthening of the deficit areas. Training provides necessary input to such people so that they can perform their best to achieve their goals and the goals of organization as well. So, training is needed to help the people and also to help organization to survive, grow and develop. The importance of training is discussed below:

- Training increases knowledge, ability, skill, aptitude of the employees to enable them to perform their assigned task.
- It improves the economic health of the employees, as the employees can increase output and can earn more.
- It helps to increase production, productivity, decrease cost of production, reduce price of sales and increase profit.
- It creates a committed, loyal, positive workforce through exposure, acquaintance with company philosophy, approach, thinking, culture, vision etc.
- Company activities can function well as the present workforce can get acquainted with methods/techniques and operation of the latest tools/devices through training mechanism.
- Employees can have thorough idea, knowledge about organizational culture through training to meet their need for creation, experimentation and contribution to the company.
- It helps to enhance the workers knowledge so that they can use latest technology in their operational activities to produce world class product.
- Employee empowerment, involvement and participation scheme of organization can be introduced easily with the use of training mechanism.
- Company can have a 'reservoir of talented and trained personnel' to meet its requirement.

- Training prepares the people to adapt to organizational environment, culture, climate, so that they feel free to exert their best to deliver goods and services.
- It moulds people's ego-state, paradigm, mindset to make complementary transactions while carrying on interactive process in organization so that sound dyadic relationship is established.
- It reduces wastes, accident rate as the employees become wellversed, acquainted with the operative techniques, methods and skill.
- Continuous and effective training increases the employees' level of morale, job satisfaction and makes them happy and contented.
- Planned and systematic training makes the company's career planning and development scheme effective.

Training, Development and Education

'Training', 'Education', and 'Development' terminologies are often used interchangeably. It is very difficult to differentiate as apparently it seems that these are similar. However, some authors have found out the differentiating aspects and have made distinction between them.

Leonard Nadler (1979) has discussed main points of differences between training, education and development. According to him, training involves learning that relates to present job, and the purpose of training is to improve performance on the present job, of the individual, while the focus of education is on learning, to prepare the individual for a different but identified job. The purpose of education is preparation of an individual for an identified job, in the not too distant future. Nadler defines development as learning for growth of the individual but not related to a specific present or future job. The main objective of development is for general growth not related to any specific job. Michael Armstrong (2000) discussed the three areas of activities of human resource development in the following ways.

Training : The planned and systematic modification of behaviour through learning events, programmes and instruction which enable individuals to achieve the levels of knowledge, skill and competence to carry out their work effectively.

Education : The development of the knowledge, values and understanding required in all aspects of life rather than the knowledge and skills relating to particular areas of activity.

Development : The growth or realization of a person's ability and potential through the provision of learning and edcuational experiences.

So, from the above it is clear that the three terms have distinguishing characteristics. However, it is felt pertinent to make distinction elaborately between 'training' and 'development' and also between 'training' and 'education' to find out the dfferentiating areas of training from development and from education in organizational context. So, the differences between 'training' and 'education', and also between 'training' and 'development' are shown in 6.1 and 6.2 respectively.

Table 6.1 : Distinction between Training and Education

Dimension	Training	Education
1. Concept:	It is a mechanism enhancing knowledge and competences of an employee to perform present job.	It is a mechanism of increasing knowledge, skill, abilities, values and understanding of employee's total environment
2. Example:	When a mechanic repairs his machine better than an engineer, it means, he is trained.	Engineer if he is not trained may not be able to repair his machine better than a mechanic, but he has knowledge and understanding of the whole course of engineering

Dimensions	Training	Education
3. Process :	It is one-time Process.	It is a continuous process.
4. Area of learning :	Its area of learning is to acquire knowledge, skill to perform the assigned task i.e. getting technical skill/ knowledge.	It involves learning on whole subject, that is, totality of the area of the subject.
5. Application:	It is practical oriented and applied.	It is generally theory based.
6. Nature :	It is specific and relates to present job.	It is broad. Learning does not relate to present job.
7. Objective :	Its objective is to prepare the employee to perform his present job.	Its objective is to prepare the employee to perform different job.
8. Duration :	It is of short duration	It is of long duration. The whole process takes much time to raise the level of understanding and knowledge of the employee.
9. Result :	It gives quick results	It takes some more time to generate results.

Table 6.2 : Distinction between Training and Development

Dimensions	Training	Development
1. Concept:	It is a mechanism of enhancing knowledge and competencies of an employee.	It is a mechansim of improving the overall personality of the employee.
2. Target group:	Target group is usually non-executives.	Target group is usually executives.
3. Objective:	The objective is to prepare the emp-loyees to perform his present job.	The objective is to prepare the employee not to perform any kind of future job.
4. Process:	It is for a stipulated period or one time process.	It is a continuous process.
5. Nature:	It is specific and to present job.	It is broad. It involves total development of the employee.
6. Need satisfaction:	It helps to satiate employees' lower level need.	It helps to satiate employees' psychological need.
7. Cost perspective:	It is less expensive.	It is much expensive.
8. Urge factor:	Urge for giving training comes from management personnel.	Urge for development comes from the indi-vidual himself.
9. Focus:	It focuses on present job performance.	It focuses on future job performance and involves personal growth of the employee.
10. Result:	It gives quick result.	It takes some more time.
11. Skill:	It improves technical/ operative skill.	It improves technical, human and conceptual skill.

Training Philosophy

Every organization should have philosophy for imparting training to its employees. Some gives much more emphasis on training as a tool for improving skill and competencies of the employees, so that they can produce quality goods and services to face the challenges in the market, and such organization for this purpose, develops policy and procedures to design and initiate course of action for implementation. Some organizations take the whole concept casually and lay stress on training when they face tough competition and feel the necessity to enhance operative skill of the employees to carry out business/production activities in a change situation. These organizations do not have any principle, policy on training on permanent basis.

Some organizations are not conscious about the effectiveness of training or the outcome/result training provides. Such organizations allocate funds in the annual budget for training but do not attach much importance for proper and effective utilization of the fund due to lack of positive philosophy on employee training.

In changing scenario, organizations pass through stiff competitive stages that demand customers' delightment through quality product and services, and this is possible if the employee producing goods and services accept changes, have acquaintances of latest technologies, have learning experiences for world class production and intend to deliver at any cost. This whole process of transformational activities of employees is generated through training. If no clear cut strong training philosophy is developed, organization may not be able to survive, grow and develop. So, organzation should develop training philosophy with the following basic elements.

- Company's long term plan, vision, mission, statements should be reflected in training projection. This area requires specific emphasis while formulating training policies.
- Changing situation, environment, future trend of activities, nature and type of participants in market should have due importance.

- Government role, intervention, policies, international relations should be thoroughly perused while developing training philosophy.
- Company should consider the latest technological advancement, research activities, innovation / introduction of behavioural theories at the time of formulation of training policies.
- Training should be based on developing 'problem-solving ethic' and 'problem-prevention culture'
- Performance management, reward management and total quality management should have priority in training design
- Training activities should be systematic and continuous.
- Each and every employee be given proper training looking to his need, requirement for excellence in performance.
- Training should be based on awareness development, self-development, role contribution, and team building of employee for creating cohesive and co-operative culture in organization.

Training Needs

It is rare to find any organization where employees do not need training for performance of present job, for discharging the function of higher jobs, new jobs. Training is, therefore, needed as a learning process to improve knowledge, skill, ability, aptitude, attitude of the employees so that they can perform existing job as also future job assigned to them. In a changing business scenario, much more emphasis has been placed by most organizations on the need for training of employees to deliver quality goods and services at reasonable price to confront challenges of the competitors.

Training Needs can be Ascertained from the following:

1. To compensate skill vacuum

When existing level of skill, knowledge, competencies of

employees falls short of optimum level of skill, knowledge, competence required for performance of present job, training is needed to compensate the vacuum of such skill.

2. To make succession planning effective

Organization needs uninterrupted business activities for survival, growth and development but there is likelihood to disturb business activities in a situation where succession planning system is not effective. To make the succession planning system meaningful and operative employees identified for higher assignments need training.

3. To change mind set of people at work

In changing scenario, organizations face stiff competition, and to confront challenges of the competitors employees need to change their mind set to accept and adopt to the new environmental situation that necessitates introduction/ use of new technologies, device, machines, techniques in organization. Such transformation of mind-set is made through training.

4. To promote team building

Employees work in a team. To achieve team goals, organizational goals employees need to develop team spirit, a sense of 'we-feeling', 'togetherness' and 'belongingness'. Training helps employees to promote team building so that they can excel in their team performance, and individual performance as well.

5. To develop competitive spirit

If the employees know the strength and weaknesses of the competitors and develop competitive spirit, it is easy to achieve .organizational goals. Training generates enthusiasm among employees, supplies necessary data, information in respect of strength, weakness of competitors and motivates them to promote competitive spirit.

6. To make employees aware of situations

If the employees can know (a) what is the strength of the company? (b) where do they stand in the competition? (c) what is their future? they can prepare themselves to fight against odds. Training makes the employees aware of the situation and develops coping capabilities to sustain.

Training Process

Process of training means stages an organization needs to follow right from analysing, studying training needs of employees to evaluating of training. It passes through different stages to make the training meaningful, effective. Most of the organizations think training is a good investment and so they attach much importance on training at the time of deciding corporate strategic plan. Such organizations give serious thought to carry out process activities in line with corporate training strategy. Some organizations are casual in approach in the area of training. So, training process of such organizations is not based on systemic planning. There are few organizations that rarely believe on efficacy of training and they do not spend money or spend a little money on 'training head'.

For smooth and effective functioning of training activities importance of stages or process of training can not be ignored. The process of training which is shown in Figure 6.1 includes the following:

Step 1 : Study/analysis of performance indications, quality maintenance etc.

Company's performance/production schedules, target, quality maintenance records, machines installation, capacity, utilization etc. give the idea whether company's production as also quality is as per expectation or falls short of expectation; if it is below the level of standard fixed training need arises.

Step 2 : Finding out/ascertaining the reason for less performance, production, low quality of product.

This is ascertained through job satisfaction, attitudinal survey, contact of supervisors etc. If the real cause is lack of knowledge, skill, competencies, attitudes, necessity to improve performances, quality, attitudes, behaviour through training is felt.

Step 3 : Indentification of employees who need training

Next step is to ascertain/identify employees who need training, through analysis of performance appraisal report, self-appraisal report, discussion with supervisors, suggestion/ recommendations of departmental heads.

Step 4 : Deciding upon the area/type of skill needs improvement through training

What type of skill employee needs reinforcement/ improvement is ascertained in this step. Generally, three types of skills are needed to perform task accomplishment. The skills are technical, human and conceptual.

Step 5 : Preparing training programme

This step decides

- Training technique
- Trainer
- Training establishment-whether external or internal training institute.
- Design of course contents, period of training.
- Facilities

Step 6 : Imparting / providing training

In this step implementation of training programme is made. The objective is to impart training to the nominated employee to develop/ improve his deficit area, so that he can manifest his change behaviour/ activities in his task performance to achieve his desired goals.

Step 7 : Evaluation of training

Whether company's training system is effective or not, that can be ascertained through evaluating training programme. A trainee's extent of learning through training mechanism is reflected in his performance and behavioural activities. In case of necessity, addition, alteration of course programme, content, periodicity may be made.

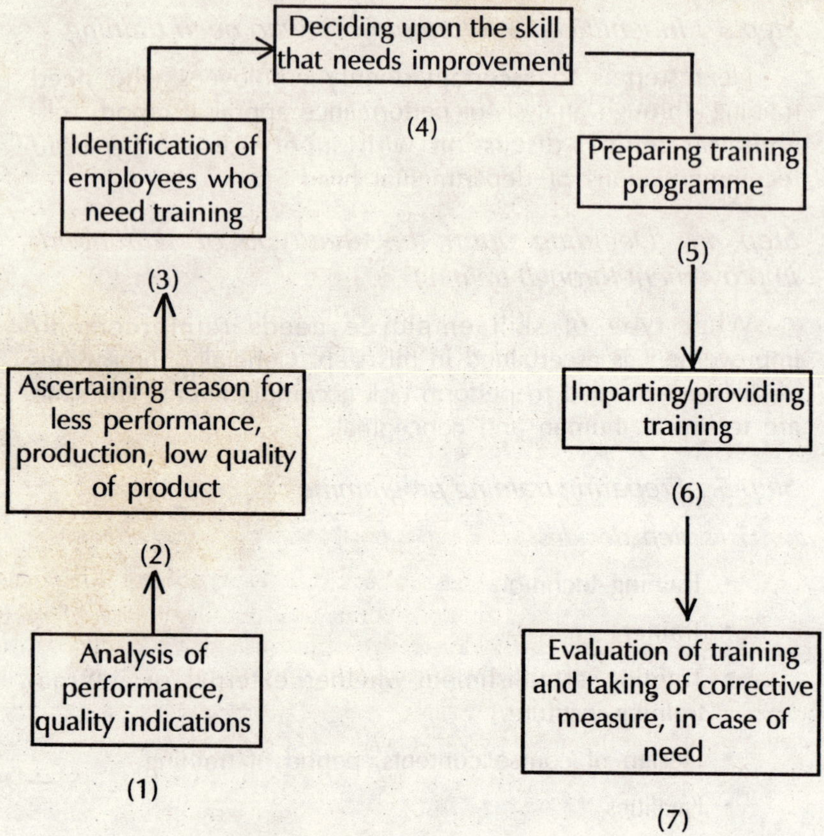

Figure 6.1 : Process of training

Training Methods/Techniques

Various methods/techniques of training are used in organizations to improve skill, ability of employees, to enrich their knowledge, to change their mind-set and behavioural pattern, so that they can excel their present performance and also can show their worth in higher positions, if assigned. The effective use of a particular training method depends on factors like

- requirement of training after training need analysis
- cost effectiveness.
- infra-structure for providing training

- mental make up, age, desire, willingness of target group of employees.
- trainer's level of competency, education, knowledge, acceptance of assignment
- training policy

After ascertaining / identification of 'training need area', company decides training location (i.e. in-company, external) and techniques. A variety of training techniques are used by different organizations and these techniques are divided into two groups viz;

- on-the-job techniques
- off-the-job techniques

On-the-job training methods / techniques

On-the-job training methods are used by companies in its workplace where people at work learn by doing. Employees are given training by their supervisors, senior workers or by some persons who are assigned for such purposes. The following are some methods introduced / practised by most companies for imparting training to its employees.

- job rotation
- coaching
- mentoring
- demonstration
- job instruction / training through step by step learning.
- committee assignment
- apprenticeship training

Job Rotation

It is rotation of employees from one job to other job or from one department / section to other department / section. This technique is much parctised in service industries specially, banking industry where employees with similar designations are moved from job to job or from department to department to gain knowledge, experience and expertise of different types of job (e.g. rotation amongst employees with designation of clerks, rotation amongst line management) Even job rotation amongst line and staff management in senior management cadre is practised.

Merits

(i) Employees can enrich knowledge, improve competence through working on different jobs, departments in organization.

(ii) Working on different jobs, departments develops feeling of 'mastery' over the whole process of activity.

(iii) It removes monotonous state of feeling.

(iv) It encourages employees to excel performance in new area.

(v) It prevents employees from developing 'hidden relationship' with customers/clients.

(vi) It facilitates promotion of employees in the next cadre.

Demerits

(i) All employees may not be able to gain adequate experience, job knowledge during specified period of time.

(ii) It may not bring results if design of this programme is faulty or irrational.

(iii) It needs tailor-made programme to suit individual employee's interest, capabilities to grasp or learn job in new area of activity which most companies ignore.

Coaching

Coaching is a method to make employees learn jobs in new area. It is a direct and man-to-man techinque which considers individual employee's competency, level of education and experience. Generally, supervisor is assigned the job of a coach or a guide who gives continuous attention and supervision of the trainees' job, corrects, modifies the operative functions, helps to improve skill, abilities of the employees so that they can excel performance.

Merits

(i) Trainees get continuous help, assistance from coach.

(ii) Coach provides constant support, positive stroke to employees to learn job at a short period of time.

(iii) Inter-personal relationship between supervisor (coach) and employees (learners) makes the learning process easy and smooth.

(iv) Immediate rectification of operative activities is possible.

Demerits

(i) Supervisor may consider coaching job as imposed assignment, so he may take it casually.

(ii) In industrial setting, coaching has been a regular and routine phenomenon and so, no emphasis is given towards quality learning.

(iii) Coaching process may take abnormally much time if grasping knowledge, skill, capability of trainees to learn new job is below the standard level.

(iv) Trainee's development of skill, ability, knowledge may not be adequate if the supervisor/coach's knowledge, skill is limited.

Mentoring

It is one of the on-the-job techniques practised in organizations. It may happen that senior employees may not have adequate knowledge, expertise in newly developed technologies, though in other areas they do not lag behind. Such employees need guidance, counselling for strengthening/ reinforcing weak areas. Mentor, who is generally company's excutive / trained personnel helps employees ('proteges') through counselling, guidance to acquire particular knowledge, skill for better performance of their work and also to reflect in the potental area for higher assignment. Mentoring is a kind of coaching to develop a specific skill. John Arnold and Karen Johnson (1997) expressed mentoring as the use of an experienced individual (the mentor) to teach and train someone (the potegee) with less knowledge in a given area.

Merits

(i) It helps to promote values, status of proteges.

(ii) Learners develop mutual understanding, personal relations with mentor through interactive process.

(iii) Employees can understand / feel corporate thinking, expectations, style of functioning and accept this technique as effective measure for sustenance, growth and development with the organization.

(iv) Empathic feeling of mentor facilitates self-development.

(v) It promotes the feeling of proteges of a sense of belongingness to the company.

(vi) It raises the level of morale of trainees.

Demerits

(i) It happens that some employees / colleagues, other than proteges, do not take this technique in good spirit.

(ii) A rift / conflict amongst porteges and non-proteges may arise out of use of this technique, as non-porteges consider that the opportunity / benefit for development of particular skill is given to some employees who are close to or in the good book of higher management.

(iii) It may create unhealthy human relations situation in organization.

(iv) Abuse of mutual tie may affect smooth running and functioning of departmental activities.

(v) Non-proteges may feel that they are ignored by higher management. Such feeling may decrease level of morale of non-trainees and productivity as well.

Demonstration :

It is a technique to make the learners/employees know the job through description / explanation of the process of operation. It is a direct process. Employees (trainees) through watching, observing and doing, learn operation. Supervisors, senior colleagues are assigned the additional duties of teaching through demonstration. This method goes through the following stages

- Description of whole operative process of the job by trainer.
- Explaining how to perform, what skill / knowledge requires to carry out the process, how much time takes to perform different processes and the whole job; what tools, devices, inputs, support require to complete the processes.
- Demonstrating operation of the whole job by trainer.
- Learning operation by doing.

Merits

(i) This process of learning is easy. Trainees can acquire knowledge, skill of operation at a shorter period of time.

(ii) It is very effective in operational area of activities where technical skill predominates.

(iii) Company does not need to spend money towards purchase of new device, tools, machines for training purpose. Trainer demonstrates on the existing machines, equipments of the company.

(iv) Employees get chance to experiment/practise on machines immediately after demonstration. So, the possibility for making mistakes is less.

Demerits

(i) It is not much effective where development of human skill, conceptual skill is required.

(ii) This method does not follow structured sequence of teaching.

(iii) Less intelligent, illiterate employees may find it difficult to learn.

(iv) Trainers may take such assignment casually.

Job Instruction/Training through Step by Step Learning

It is a direct process of training. Trainers are generally supervisors, experienced workers or skilled identified personnel. They train employees as coach, guide through instruction, explanation and demonstration. The success of this method depends on

- trainees' aptitude, desire for learning, grasping capability and level of competency
- trainers' ability, workload, willingness to taking up such assignment
- training materials, contents, environment, trainer-trainee relations, training duration
- company's policy, management support, attitude towards employee training especially training through step by step learning
- approach to job analysis, process of job analysis
- emphasis on training evaluation, cost-benefit analysis.

This technique of training gives trainees the ideas of the job, its different steps of operation, process of performance/operation in different steps and working with the machines/equipments in various steps. The whole process of training covers

(i) Preparation of congenial climate for training, mind-set for acceptance of learning, awareness / clear perception of job description.

(ii) Job instruction through step by step (i.e. description of whole process of activities, explanation of process/es/ operations to be performed, demonstration of activities.

(iii) Use of machines/tools, equipments by learners to find out as to how much they have learned and the areas where they lag behind.

(iv) Guidance of instructor to perform job as per standard/ to excel the area of performance.

(v) Repetition of activities by learners till optimum level of performance is reached.

Merits

(i) It helps the learners acquire knowledge, skill of the job, at short period of time.

(ii) Competency level of trainees is developed through process of experimentation, exposure to different situations and rectification of mistakes resulting in acquisition of thorough knowledge, clear concept of perfomance activities.

(iii) It helps to establish healthy inter-personal relations between trainees and supervisor.

(iv) This method is simple for transferring knowledge to employees (trainees).

(v) This is less expensive. Trainees learn while working.

Demerits

(i) It distrubs production activities of organization as during training machines / equipments are used for training purposes only.

(ii) Quality of training is affected if supervisor lacks adequate knowledge / level of competency to excel performance of job.

(iii) Trainer may be biased / influenced by some trainees when both the parties develop inter-personal relation through interactive process.

(iv) Learners may develop fear psychosis to operate machines.

(v) This method may not be useful when theory-based learning is required.

Committee Assignment

Under this method of training, employees (trainees) are given some common assignment which is required to be performed jointly by them. The whole process of activities covers the following :

- identification of trainees to work as a team
- ascertainment of task for performance by team members.
- investigation / application of skill, knowledge to find out genesis of problem / issue
- searching out ways and means / alternatives to sort out problem.
- discussion / interactions amongst team members over the issue.
- offering suggestions, recommendation, opinions by trainees
- reaching at conclusion
- submission of report / solution to the management

Merits

(i) It helps to increase trainees' level of judgement, reasoning and expression.

(ii) It develops a sense of belongingness, 'we feeling', 'togetherness' and team spirit.

(iii) It facilitates to improve morale level of the trainees.

(iv) Trainees may feel encouraged to change mental set up and to frame a new mind-set as per team requirement.

(v) It is an easy method of training which does not involve much cost.

Demerits

(i) Junior employees may feel it difficult to adjust with the new environment.

(ii) If the whole team consists of new entrants quality of report / suggestion may not contain substance.

Apprenticeship

Apprentice is a person who undergoes apprenticeship training in a designated trade in an organization. Company arranges to give training to the people in different trades in terms of policy framed therein or in pursuance of a contract of apprenticeship under Apprentices Act. 1961. Generally, apprenticeship training is given for a specified period of time, that ranges from 2 to 5 years, to learn the job of printers, weavers, electricians, carpenters, machinists and in other areas of trades, crafts. Apprentices learn job by doing. Skilled employees, supervisors coach the apprentices through demonstration, explanation and description of job activities. People who undergo training get stipend which is much less than the wages of workers to those trade, crafts.

Merits

(i) Labour cost is much less as compared to production/ service rendered by the apprentices.

(ii) It meets up some part of social obligation to serve society through the process of creating a trained workforce for utilization of services as per needs of different organizations.

(iii) Company can meet up demand for human resources.

(iv) Training cost is minimum.

Demerits

(i) Since rate of stipend is minimum apprentices feel dissatisfied.

(ii) Duration of training for all apprentices in a trade is fixed. Hence, the intelligent, capable apprentices who excel in learning get frustrated as they are required to stay with the organization, even after knowing operation.

(iii) There is no system / arrangement to continue training for the apprentices who can not complete learning during stipulated period of time.

Off-the-job training methods / techniques

Off-the-job training means, training away from work place. It may be in-company or external training. It has no relation with performance of work while learning. Organizations use these methods

- to change attitudes, behaviours of people at work
- to improve human skill
- to develop skill in conceptual aspects
- to enrich knowledge in specific field
- to improve communication skill
- to develop skill for effective administration and management
- to improve analytical skill
- to mould mind-set of employees
- to make people know/aware of different techniques of motivation
- to make employees acquainted with latest rules, regulations, methods, policies, procedures of the company.

The following are the off-job-training methods generally used in different organizations.

1. Vestibule training
2. Lecture method

3. Role playing
4. Case method
5. Conference
6. Programmed instruction

Vestibule training

It is one of the off-the-job training methods. Under this training method employees receive training away from their workplace and in training centre they use the same machines, tools, equipment what they will be given for work at workplace, for learning purpose. When large number of employees mostly clerks, operators are required to be trained at a short period of time, a simulated workshop/workplace is created in the training centre and training is imparted through demonstration, discussion, role playing, case studies, and lecture methods.

This training method helps the trainees to learn operation (i.e., 'learning by doing') and also to have theoretical concept of the job for smooth performance. Since, the learners give some production/service while practising it helps to reduce cost of training which is expensive. However, the effectiveness of training depends on course contents, quality of faculty, machines/equipment used, opportunities available for learning operations, course duration etc.

Lecture Method

Lecture is an old and direct method of training used in most organizations. Where number of trainees is large and training is required to be given at a short period of time, this method is used.

Lecture method includes the following :

- talk
- discussion
- Film shows, overhead projector

- feedback
- explanation

This method is less expensive as per trainee cost is minimum. It is effective where organizations need

- to make participants aware/know its rules, regulations, procedures
- to improve human skill and conceptual skill
- to develop analytical ability
- to promote communication skill, negotiation skill, presentation skill
- to change attitudes of trainees.

The effectiveness of this method depends on participants, their seriousness, sincerity, listening and also trainers-their method of presentation, talk and use of techniques. In this method a large groups of trainees can have the opportunity to learn within a short period of time. However, this method can not be of use when trainees need to know operation aspects of different processess of a job.

Role Playing

It is a class-room training method. Under this method trainees play the role of other characters to feel the situation, difficulties, inconvenience other personalities face while interacting with them during normal course of transactions/activities, and to develop/improve their behavioural attitudes.

This method covers the following:

- selection of trainees in terms of behavioural evils like lack of sympathy/empathy, mal-adjustment, misbehaviour, ego centric, use of abusive language, impatience, intolerance and so on.
- preparation of note by trainer for each participant mentioning background of situation and role to be performed by each trainee.

- explanation of the whole matter by trainer.
- creation of a realistic situation for role performance.
- commencement of role playing by participants.
- observation, constructive criticism by other trainees, positive stroking, guidance by trainer.

It happens in organization that some employees cannot render proper service to their customers or can not perform their work due to inter-personal/attitudinal problems. These employees cannot feel the difficulties/trouble which customers bear because of their illbehaviour/ego contamination. To feel and understand the others' difficulties, problems, such employees are assigned the role of other personalities to play, like a bank's cashier playing the role of a customer, a sales executive playing the role of sales supervisor, a superior taking the role of his subordinate.

It is effective

- to improve interpersonal relations
- to develop understanding
- to enhance human skill
- to mould mind-set
- to change attitude and behaviour of the trainees.

But, this method may not give result if the trainees do not mainfest their 'real' behavioural activities.

Case Method

It is one of the methods under off-the-job training. Whole incident or set of circumstances is presented before the trainees for finding out causes of problem, genesis of issues and for submitting solution, alternatives. The incidents, circumstances are job related which the trainees may encounter in the process of their performance activities.

This method helps

- to improve analytical skill

- to develop judgemental ability
- to make conscious about circumstances / situations cropped up in organization and to take pre-cautionary measure
- to increase power of observation

The effectiveness of this method depends on (i) trainer's knowledge on subjects and area of operation, skill and ability of presentation of cases, (ii) case preparation, relevance of cases with 'real life' situations, (iii) trainees' willingness, desire for participation, (iv) selection of participants.

Conference/Discussion

It is an off-the-job technique. Under this method topics for discussion are decided beforehand. Trainees learn subjects/ conference theme, sub-themes through active participation in discussion / conference. *This method includes the following:*

- selection of topics which needs discussion
- identification of participants / trainees and also experts in the concerned areas
- structuring time to enable participants to discuss, present their thinking, ideas on the subject
- creation of climate for making direct questions by participants
- ensuring active participation of all trainees and that question-answer session is not dominated by a section of trainees
- arriving at conclusion of issues discussed

It helps trainees to:

(i) improve communication skill

(ii) develop idea, understanding, concept on topics discussed threadbarely

(iii) develop conceptual skill as they get to know viewpoints of experts in the field.

(iv) change / mould their behavioural activities

This methods has some limitations. They are:

(i) time allotted to each participant is short. Hence, participants do not get opportunity to express their view points.

(ii) large number of participants may make conference a mess

(iii) if topics selected for discussion are irrelevant and do not have link to job problems, trainees may not find interest to participate.

Programmed Instruction

It is a method which makes the trainees learn operations, procedures, rules, regulations through teaching machines or programmed texts manuals. This is also called 'self learning' or learn by self method. It does not require participants to attend classes to receive training. They learn at home during their off-time/leisure period. Some say programmed instruction is 'trainee paced'. Trainees complete learning at their own speed.

Programmed instruction method includes the following:

(i) identification of areas where training need is felt i.e., training coverage

(ii) analysis of subject matter/training areas to make into units that can provide frame of instructional programme

(iii) preparation of text materials looking to logical sequences like feedback sequences for trainees to have idea regarding their extent of learning.

Under this method participants are given training through programmed texts which contain facts, problems, short questions. After going through text materials/facts trainees are required to answer questions given in Text Units and they get nearly instanteneous feedback about their response whether it is correct or not.

Merits

(i) This method is effective when participants are well aware of information relating to rules, regulations, policy courses etc.

(ii) Since trainees are not required to attend classes, they save time.

(iii) It motivates trainees as the learning method is not complicated and they can do it at their own time.

(iv) Feedback arrangement encourages trainees.

Demerits

(i) Application of this method is limited.

(ii) Preparation of texts needs specialized knowledge and skill.

(iii) It is not easy for all participants to follow instructions.

(iv) Preparation cost of programmed instruction is very high.

(v) Efficacy of this method depends on quality of materials, trainees' seriousness, willingness and also speed of training institute.

Training Need Analysis (Discovery of Training Needs)

Before designing training programme company needs to find out 'who need training' and 'what training'. That means training need analysis is required. Different authors / experts have suggested various mechanisms to discover training needs. Gary Dessler (2000) has prescribed 'task analysis' and 'performance analysis' as two main ways of identifying training needs, while Michael Armstrong (1999) proposed following four methods of training need analysis.

- analysis of business and human resource plans
- job analysis
- analysis of performance reviews
- training surveys.

However,looking to viewpoints of various researchers, authors and also analysis of survey reports conducted on such area, it is felt that the following methods may be used to identify/ discover training needs of an organization.

(i) Organizational analysis

(ii) Job / task analysis

(iii) Performance review analysis

(iv) Other methods

(a) Management requests

(b) Observations

(c) Attitude survey

(d) Questionnaires

(e) Employee suggestions

(f) Incidents analysis

Organizational analysis

Training needs can be ascertained through organizational analysis that covers (i) analysis of corporate business strategies/ plans (ii) HR strategies/plans (iii) analysis of HR utilization in different departments (iv) equipments / machines used (equipments/machine analysis)

The above analyses, may help to know the number of people who need training to develop level of competencies.

Job/Task Analysis

Training needs can be ascertained through job / task analysis. Task analysis involves:

- job contents-job details
- quality and performance standard
- skill and knowledge requirement

Job analysis helps (i) to identify / indicate areas where knowledge and competency levels are not upto mark. (ii) to specify areas where employees find difficulty to operate/give standard performance (iii) to indicate type of training needed for performance of job (iv) to know nature of problems faced by employees to give standard quality and quantity of performance.

Job analysis method is effective for determining training needs of employees, who are not very much experienced.

Performance Review Analysis

Performance review is a part of performance management that is concerned with managing and improving individual and team performance in a continuous system. Necessary measures are taken to improve performance by providing counselling, solving performance problems, giving feedback and developing skill, knowledge, competencies of employees. Performance review is made at the end of the specified period to ascertain performance level (i.e. extent of achievement), areas where shortfall is noticed, problems faced by employees in the process of carrying out performance and to reinforce the deficit/weak areas through learning process.

Analysis of performance review helps to know about employees' performance as compared to standard fixed in terms of quality and quantity, the reasons for not achieving targeted performance and type of training needed (whether training required to improve conceptual skill or human skill or to increase operational knowledge).

Performance review is an effective technique to understand training needs of employees as this is a continuous process that can evaluate performance/achievement more or less perfectly and accurately. Training needs can also be ascertained from self-appraisals.

Management Requests

Sometimes, line management particularly supervisors request higher management by way of sending suggestion or by placing nomination in training meeting for arranging training programme for some employees working in the respective departments. Areas in which training is required to be imparted are specified/ recommended by the supervisors.

Discovery of training needs by first line management brings accuracy and perfection, as employees are directly working under them and it is supervisors who know in which areas concerned employees are weak and need training. However, this technique may not be effective if nomination for training is biased.

Observation

It is another method of identifying training needs of employees by management. Supervisors/managers under whom employees work pay constant look and careful observations on employees while working, and through such observation they ascertain quality and quantity of performance and also weak areas, if any, that need reinforcement through training. If training need is felt by management, nomination is suggested.

Attitude Survey

Attitude survey helps management to know/understand about employees' perception towards supervisors, work, promotion, working conditions, pay, training and developmental aspects etc. Through behavioural mainfestation and interactions employees' satisfaction, dissatisfaction on different areas can be ascertained. Hence, the weak areas which need reinforcement/ training can be identified.

Questionnaires

This is another tool used to identify employees' need for training. Questionnaires are prepared covering areas like compensation packages, welfare benefits, promotion, supervisors, company policies, strategy, objectives, mission, career planning, and development, training and other aspects. Questionnaries are given to employees with an advice to return them to the management/sender after eliciting their opinions.

The weak areas of the employees as opined by them can be identified and type of training needed can be ascertained.

Employee Suggestions

Sometimes, employees themseleves suggest the kind of training they need. It occurs that employees can not give standard production / service for not having thorough knowledge in operational process and activities, though they are very much willing to give their best. Employees confess before supervisors/ management personnel about their weaknesses and need for training in the concerned area for improvement of their knowledge and competencies.

Incidents Analysis

Training needs are identified through analysis of the following:

- productivity rate of employees when it is below the standard rate.
- accident rate when it is higher than normal and it is due to employees' negligence or not knowing safety rules / regulations, or for not having knowledge on operational activities.
- wastes / scraps when percentage / quantum of wastes, defects is considerably higher due to lack of knowledge, skill and competencies.
- labour turnover rate (when it is much more than standard rate) that requires the present employees to know the job as fallen vacant
- indisciplined activities of employees due to lack of adequate skill in human relations area.
- alarming number of unsuccessful employees in promotion test due to lack of knowledge / idea on operational and other subjects.

The above incidents / occurences help management to discover training needs of employees.

Evaluation of training programme

It happens that some employees lack knowledge, skill, ability as required for performance of job, and company nominates them for training to reinforce their weak areas so that they can perform well. Now, the question arises wthether the training programmes designed for employees give results and contribute to the company in terms of quantity and quality of production (i.e. increasing production, improving quality of goods), reducing accident rate, waste rate, absenteeism rate, turnover rate and the like. To know these, it is necessary to evaluate training programmes organized by the company.

Various authors, experts namely Gary Dessler (2000) Hamblin (1974) Kirkpatrick (1994), Decenzo and Robbins (1998) and others, suggested different methods to evaluate training effectiveness. Some important methods as prescribed by above experts and other contemporary authors are discussed below for evaluating training programmes of a company.

(i) Test-retest method

Under this method employees who are selected for training are given a test (a series of questions, problems etc. intended to measure the extent of knowledge, aptitudes, intellegence and other mental traits) before training starts. The same batch of employees (trainees) after training is over retake the test. The scoring of such employees in both the tests indicate training effectiveness if retest score is on the higher side.

However, the criticism crops up on the point that high scoring in retest may not be due to the effects of training but for some other factors.

(ii) Reaction

Questionnaires are prepared and given to trainees immediately after the training is over or on the same date, at the close of training.

Questionnaire contains a series of questions to know reactions of trainees on

- training duration
- course materials

- course coverage
- value of course content to current job
- linkage of training with job performance, improvement in confidence
- trainer's ability, skill, communication knowledge on the subject, responsiveness to the trainees
- level of satisfaction in respect of training
- objectives of the programme
- extent of learning
- method of presentation
- facilities

Reactions of trainees give the idea about effectiveness of training programme.

(iii) Learning

Extent of learning indicates efficacy of training. Learning relates to acquisition of knowledge, skill, ability through training mechanism. If employees learn more in training, it means training is successful in transforming knowledge, skill of the trainees. The magnitude of learning is reflected in performance and attitudinal areas of trainees.

To measure the extent of learning, test is taken before employees go for training and again after training. The difference of score in tests indicates extent of learning and also effectiveness of training.

(iv) Behaviour

To know change of behaviour of employees if occurred, due to training questionnaire is administred before and after training.

Questionnaire contains mostly questions relating to behaviour, attitude, problems of team working, team building, interpersonal relations. The difference of score in pre-training test and post training test tells the company, whether training has made some changes in attitudinal behaviour of employees who received training.

(v) Results

Whether training programme is effective or not that can be evaluated/ascertained from the results like

- increase in production
- decrease in wastes rate, defects, scraps
- increase in productivity
- increase in customers' delightment
- decrease in accident rate
- increase in sales
- change in attitudes and behaviour

Data/information have to be collected before the employees are sent for training and again after they come back from training. The technique of collecting information used in organizations is through questionnaire, test, developmental records. However, difficulty arises to evaluate training programme when results relate to quality, change of behaviour, attitude etc.

(vi) Experimentation method

This evaluation method is effectively used in various organizations. For evaluating training efforts two groups of employees are created-control group and experimental group. Control group consists of employees who do not go for training while experimental group includes employees who receive training. Before experimental group is sent for training, performance, attitudes, bahaviour of employees of both groups are measured and data/statistics to this effect are recorded. After employees of experimental group (trainees) come back from training, both groups are again evaluated and difference is ascertained. If the data reveal that there is much improvement in experimental group as compared to control group, it can be assumed that the training programme is effective.

(vii) Performance method

This method relates to measurement of performance of trainees. Effectiveness of any training programme to increase production can be ascertained through this technique. Before an employee receives training, his production quantum is measured and after his returning from training his production capacity is noticed to find out whether there is an improvement in production. If production has increased, it is a considered that increase is due to training, the employee concerned has received.

This method is useful when job can be quantified; but care should be taken to notice that, during the period of training the trainees have not been under the influence of any pay hike, incentive, reward or any increase in compensation package.

(viii) Interview Method

Under this method supervisors are interviewed with regard to performance of employees who have resumed work after training. Supervisors' analysis, opinions suggest efficacy/ineffectiveness of training programmes.

Books Recommended

1. Michael Armstrong : A Handbook of Human Resource Management Practice (Kogan Page Limited, London 2000)
2. Raymond A. Noe, John R. Hollenbeck, Barry Gerhart and Patrick M. Wright ; Human Resource Management-Gaining a Competitive Advantage, (2nd edition, The Mc Graw Hill Companies, Inc, 1997)
3. O. Jeft Harris : Managing People At Work : Concept and Cases in Interpersonal Behaviour (John Wiley & Sons, Inc. New York, 1976)
4. Leonard Nadler : Developing Human Resource (2nd Edition, Austin : Learning Concepts, 1979)

5. R. F. Lynton and U. Parekh: Training for Development (Taraporewala, Mumbai, 1973)
6. D. L. Kirkpatrick : Evaluating Training Programs (Berret - Kochler, Sanfrancisco, 1994)
7. A. C. Hamblin : Evaluation and Control of Training (McGraw-Hill, Maidenhead, 1974)
8. R. Harrison : Employee Development (2nd Edn. Institute of Personnel and Development, London, 1997)
9. Rackham, N, Honey, P and Colbert M : Developing Interactive Skills (Wellens Publishing, Northampton, 1967)
10. Manpower Service Commission : Glossary of Training Terms (3rd Edn., HMSO, London)
11. Gary Dessler : Human Resource Management (Prentice-Hall, Inc. Upper Saddle River, New Jersey, 8th Edition, 2000)
12. John Arnold and Karen Johnson : Mentoring in Earl career (Human Resource Management, Vol. 7, No. 4, 1997)

Questions

1. Define the term 'training'. State the objectives of training.
2. Explain Leonard Nadler's views on 'training' 'development' and 'education'.
3. Do you think the terms 'training', 'development' and 'education' are the same? - Discuss
4. 'Every organization has philosophy to impart training to its employees'. Discuss in this context training philosophy with basic elements.
5. 'It is rare to find any organization where employees do not need training for performance of present job' - Explain in this context importance of training in an organization.

6. 'For smooth and effective functioning of training activities importance of training process can not be ignored' - Discuss in this connection the training process an organization needs to follow.
7. What is 'on-the-job' training? How does it differ from 'off-the-job' training?
8. Do you agree 'on-the-job' training methods are more useful than 'off-the-job' training methods?
9. What is 'off-the-job' training? Discuss any three 'on-the-job' training methods with advantages and disadvantages of each method.
10. Do you feel training need analysis is a necessity before designing a training programme? - Discuss.
11. Explain in brief three important methods of training need analysis.
12. Discuss in short the different methods used in organization to analyse need for training of employees.
13. Why do the organizations intend to evaluate training programmes participated by the employees?
14. Explain in brief the different methods used in organization to ascertain efficacy of training programmes.

Case Study No. 1

Mr. Ramesh Mahajan has recently joined a medium size factory at Gaziabad as Human Resource Manager to manage and develop the human resources of the company. Prior to his joining Mr K.P. Panwar, Production Manager was looking after HRM Department in addition to his own portfolio. Total employee strength of the factory is as follows :

Workers	:	2000
(including maintenance staff, watch and ward personnel and peons)		

Clerical staff	:	50
Supervisors	:	20
Executives	:	80

Four years back the company had made an agreement with the recognised workers & Staff Union with regard to promotion and training of workers and clerical staff of the factory. Mr Panwar was assigned the task of negotiating with the Union on their above agenda issues.

The salient features of the agreement, inter alia include

(i) expiry period : The agreement remains effective for a period of four years. However, for a fresh agreement either party needs to inform its intention at least 3 months ahead of the date of expiry of the agreement. If, no communication is made by any party for change of agreement / fresh agreement the settlement remains in vogue. (This agreement has another 6 months time to expire.)

(ii) training : All workers and clerical personnel should be given training. Arrangement of training should be made in such a way, so that there cannot be any backlog of training after four years.

(iii) promotion of clerks to supervisory / executive cadre : Fifty percent of recruitment in the supervisory / executive posts should be made internally. Weightage be given on seniority. Out of 100 marks, 50 marks be alloted for seniority and rest for personal interview and performance rating.

You are advised to discuss the following :

(*a*) What should be the role of Mr Mahajan as HR Head with regard to the agreement already in force? How will he tackle this issue?

(*b*) Do you think that the training matter has been rightly incorporated to reflect company's training policy? What should be the policy on training to achieve organizational goals?

(*c*) Can Mr Mahajan ensure that the present agreement on promotion helps the development of the people at work and the organization as well? Is it essential to recruit people internally?

Case Study No. 2

Mr A. P Jain has been working as HRD Executive in a Tea Estate near Jalpaiguri, (West Bengal) where nearly 2500 employees are working. The Company has started business activities five years back. The Head Office of the Tea Estate is in Kolkata. The Company has no arrangement to impart training to its employees for improving their skill, ability and attitudes. The company has introduced attractive compensation package, scheme to provide fringe benefits and social security to its employees. It has also designed a career planning and development programme for its employees. After spending a colossal amount towards social security, welfare benefits, recreational activities and various employee benefit programmes the company observes that the production of some workers remain static, no improvement in quantity and quality is noticed, rate of accident and wastes is on the higher side. It is now felt that the company should develop a system to train its employees. Mr. S. P. Dey Managing Director of the company wants a detailed report from Mr Jain to this effect for placing the same before the Board. Mr Dey also asks Mr. Jain—

(*a*) to give his views whether training of employees will bring any change in behaviour and performance activities of employees.

(*b*) to submit suggestion in respect of training method he recommends for introduction.

(*c*) to submit action plan for ascertaing effectiveness of training programmes.

(*d*) let him know the mechanism he suggests for identification of training needs of employees.

Now, as HRD Executive of the above company, in place of Mr. A. P. Jain how would you react to all queries made by the MD? Reply to all the questions in seriatim and also submit a report on the usefulness of training.

7

Management Development

Meaning of Management Development

Management Development means development of people in managerial cardre, so that they can excel in their present performance and future performance as well. So, it is a process to improve knowledge, skill, abilities and attitudes of managers/executives for better performance of the job. Management development programme is designed looking to the objectives/strategy of the company and necessary measures are taken to impart knowledge, to improve skill, abilities and to change attitudes of the executives. In management development programmes, much more emphasis is given towards enhancement/development of such knowledge, skill, abilities, attitudes of managers which help to excel in future performance. So, management development is basically future-need oriented educational programmes for managers to develop them in all perspectives so that they can competently and effectively confront challenges and achieve organizational goals for survival, growth and development. However, the details of objectives of management development programmes are given, herein below:

(i) Identifying potential executives and developing them

Development programme helps the company to identify the executives who are potential and performers. Potential managers are given special care to improve their skill, ability and knowledge through participation in tailor-made training programmes.

(ii) Enhancing knowledge, skill, ability for performance of present job

For performing present job officers need to increase their knowledge, level of skill, ability. Management development programme is organized looking to needs of such officers/ managers of the company.

(iii) To create a dynamic management pool

In the changing scenario, organization needs to have dynamic management force so that organization can face challenges, and it is possible if, suitable development programme is organized for the managers.

(iv) To increase proacting capabilities of managers

Management development programme enhances visionary and strategic skills of the managers that help to develop their proacting capabilities.

(v) To develop conceptual skill of higher executives

Higher executives should have thorough knowledge, idea regarding the organization, its activities, relationship with functional units. All such skill which is termed as conceptual skill needs for effective functioning of organizational work. Management improvement programme helps to increase conceptual skill of higher management.

(vi) To improve human relations skill of managers

Human relations skill is needed for all cadres of management and through development programme such skill of managers is promoted.

(vii) To prepare managers to act as change agents

In today's competitive age every organization needs to introduce change in device, production method, technique, equipment etc. to confront challenges, and all this is possible if the managers can act as change agents. Specific management development programme may bring a total change in the mind-set of managers.

(viii) To keep the organizational activities running through provision of replacement

Organizational activities may be affected if suitable replacements are not provided in vacant positions of higher executives. Management development programme, as a measure of succession planning prepares the middle-level executive to occupy the vacant higher positions.

(ix) To identify individual learning needs and to meet them

Learning needs of managers vary from person to person. Hence, tailor-made individual programme, is required to be designed and imparted for growth, development of the individual executive.

(x) To keep the morale level of executives high

A lot of developmental programmes bring a change in the attitudes of management personnel that tend to increase the level of morale of such managers.

(xi) To encourage management personnel to prepare and implement personal development plans

Management development programme encourages potential managers to prepare personal development plans to cope with changing situations.

(xii) To increase problem solving skill, skill to study situational and analytical skill of managers

Management development programmes increase skill of management people to solve problems, to analyse critical events and to study different situations of organization.

Need for Management Development

The survivality, growth and development of any organization depends on the quality of workforce it has, and the quality of such workforce depends on the quality of management personnel (that means skill, knowledge, ability, attitudes of management people) of the company. Since, procurement, motivation, development of workers are part of managerial functions, qualitative functioning of such activities are influenced greatly by degree and qualities of skill, ability, competencies and attitudes of such managerial personnel. Hence, management development programmes are needed to compensate and strengthen the deficit areas of knowledge, skill, abilities of the executives so that they can perform their present job well and also future job when assigned in terms of objectives / strategies of the company.

However, the need for management development can be ascertained from the following :

(i) Social obligation

Organization is a part of society. Society has expectations, demands for its growth and development from societal members including organization/s functioning in the society. Organization can fulfil societal demands / requirement if managers are capable enough to analyse social obligations to present cases as spokesperson of the society to the company, to develop a bridge between company thinking and societal expectations, to make the society aware of contributions company made for amelioration and well-being of the members of the society. Hence, management development is needed to prepare capable and effective managers.

(ii) Effect of globalization

Because of globalization, multinational corporations (MNCs) and trans-national corporations (TNCs) have entered in the market resulting in, stiff competition amongst the market players. In such a situation, it becomes difficult for the domestic companies to survive in the context of quality goods they supply and the price they fix for the customers. It is, therefore, imperative need for the companies to have world class workers for production of world class product at resonable cost; and the companies can have such dynamic workforce if, they have highly skilled, committed, dynamic pool of management personnel who can prepare the workers' community according to need, requirement of the companies. So, here is the necessity of management development to face the challenges emanated from the globalization.

(iii) Effective functioning of line management

Line management/technocrats are well conversant with technicalities of production activities but, they may lack adequate skill, abilities in human relations development and conceptual areas of the company. For effective functioning of their work they need improvement, development of their skills in those areas where they lack.

Hence, management development programmes are required to be conducted to promote enhancement of human skill and conceptual skill of technocrats, line managers of organizations so that, they can perform their job better in terms of need, requirement of the companies.

(iv) Excellent quality of work of non-technical higher management

Technical skill is required for excellent performance by non-technical managers. Requirement of technical skill of management personnel varies in degree considering grade/strata a of the management to which they belong. Higher level management may need some knowledge/skill in technical areas and so, for better functioning they need to acquire skill in this area. Management development programme designed to impart technical skill to such non-technical higher management personnel may facilitate to deliver excellent quality of work by them.

(v) Use of latest technologies

Every organization needs to use latest technologies in its operational and service activities so that, quality goods at minimum cost can be produced to face competition with the market players but, these latest technologies can not be effectively used if, the managers are not given proper training to have aquaintances with technologies, its operative areas, use, effectiveness, probable problems, etc.

(vi) Change in economic policy

Change in economic policy creates a new business climate and work culture in organization where re-inventing of management practices appears to be of much necessity. New areas are required to be explored for expansion and diversification of business; continuous improvement of quality in services and products needs to be emphasised; issues like retention of customers and search out for new customer be prioritized. For all these, executives need an enrichment of knowledge, specific thought pattern, creative thinking, analytical ability, meaningful vision and foresightedness, and this is possible through organizing tailor-made development programmes which may enable higher management to explore new areas and to practice in the company to confront changes.

(vii) Smooth and effective functioning of business activities

Workers perform business and industrial activities under the guidance and supervision of management. Management personnel play the role of guide, coach, motivator, leader of the people at work. Workers can be effective if the decisions, directions, guidance of the management are proper, perfect and accurate. So, for smooth, effective and uninterrupted functioning of business activities managers should have leadership qualities, proper knowledge, skill in decision making and also should introduce schemes like employee involvement, empowerment and participation in organization. For all this, management development programme should be of much use.

Steps in Organization of Management Development Programme (Process of Management Development)

To develop skill, knowledge, abilities and attitudes of managers/executives and to design programmes for the purpose of such development, some steps are needed to be followed. They are discussed below in brief.

(i) Ascertainment of objectives/strategies of the company

The first step of management development is to know the objectives/strategies of the company. That means, company's plan, programme, policies, thought process, should be clearly ascertained. Whether, the company goes for expansion, diversification or reduction of business can be known from its objectives. So, the objectives/strategies tell, how many and what kind of management personnel will be required for the company. It gives a framework of management personnel requirement for future activities.

(ii) Analysis of organization's total need for management personnel

Total need for management personnel includes present need for management personnel in terms of present activities and future needs in terms of development activities. Present needs can be ascertained from

- organizational structure
- departments, sections, divisions
- span of supervision, delegation of authority, accountability, responsibility
- job role, job analysis, job description, work load, job specialization
- executive position

Analysis of the above factors would indicate whether, the company has right number and right kind of executives for present performance.

Future needs for management can be ascertained from the analysis of company's objectives/strategies.

(iii) Appraisal of current management resources

In this step current management talent is assessed. It is seen whether, company's own management team has desired skill, ability, attitude, knowledge to perform present job and has potential for development need of the company. An estimation of potential mangement personnel is made to ascertain the future requirement.

(iv) Preparation of management inventory

After estimation of potential management personnel, a management inventory is prepared to find out individual manager's strength and weaknesses so that, necessary developmental process can be initiated to make him competent and effective. Management inventory contains information / pa rticulars pertaining to each individual manager. Some of such information are given below:

- educational background
- age
- professional distinctions, if any, experience in different grade
- performance ratings
- training/development programme attended
- length of service
- achievements
- prize/rewards awarded
- transfer details
- specific aptitude
- different test results
- health records
- past promotions
- marital status
- present assignment
- interest in any field of activities

The above information help the company to know:

a. skill deficiency of manager's in term of future need
b. details of capable, competent managers for higher assignment.
c. need for training / development for future work.
d. shortage of managers for higher jobs.
e. strength and weakness for effecting succession planning.

On the basis of information available from management inventory, organization sets standard/criteria for nomination of managers for management development programmes.

(v) Deciding individual development needs

Individual manager's needs for development are determined on the basis of knowledge, skill, ability and attitude he has. Some managers may lack knowledge, skill, ability which they need to acquire, while others may lack attitudes which they need to change. So, development needs differ from individual to individual. To ascertain individual needs for development use of assessment centre/development centre can be made. Analysis of performance ratings also helps to indicate the weak areas of the individual managers that need development.

(vi) Organizing development programmes

On deciding the development needs of individual managers it is essential to prepare development programmes on the basis of such needs. Generally, in organizations HRM/HRD department designs different programmes suiting individual managers' needs and organises such programmes.

(vii) Evaluation of development programme

Whether, development programmes are effective or not that is evaluated after programmes are over. Change of behaviour of managers, organizational performance/results, promotion of healthy industrial relations, reduction in industrial conflicts, higher level of employees' morale are some indicators of development programme effectiveness.

Methods of Management Development

Today, mostly all organizations have realized the importance of training to develop skill, abilities, knowledge and attitudes of management personnel. So, training system has been accepted by the companies to conduct management development programmes through 'on-the-job' and 'off-the-job' techniques. Earlier, companies had much more reliance on external establishments like B-schools, training institutes / colleges for the training of their executives. Now, the situation has changed greatly. Big companies have set up their own training institutes / colleges at zonal or corporate level where executives are deputed for training. Some executives are assigned the job of Training Officers / Training Managers to (i) arrange for conducting programmes (ii) prepare training calendar (iii) design course contents with the help of subject experts, line management and HR specialist (iv) bring guest lecturers to provide faculty support (v) arrange for nomination of executives from different departments / regions (vi) impart training on the subjects on which they have expertise. Such training officers/ managers are also responsible for supervision, administration for running training institutions / colleges, preparation of budget for approval of the higher authority etc. However, for training in specific field/areas companies send executives to outside establishments.

Methods of Management Development

On-the-job	Off-the-job
1. Coaching	1. Role playing
2. Job rotation	2. Case Method
3. Understudy assignments	3. Intray/In-basket
4. Multiple Management	4. Sensitivity training
5. Committee Assignments	5. Syndicate Method
	6. Incident Method
	7. Johari Windows
	8. Problem-oriented projects
	9. Transactional Analysis
	10. Behaviour Modelling
	11. Lecture
	12. Conferences
	13. Programmad Instruction
	14. Films
	15. Business Game

All the methods of management development are discussed herein below in short :

Coaching

It is an on-the-job technique used for development of managerial skill, knowledge, ability so that assigned job can be performed well. Under this method, officer obtains coaching, guidance, instructions from senior officer to enhance, acquire knowledge, skill to perform job better. Coach/guide keeps continuous vigil, supervision on the performance of trainee officer and corrects, rectifies wrong doing, methods of operation. Trainee officer is involved in problem solving exercise, decision making process to develop his skill and confidence in performance.

This is easy, simple, inexpensive method of developing ompetence, knowledge of officers. This can be an effective method if competent, experienced, willing and expert coach is available.

Job rotation

It is a rotation of manager/officer from one job to other job, from one department to other department or from one place to other place in a systematic way. The objective of job rotation is to make the manager know the job so that he can excel in his performance. Through this method manager can make mastery over the jobs of different departments, units and can effectively perform the job of higher responsiblities. It gives a chance to the trainee manager to gain experience of working in different situations, environment, culture and of dealing with issues, problems of varied nature. All this broadens outlook of the manager, promotes human relations skill and develops problem solving skill.

Understudy assignments

This is a method of preparing potential officer, manager to perform the job of his boss that he holds. 'Understudy' means a person prepared to perform the work or fill the position of another. Manager watches and observes the style of functioning of his boss, his method of solving problems, dealing with customers, peers, suborodinates and his decision-making role in organization.

When potential manager's boss remains on leave or is away from headquarter for some work, potential officer is given a chance to officiate in place of his boss with the objective of making him permanent in that post. Through working in higher post during leave vacancy, manager gathers experience of working, acquires thorough knowledge of job, develops confidence of performing job of higher responsibilities. However, this method may not be helpful if boss does not cooperate with his suborodinate to learn the job as a whole and for not knowing completely/perfectly the job potential manager may make a lot of mistakes which may indicate that such method is ineffective to develop skill, ability of the potential manager.

Multiple Management

It is one of the on-the-job techniques used in organizations for the purpose of developing skill, abilities, attitudes, knowledge of the management.

Multiple management is a kind of committee / board of junior executives which conducts survey, studies problems on important issues, discusses thoroughly, makes interaction between members and submits recommendation to the top management.

This forum gives an opportunity to the junior executives to

- promote self-development
- develop team spirit
- prepare mind-set of accepting need for cooperation
- adjust to situations of group working
- develop human relations skills through interactive process
- enhance analytical ability
- acquire knowledge on different aspects of organization
- develop problem-solving skill
- improve knowledge/understanding on decision-making process

This method helps to identify the executives who can be successful in future assignment. It is a very useful technique to groom executives for senior positions at a reasonably lesser period of time with practically no additional cost for development.

Committee assignment

Under this method potential executives are taken in committee as members for enhancing knowledge, idea on problematic issues and gaining experience to find out solutions and alternative means for redressal. This committee may be constituted for a limited period on ad-hoc arrangement for ascertaining real issues through investigation, study, observation and submitting suggestions, comments, views on the problems to the higher management. It may have also permanent nature of activities where a large number of executives can be brought under the management development programmes.

Some of the merits of this method are mentioned below :

(i) Members can broaden their outlook and understanding for redressal of the issues

(ii) It helps to develop mutual understanding, faith and confidence between committee members.

(iii) It promotes human relations skills of managers

(iv) It increases skill of interaction, presentation, communication, argument for reaching to an agreement.

(v) It is inexpensive and easy method for development of executive.

Role playing

It is an off-the-job technique used in organizations for development of managerial skill, attitudes by allowing the executives to play the role of some other personalities. It happens that senior executives ignore junior executives' problems, inconveniences, difficulties faced by them in the process of performance of their work, and as a result such senior executives may not be able to develop mutual understanding and confidence between them and their subordinates. It also happens that senior executives because of their attitudinal problems can not make positive/conducive interaction with their subordinates. Hence, to understand emotion, feeling, difficulties, inconveniences of subordinates and also to change their own attitudes for better interaction with subordinates, senior executives play the role of subordinates. A sales manager playing role of sales supervisor, a bank manager playing role of a bank officer become exposure to real life situation as others perceive it.

In role playing session each player is given a role to play. He is briefed about his role, the description of problem/incident is written up and given to him. Each player is asked to play the natural role of the position he is given to act. During role playing activities other trainees watch, observe and note the area of undeserved activities of role players. In subsequent discussion, trainer focuses the point of differences and allows other trainees to deliver their suggestion/arguments. Through such interactive process, role players can experience the truth and develop their attitudes and promote learning.

Role playing helps to

- mould attitudes/mind-set of trainees
- improve skills of executives for interaction
- develop human relations skills
- develop sense of 'we feeling', 'togetherness'
- understand others' feeling, emotions
- make more sensitive about problems/perspectives of other people.

This method can be effectively used in organizations for the purpose of changing attitudes and developing skill, competencies of executives if, role players manifest their real behaviours, do not overact or do not take playing casually.

Case Method

Under this method cases are prepared and given to trainees by trainer for study, discussion, analysis of problems, finding out genesis/causes of problems and for determination of solutions, alternatives. A case is no more than a set of circumstances or description of events. A central theme of case study is to bring out real incidents, problems of the company which the executives are likely to face and to present these before the trainees to develop their skill in the area of decision making, problem searching/analysis and problem solving through study, discussion, enquiry, exchanges of ideas and analysis of incidents.

This method is of great use in developing decision making, analytical and judgemental abilities of the executives, but it may not generate interest, inspiration amongst trainees if cases are imaginative having no expression of real life situations of the company.

In-tray/Inbasket

This is one of the off-the-job techniques that develops decision making, problem solving and analytical skills of the executives.The main activity of the manager/senior executive is to get the work done with and through the people. Hence, for accomplishment of task/job it needs allocation of responsibilities, team management, overall supervision, coordination with the different functionaries, problem analysis and decision making. What a manager is required to perform is decided by him looking to the information contained in the papers like letters, reports, statement, documents, complaints, message. Orders/ instructions of higher authority and also other papers are received by manager/executive daily from his 'in-tray'/'in-basket' meant for incoming mails.

Trainer collects few days' mails from the managers of those organizations from where executives are deputed for training, and gives the same to each trainee for disposal of issues mentioned in the papers within a scheduled period of time.

Trainer provides background brief of the issues to the trainees to facilitate them to work. Trainee's activities include :

- prioritisation of issues (giving much more priority on urgent issues than routine issues)
- preparation of time-frame for completion of tasks
- obtaining comments / reports from other officers / personnel
- analysis of problems and also suggestions, comments, reports received from other officers / personnel
- decision taken for execution of work
- assignment of work to junior executives and to get the work executed through them within a seheduled period of time.

After participation of all trainees in such exercise is over, review of individual trainee's work is made.

Merits of In-basket/In-tray method

(i) It increases analytical ability of the executives as they need to analyse the issues to find out causes/origin and to suggest solutions.

(ii) The executives can come to know the area of activities they would be required to perform. So, they can take initiative beforehand to increase skill in those areas.

(iii) The executives through interaction and presentation of their analysis and suggestions can get to know the right method of collecting information and the right solution of the problems.

(iv) It improves decision making and judgemental skill of trainees.

(v) Executives become familiar with real life situations that help them to measure their strength and weaknesses for confronting situation. Hence, trainees' capabilities can be judged through this technique.

(vi) Since, most of problems are taken from the same organization where trainees work, it generates a lot of

interest amongst trainees for involvement and effective participation in the training programme. So, training becomes useful to promote learning of the trainees.

Demerits of In-basket/In-tray method

(i) Executives may take the whole training programme casually when they perceive that problems are not related to real life situations of the company.

(ii) It is not effective when trainer is not well coversant with the nature of duties, responsibilities of the potential managers.

(iii) Trainees may not have effective learning from this exercise when imaginary problems are given for discussion, study and suggestion for redressal.

(iv) It may not be meaningful for those trainees who lack human skill as this method has no scope to promote human relation skill.

Sensitivity training

This method is also called T-Group (T'stands for training) or L-Group ('L' Stands for Learning) training. This training method is used to change attitudes and behaviour of trainees through group interactions.

All individuals are not same in respect of temperament, disposition, feeling, emotions. Some are rough, harsh, insensitive, impatient, intolerant while others are cool, calm, rationale, amiable, sensitive. The first category of people may face difficulty to develop interpersonal relations, mutual understanding and mutual faith between each others as they lack human skill. These type of people are not rare in the executive cadres who need change of attitudes and behaviour for development of human skill. This change is possible through sensitivity or T-Group training.

Salient characteristics

(i) This development programme relates to change of behaviour and attitudes of executives.

(ii) It has no fixed agenda for discussion, participation. No formal training is given by trainers, as there is no course content designed for the purpose of imparting the same to the trainees.

(iii) It is a leaderless, unstructured programme conducted by the participants. Trainees are the objects of study by themselves.

(iv) Participations in the training programme who are 10 to 15 in number form a small group for interaction by themselves.

(v) Trainer tells the participants about the objective of the programme, creates an opportunity for the trainees to carry on their transactions (that is exchange of stimulus and response) to manifest each other's behavioural attitudes.

Through this group process each participant gets to know / perceive the attitudinal / behavioural problems of others; and this experience is communicated to each other for rectification, changes of attitudes.

(vi) Trainees are given the message that they should feel free and frank; and with open mind they should interact with each other. They should not have ill feeling for pin-pointing their weak areas by others.

Merits of sensitivity training

(i) Potential managers may get to know their 'blind areas' which may stand in the process of their development, elevation. Such officers may take necessary measures to rectify / strengthen those areas.

(ii) It helps the trainees to be tolerant, patient and develops a skill of active listening.

(iii) It creates a feeling of openness, co-operativeness and team development.

(iv) It develops the skill of the trainees to perceive others accurately that helps to establish mutual understanding, confidence and faith.

(v) It facilitates change of attitudes of the trainees as open discussion, interaction, identification of each other's limitations, weakness urge upon them to mould their behavioural pattern.

(vi) It develops the skill to remove differences, redress misunderstanding and to settle conflicts.

(vii) It is very useful for the trainees who are liberal, enlightened and healthy personalities.

Demerits of sensitivity training

(i) All the trainees may not be open, freeminded for interaction. Hence, the method may become ineffective.

(ii) The trainees with excessively high degree of 'evil-traits' may be found to be incorrigible.

(iii) It may be difficult to create an atmosphere of open interaction if participants do not take such exercise seriously.

(iv) The skill acquired through interaction may be found to be meaningless if, the same can not be transferred to the work situation. The possibility of emerging such a situation may not be ruled out.

(v) The interaction between participants may create an unhealthy, inconducive atmoshpere that may stand in the process of conducting such programme. Hence, this method may prove to be ineffective.

(vi) This method is expensive and time consuming.

Syndicate Method

This is one of the methods used in industrial settings for improvement of skills of its executives, so that, their potentials can be utilized by way of assigning higher responsibilities to them. The objectives of such training programme are:

- to update the knowledge of the trainees
- to expose trainees to various problems cropped up in industrial situations

- to know solutions of problems
- to enhance analytical ability of the trainees
- to make the trainees effective as leaders
- to make the participants team-friendly
- to improve human relations skill

Salient charcteristics

(i) Trainees are divided into small group which are called syndicates. Each syndicate has leader or chairman to represent the group.

(ii) Members of the syndicate selected by the trainer are taken from different functional areas where they are already recognized as performers. The group has heterogeneous mix of executives.

(iii) Each syndicate is given a task which is spelt out in terms of briefs and background papers prepared by trainer.

(iv) The subject matter of the assigned task varying from group to group is chosen for the group looking to the availability of the competent, matured trainee executives in the group.

(v) Each syndicate member is required to work as leader/ chairman of the team during the period of his training.

(vi) The group members discuss issues thread-barely, analyse them to find out genesis, suggest solution and prepare report for presentation. The group leaders of individual groups present papers before all the groups and reply to questions/queries of members / leaders of groups.

(vii) Trainer acts as guide, gives less direction for solving issues.

This method is useful for developing human skill to promote inter-personal relations, analytical abilities, problem-solving skill and leadership qualities of executives.

This training technique may not be effective if,

- briefs, background papers are prepared on the basis of imaginary information not having link/relevance to real life situations.

- selection of syndicate members is not perfect.
- trainer lacks competence to conduct such programmes.

Incident Method

This is an off-the-job technique developed by Professor Paul and Faith Pigors at the Massachusetts Institute of Technology. Under this method, trainees are given some information about incidents / cases and are asked to give their suggestion / decision. Incidents may be short interactional activities between boss and subordinate relating to improvement of quality of goods or reducing rate of defect products.

The objectives of such training programme are :

- to develop inquisitiveness amongst the trainees so that they can activate their mental faculty to put various questions to the trainer for collection of data / information etc.
- to promote self-development of trainees
- to increase diagnostic skill of participants
- to develop skill of executives to make them understand/ aware of their limitations, weakness for solution of problems.
- to improve judgemental skill of trainees
- to promote human skill of executives

Features

(i) Each trainee obtains outlines of issues / incidents from instructor / trainer. Incidents are real life situations.

(ii) The trainer supplies details of incidents to the trainees if, the same is asked for.

(iii) The individual trainee analyses data, information in order to find out causes of problems and to arrive at a decision.

(iv) The like-minded trainees form group/s and select group leader / spokesperson.

(v) Individual trainee's analysis of problems, suggestions, opinions are discussed and group decision is taken.

(vi) Spokesperson of each group presents its position in respect of data / information collected from the trainer and also suggestions for solution of problems/issues taken by the group.

(vii) The trainer tells decision of problems to the trainees.

(viii) In this method different group members can ascertain strength of collection of data (i.e. extent of data, information collected) from the trainer and their decision making ability.

Efficacy of the technique

This technique is of great help

- to promote mental faculty and emotional effectiveness of trainees, to collect appropriate information to study and analyse situations
- to develop skill to promote 'self-concept' of executives so that, they can learn by developing themselves.
- to improve creative ability and thought process for application of data/information for arriving at decisions.
- to make the trainees acquire knowledge, skill, ability · to understand where do they stand in respect of their collection/analysis of data and their judgement on the issues/problems.
- to develop mutual understanding and confidence amongst trainees
- to enhance leadership qualities of trainees

This training method may not be effective if,

- trainer is not competent
- trainer does not have skill, ability to conduct such programme

- incident, problems are not taken from real life situation
- trainees do not have potential for taking higher responsibilities
- trainees take the whole matter in a casual manner.
- group members are not cooperative.

Johari Window

Johari Window is a conceptual framework used by organizations for increasing personality of executives. The framework developed by Joseph Luft and Harry Ingham (taken from the first names of its authors) gives an idea that attitudes, behaviour (i.e, form of personality) of individuals manifest in four ways as shown in Figure 7.1, and such depiction/ manifestation is due to, self-perception of individuals and perception of others.

Under this framework, four parts of personality of executives/ leaders are :

- Public arena i.e. that part of personality (attitudes, behaviour) of executives which is known to self and also known to others like peers, subordinates, boss.
- Blind arena meaning that part of executive's personality, (attitudes, behaviour) which is unknown to self (executive) but known to others. It is unknown to executive because the executive has been unwilling to get feedback from others or has been unable to study indications/ message of people about feedback.
- Private arena i.e. that part of executive's personality which is known to self but unknown to others. Other people may not come to know the executive's attitudinal/ behavioural manifestaion probably because the executive has been unwilling to get the people know or the people have been unable to pick know or the people have been unable to pick upresponses of executive to know this arena.
- Unknown arena meaning that part of executive's personality which is not known both to executive and to others

	Known to self	Not known to self
Known to others	Public	Blind
Not known to others	Private	Unknown

Figure 7.1 : The Johari Window

Features :

(i) Trainees are given thorough idea about concept, uses and utility of this method.

(ii) Necessity of getting feedback from others to expand 'public' arena of the trainees in order to reduce the 'blind' arena is emphasised.

(iii) It enhances knowledge, understanding of the executives through disclosure of private arena to others by way of extending the 'public' arena and reducing the 'private' arena.

(iv) In a situation, where there is simultaneous feedback and disclosure between leaders / executives and the people with whom they work, the 'public' arena begins to extend itself into the blind and the 'private' arenas, and there is high probability that some of 'unknown' arena will begin to surface into the 'public arena (Paul Hersey and Kenneth H. Blanchard 1980)

This is an effective technique to develop human skill of executive but this framework may not bring any result in a situation where dispositional / temparamental conditions of executives and the people with whom executives work are not conducive for change / alteration. Besides, some trainees may not accept this technique wholeheartedly as they do not want to disclose their private arena to others.

Problem-Oriented Project

This is a method of developing analytical ability, judgemental skill and problem solving ability of the executives who are identified as potential managers of the company.

Under this method, problems of the company are collected by the trainer and are written up by him for obtaining suggestions/ solution from the trainees. Some examples of projects are :

- reorganization of departments
- designing and developing performance appraisal format
- ways and means to reduce absenteeism and labour turnover
- changes in operation techniques, device.

Process

(i) gathering / collecting information from the company by the trainer / instructor with regard to problems confronted by it for which changes are needed for removal of problems.

(ii) writing up of projects on different areas of activities by trainer for trainees

(iii) forming of some groups of trainees and assigning of specific task / problem to each group with necessary details/materials available with trainer

(iv) studying, investigating and analysing by each group separately and preparation of report by the group

(v) presentation of reports by groups

(vi) discussion, clarification on issues

Merits

(i) It gives a thorough idea on the subjects on which project work is carried on by the trainees. In the process it improves conceptual knowledge of the executives.

(ii) It enhances problem-solving skill of the executives as , the groups consisting of trainees are required to submit reports containing suggestions and recommendations of trainees for solution.

(iii) Trainees can get to know the real life situations of the company. So, they undertake project work with great interest and involvement

(iv) It promotes analytical ability, judgemental skill of trainees.

(v) It helps potential executives to know right solution and also to ascertain their strength and weaknesses for redressal of problems.

(vi) It helps to develop team-building skill as the trainees work in a team and each trainee's success depends on how he contributes to the team work.

(vii) It improves human skill of the trainees to develop understanding, confidence amongst team members.

Demerits

(i) As the trainer writes up problems for trainees he needs competence, special skill for designing and setting problems. Hence, trainer without such skill may not be successful.

(ii) If trainees lack adequate knowledge, skill for higher assignments, this method may not be effective.

(iii) The trainees may not take interest to carry out such task if, the project topic is imaginary and has no relevance to company's activities.

Transactional Analysis (TA)

It is an off-the-job technique used by organizations to analyse and understand behavioural pattern and activities of executives that helps to develop their interpersonal competence. TA has been developed by Eric Berne. According to him, the unit of social intercourse is called a transaction. If two or more people encounter each other in a social aggregation, sooner or later one of them will speak or give some other indication of acknowledging the presence of the others. This is called transactional stimulus. Another person will then say or do something which is in someway related to this stimulus and that is called the transactional response. So, stimulus response relationship between two individuals is a transaction. Each person irrespective of age has three ego states (Parent, Adult and Child) which are distinct sources of behaviour. An ego state is a consistant patten of feeling, experiences and behaviour/activities manifestation.

Parent Ego

This is that part of the ego state which an individual acquires from his parents and parent substitutes during the entire peiod of childhood, especially during the formative period of childhood. Considering different types of stimulus provided by parents and perception held by the child in regard to parents as stimulus supplier, the parent can be characterised as critical parent and nurturing parent.

A critical parent makes critical evaluations and assessments of each and every activity and provides stimulus to the child. He supplies negative stimulus through abusing, criticizing, rebuking and reprimanding. He thinks himself supreme in every aspect and considers him to be the one who knows everything. With continuous inflow of negative stimuli from the parent during development period, child forms some idea about his parent which subsequently dominates his ego pattern.

Nurturing parent takes excessive care of the child than needed. He seldom allows the child to be exposed to the vagaries of the environment. He sets a list of do's and don'ts for the child.

Adult Ego

It is the most important ego state of the individual. Supply of stimulus, response to stimulus, action, interaction and all other activities a person requires to pass through during the course of transaction are integral part of functional activities of adult ego. The activity part of this ego state includes:

- Collection of data from primary as well as secondary sources
- Storing of data in the data bank
- Processing of data to suit requirements
- Examination, scrutiny and analysis of issues/situations to provide stimulus, response to stimulus.
- Objective assessment/evaluation of issues/situations
- Thorough finding and refinding of genesis of issues/ situations
- Ascertainment of probable effect of issues
- Application of a rational and judicious decision making process
- Proper and unbiased judgement.

The adult ego provides rational judgement on issues if, it functions on its own, but adult ego states in most individuals are contaminated either by the child ego or by the parent ego or by both ego states and as a result, the adult ego cannot work effectively unbiasedly.

Child Ego

This ego state is formed during the period after the child comes out of mother's womb till the expiry of childhood. So, long child remains at mother's womb, he gets influenced by mother's behaviour-physical, physiological and psychological.

According to Muriel James and Dorothy Jongeword (1971) the child ego state includes impulses that come naturally to an infant, recording of the child's early experiences, responses to those experiences, decisions made about himself and other people surrounding him. When a person feels and acts as he did when he was a child, he is in the child ego state.

The child expresses his behavioural activities during his evolutionary period as 'natural' child, 'trained' or 'adapted' child, and 'witty' child or 'little professor'.

The structure of different ego states is shown in

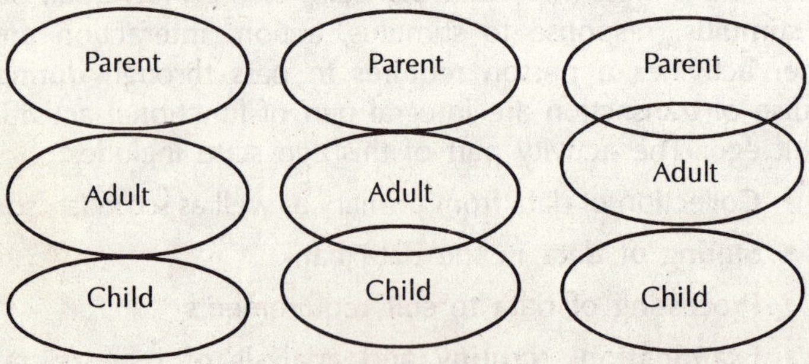

Figure 7.2

1. Balanced Ego State
2. Adult Ego State contaminated by child ego.
3. Adult Ego State conaminated by parent ego.

Figure 7.2 : Structure of ego states

Merits

(i) This is an effective method to analyse and understand behaviour of executives

(ii) This enhances confidence of executives to deliver quality service.

(iii) This facilitates executives to mould their mind-set/ behavioural attitudes to make perfect and speedy decisions.

(iv) This method helps executives develop special skill and ability to study, understand ego pattern of subordinates and also to change their attitudes/ego state for excelling in their performance.

(v) Interpersonal relationship can be developed through identification, reinforcement of areas disturbing relationship.

Demerits

(i) This method may not bring result if, trainees do not have confidence over working of such method.

(ii) It is a very time consuming and expensive mechanism to change all the subordinates' mind-set.

(iii) Subordinates' cooperation for changes may not be available if, they are not happy with their superiors.

Behaviour Modelling

This is a method of improving behaviour, attitudes of executives through video tapes, films that display effective handling / solution of problems in real business situation by model persons in organizations. It occurs that some executives may not have proper skill to deal withproblems particularly inter-personal problems, and to develop such skill, use of videotapes, films is made to show how successful executives tackled/handled problems in different real situations.

Trainees watch videotapes, films that show model persons' activities, acquire knowledge, idea about technique used for solution of problems, practice till thorough idea/skill developed and get feedback about performance.

Thus, behaviour modelling involves getting the trainees know the right way of working, providing them opportunities to practise and giving them feedback about their performance.

Process

Steps of behaviour modelling are as follows :

(i) Modelling

Trainees are shown through films, videotapes as to how model persons are behaving effectively in a problem situation. The main idea of this activity is to make trainees know the right way of handling problems by senior executives.

(ii) Role Playing

Trainees are given the roles of specific executives to play in simulated situation which they practise and rehearse in the same manner as demonstrated by the models.

(iii) Discussion and reinforcement

In this step trainer discusses with trainees about their role performance. Each trainee's defect/shortcoming and also outstanding performance areas are pointed out. To rectify the weak areas the trainer makes the trainees rewatch films/ videotapes and see attentively how model persons deal with issues and behave in a problem situation. For outstanding performance positive stroke is given to the concerned trainees.

(iv) Transfer of learning

Trainees are encouraged to apply their new skills when they are back on their job.

Merits

(i) It enhances problem-solving skill of trainees

(ii) Trainees get to know the right ways to deal with problems.

(iii) Under this method trainees play the roles of specific executives in a simulated situatioin to acquire skill and ability to confront problems and solve them.

(iv) Trainees get the chance to practise and rehearse the use of skills on the job and in the process can develop 'self-efficacy'.

(v) It develops human relations skill to behave effectively with subordinates.

(vi) Behavioural approach, skill, tact of model executives used for handling problem situations effectively may develop a mind-set of 'must win' 'must achieve' 'must succeed'.

Demerits

(i) This method may not be effective if, the trainees are reluctant to participate and take it very lightly and casually.

(ii) If, potential executives are not nominated for training, this method may not be useful to yield results.

(iii) Since, issues, problems of companies are numerous, it may not be possible to demonstrate dealing, tackling, handling of all problem situations to the trainees, as a result learning of trainees may become incomplete.

Lecture (Already discussed in Training Chapter)

Conferences (Already discussed in Training Chapter)

Programmed Instruction (Already discussed in Training Chapter)

Films

Films are used in training programme in India for a long time. These are prepared on different subjects and trainer selects specific subjects which are useful for trainees. Films are shown to the trainees to let them know how problem situations are handled by executives.

Features

- It is one of the methods used by trainer to provide knowledge, idea to the trainees about the problems faced by senior executives in organization and also situations tackled/settlement made by them.
- Trainer ascertains subject areas on which trainees lack requisite skill, ability and need reinforcement.
- Trainer may use films for different purposes viz., giving detailed information about various problems relating to IRs., HR, developing inter-personal relations by letting the trainees know the behavioural techniques used by senior management people to improve performance, etc.
- This method may be used along with other techniques like lecture, discussion, conferences to make the trainees understand clearly the whole exercise.

Merits

(i) It is simple and quick method of learning.

(ii) Trainees learn techniques of solving problems which they can use on the job after they are back from training.

(iii) It helps trainees to develop a spirit of self-determination to do, to achieve.

(iv) This method helps the trainees to keep the learning in their memory for a long time.

(v) Trainees may give their best for excellent performance if, they are influenced by the activities of senior executives demonstrated in the films.

(vi) This method can provide knowledge to a large number of trainees.

Demerits

(i) This method is exepensive as films on different subjects, problems need to be prepared.

(ii) It may not be possible to prepare films on all problem situations, issues of organizations. Hence, trainees may not get knowledge, idea on all organizational problems, issues dealt with by senior executives.

(iii) Since there is no arrangement of practising, rehearsing skill, knowledge acquired through observations, watching of films in the training system can not be experimented. Thus, the learning process becomes incomplete.

(iv) Participants may not take this method seriously.

(v) This method may not be effective if, quality of trainees is sub-standard, below average.

Business or Management Game

Business game is a simulation exercise of business situations used in training programmes to develop skill, competencies of executives in organizations. It is a popular training method used in India, for many years.

This kind of simulation exercise has following activities:

- Making of some groups

Trainees are divided into some groups consisting of two or more members. Each group represents an imaginary company. All groups are competitors to each other in a simulated market place and objective of each group is to become the number one company in the market, to dominate over other competitors.

- Ascertainment of games

Trainer decides what type of games the trainees are required to play in the training session. Games may relate to marketing, advertising, production, inventory maintenance and the like.

- Supply of data, information to the groups

Trainer collects data, information from organizations regarding production, sales, finance, human resources, advertisement, price, inventories, organization structure, company details, strategy, mission etc. and supplies relevant information to the groups.

- Setting of game periods

The game may be for 3 or 4 periods duration and a week may represent two periods of 6 months duration. So, the whole game exercise may be over within a period of 1½weeks or 2 weeks.

- Group decision

Each group works out action in detail for each period and details of action for 3/4 periods are incorporated in the prescribed format to find out final results.

Final results of each group are compared with those of other groups.

Merits

(i) It enhances problem-solving skills of trainees.

(ii) It helps develop conceptual skills of executives who participate in business games.

(iii) Trainees get opportunity to play pro-acting role that helps improve pro-acting capability of the trainees.

(iv) Trainees can get thorough knowledge about planning, organizing, directing and controlling through their direct involvement, participation in basic business activities.

(v) It creates competitive spirit amongst trainees. So, after they are back to workplace, they may go for aggressive business for achievement of their goals.

(vi) Trainees are required to analyse the data, information supplied by the trainer for making decisions on different subjects, and in the process trainees develop analytical ability.

(vii) Decision making process of trainees enhances problem-solving skills.

Demerits

(i) Since business game is a simulation exercise it may not be effctive to yield result in real business situations.

(ii) Trainees may take it casually as they think that this exercise is childish exercise.

(iii) Business game writing is a difficult task that needs experience and field study.

Development Centres

Development centre is a platform where executives get opportunity to know their present level of competence, potential competencies and level of competencies needed for higher positions. This understanding and acquisition of knowledge they get through awareness programmes of development centres.

In some areas development centres have similarities with those of assessment centres. They are as follows :

- Both the centres make the participants know the present level of competence and also potential competencies
- Much more emphasis is given on behavioural dimensions by both centres
- Most of competence assessment methods are common in both centres
- Principles, norms followed for engaging assessors in both centres are same.

Differentiating areas of development centres from those of assessment centres are as follows :

- In development centres feedback exercise is made at the end of each exercise whereas in assessment centres feedback review is arranged just before conclusion of the programme.
- Self-assessment is one of the basic activities of development centre which is absent in the process of assessment centre activities.
- End result of assessment under assessment centre is used by companies whereas, results of development centre remain with participants.

- Development centre is used as a tool for total development of participants whereas, assessment centre is used as a selection/promotion tool of the company.

Development centre helps the executives to know the shortfall in their competency level for performance of the present job and also for future performance and accordingly executives prepare personal development plan. Different simulation exercises are conducted to improve weak areas of participants and at the end of each exercise counselling, feedback reviews, guidance, behavioural orientation, coaching are arranged.

Books Recommended

1. Eric Berne : Games People Play : The Psychology of Human Relationships (Penguin Books Ltd. Harmondsworth, Middlesex, England, 1980)
2. Ajit Kumar Ghosh : Managing Human Resources : Strategic Approach to Win, (Manas Publications, New Delhi, 2002)
3. Muriel James and Dorothy Jongeward : Born to Win (Mass : Addisonwesley Publishing Company, 1971)
4. Gary Dessler : Human Resource Management (Prentice-Hall International Inc. London, 2000)
5. R. Harrison : Employee Development (Institute of Personnel and Development, 2nd Edn. 1997, London)
6. A. Mumford : Management Development : Strategies for Action (Institute of Personnel Management, London, 1994)
7. R. W. Revans : Developing Effective Managers (Longman, Harlow, 1971)
8. U. Pareek and T. V. Rao : Designing and Managing Human Resources System (Oxford and IBH, 1981, New Delhi)
9. C. Argyris : On Organizational Learning (Blackwell, Cambridge, Mass, 1992)
10. R. M. Gange : Conditions of Learning (Holt, Rhinehart and Winston, New York, 1965)

11. Paul Hersey and Kenneth H. Blanchard : Management of organizational behaviour : Utilizing Human Resources (Prentice-Hall of India Private Limited, New Delhi, 1980)

Questions

1. What is management development? What are the objectives of management development pogramme?
2. "Management development programmes compensate and strengthen the deficit areas of knowledge, skill, abilities of the executives" Do you agree? Discuss
3. Explain the need for management development.
4. "Various programmes are designed to develop skill, knowledge, abilities and attitudes of managers and for such purpose some steps are needed to be followed" - What are those steps? Discuss.
5. "Training system has been accepted by most companies to conduct management development programmes through 'on-the-job' and 'off-the-job' techniques" - Give a brief outline of the techniques generally used by the companies for developing managerial competencies and behaviour.
6. Do you think 'on-the-job' training methods are more effective for improving managerial skill than 'off-the-job' training methods? Explain your views in this context
7. What is Johari Window? Is it considered a technique to improve executive skill? - Discuss
8. What do you mean by Transactional Analysis? How does this technique help the managerial personnel to change their behavioural pattern?
9. What is Business Game? State the difficulties some training institutes face to conduct such programme?
10. What is Development Centre? Is there any difference between Assessment Centre and Development Centre?

Case Study

ABC Bank Ltd. has 1500 branches across the country. It has four Regional offices which are situated in Kolkata, Mumbai, Bangalore and Delhi. The Head offfice of the Bank is in Pune. The branch activities are controlled and monitored through respective Regional offices headed by Regional Managers who are in the rank of Dy General Manager.

The overall control of the Regional offices is made by Head office through General Managers of different portfolios who are directly accountable to Chairman cum Managing Director, for the business activities of the respective regions. The Bank has four Regional Training Centres (RTC) under the control of respective Regional Manager. Apart from RTCs the bank has Staff Administrative College in Pune which is used as Training cum Development Centre to facilitate change in the behavioural activities of those officers whose change is needed for performance of the present job and future job also. The Staff Administrative College is under the direct control of GM (HRM & General Administration). Generally, human skill and conceptual skill developement of officers is done through this college after proper analysis of the training/development need of the concerned officers is made.

In the instant case Mr Harihar Chakraborty Accountant has been working in Jadavpur Branch of the ABC Bank Ltd. under Kolkata Region. The administrative set up of Jadavpur Branch is like this:

Mr. A. K. Banerjee, Sr. Manager (HRM) of Kolkata Region has received a complaint from Sr Branch Manager, Mr Ajoy Paramanik of Jadavpur Branch against Mr Harihar Chakraborty, Accountnat who picks up quarrel with officers, customers and even with him on filmsy ground, creates unhealthy environment in the banking hall and tarnishes the image of the institution. In a recent event Mr Charkraborty got furious and created a nasty scene in Sr Branch Manager's chamber when he was advised by Mr Paramanik to head the Deposit Mobilization Team consisting of 3 officers (including Mr Chakraborty) and 2 clerks and to put in efforts so that maximum deposit could be modilized. Mr

Organizational Structure of ABC Bank Ltd is given below:

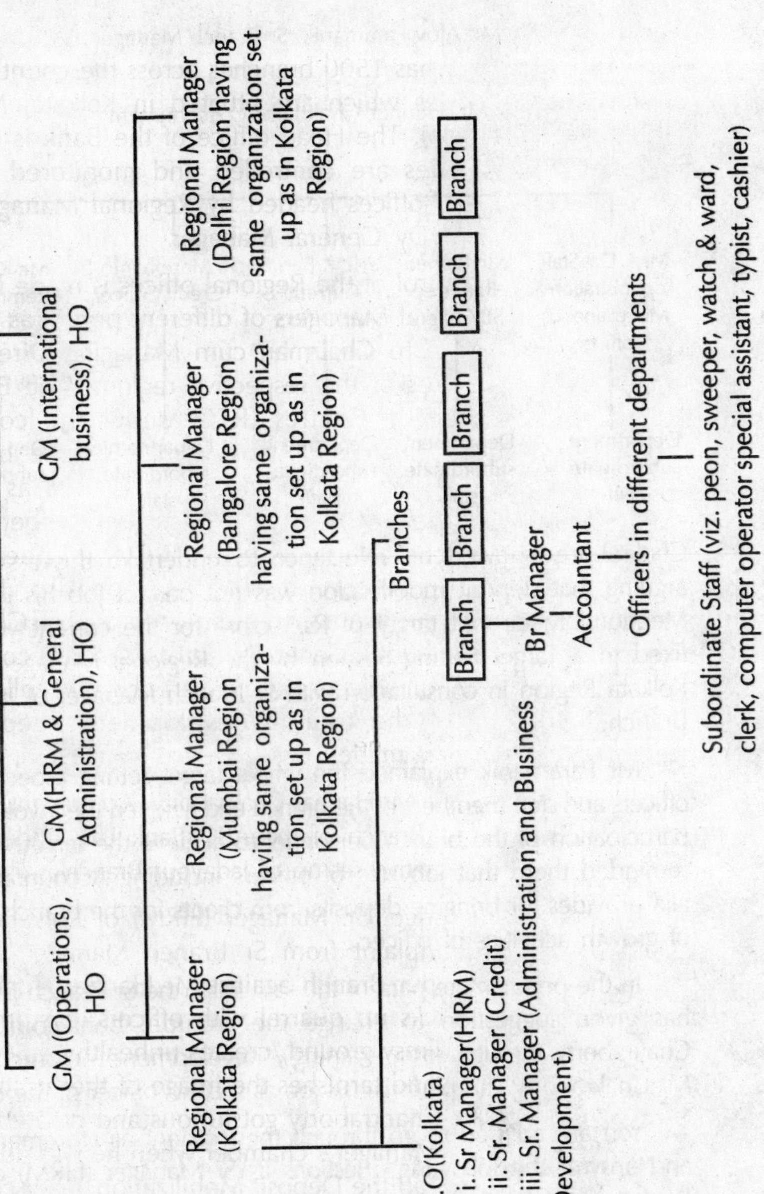

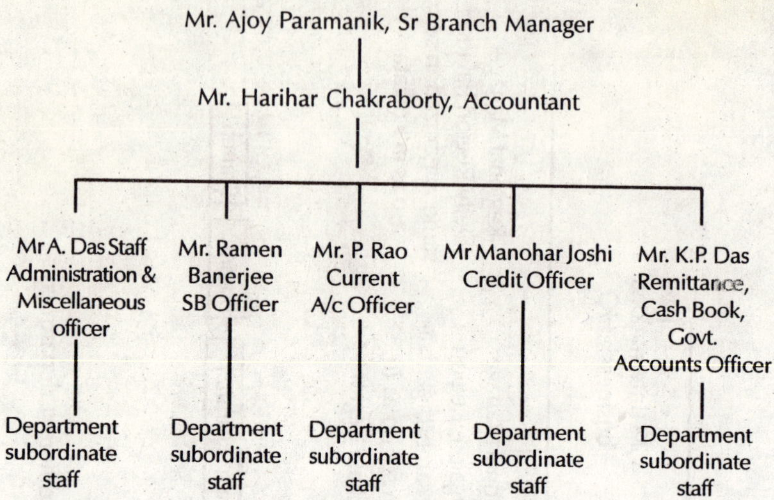

Chakraborty showed his reluctance to undertake this assignment arguing that deposit mobilization was not part of job his job role. Mentionably, deposit target of Rs.5 crore for the current year was fixed in a Target Setting Session by the Regional Manager of the Kolkata Region in consultation with Sr Branch Manager of Jadavpur Branch.

Mr Paramanik explained the whole target setting aspect to the officers and staff members of the branch and asserted the involvement/participation of the branch personnel to achieve the target. He also reminded them that job role of officers including Accountant inter alia provides for bringing deposits from clients for the branch as part of growth activities of officers.

In the penultimate para of the said letter the Sr Branch Manager has given suggestion to change the attitude, behaviour of Mr Chakraborty through some training / development measure so that Mr Chakraborty can perform his job as second officer of the branch.

You are advised to go through the incident as aforementioned and answer the following questions as Sr Manager (HRM) of ABC Bank Ltd., Kolkata Region.

(i) Do you feel Mr Harihar Charkraborty needs training to improve his behaviour? If so, what training/development

method you would suggest for Mr Chakraborty? Discuss the details of such training method.

(ii) How does the behavioural problem as revealed from the activities of Mr Chakraborty affect the branch functioning? Apart from training what other measures can be taken for improvement of behaviour of Mr Chakraborty?

(iii) Do you think Mr Ajoy Paramanik, Sr Branch Manager has not done right thing in assigning the task of heading Deposit MobilizationTeam to Mr Chakraborty?

(iv) Under what circumstances you can take the help of Development Centre?

8

Performance Appraisal

Meaning of Performance Appraisal

Performance appraisal is a development activity undertaken by the company for improvement of the skill, knowledge, ability, personality of the people at work. After procuring people, organization finds whether output/service of the people is as per standard set or below the standard. In case of a situation, where performance of people is less than the standard set, organization provides counselling and feedback to such people for reinforcement of their weak areas. The mechanism of appraising performance of an employee relative to his standard set for performance is called, performance appraisal. So, performance appraisal may be defined as a systematic and planned process of evaluating performance of an employee, relative to his/her standard set for performance.

Performance appraisal involves the following basic activities :

- Setting standard/goals
- Internal discussion
- Appraising/measuring performance relating to standard set
- Interface discussion

- Providing feedback, counselling to improve weak areas, or stimulating performers, achievers for maintenance/ continuance of the present level of performance.

Features of Performance Appraisal

Salient features of performance appraisal are as follows:

1. Continuous approach

Performance appraisal is a continuous approach. It is not that evaluation is made for the performance for a particular date. The employees' performance for the whole review period is assessed. So, assessment of job is continuous.

2. Systematic Process

Assessment activity is carried on a definite plan, programme. Review period, reviewing authority, reviewing method etc. are pre-determined and the whole performance assessment work follows a clear-cut, definite process.

3. Periodicity

It follows a definite period for the assessment of employees' performance. Evaluation may be made for the performance of six month's period or for the whole period of twelve months.

4. Basis of assessment

Assessment is made on the basis of standard set earlier. Quantum and quality of performance is judged looking to the goals, standard fixed earlier.

5. Reinforcement activity

Performance appraisal system includes reinforcement activity to strengthen weak areas of reviewees. Reviewing authority tells reviewee the weak areas that need improvement. He also ascertains reasons for less performance and provides counselling, coaching and feedback to strenghten the weak areas. The employees who perform much more than the standard set are given positive stroking, stimulation to maintain.

6. Potential assessment

Performance appraisal has many activities. It identifies:

- People who are non-performers, below standard
- People who are performers, excellent
- People who have potential to occupy higher positions and to shoulder higher responsibilities

Under this system potential appraisal is made along with evaluation of present and past performance of employees.

7. Chain activity

Activities under this system follow each other. Performance appraisal is like a chain activity which is shown in figure 8.1

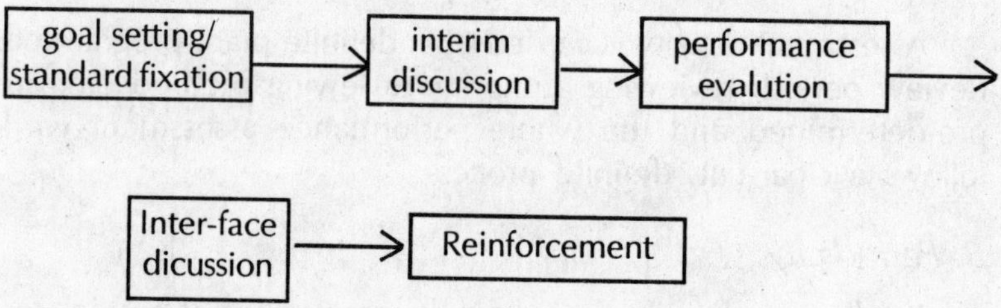

Figure 8.1 : Chain activities

8. Formal/Informal Assessment

Performance appraisal could be formal or informal. In case of informal assessment, supervisor/boss observes working, performance of employees working under him and provides feedback, counselling to perform as per standard set. So, this is a continuous method of looking at job behaviour of employees and of providing annually input to employees by boss for improving performance. In case of formal assessment boss assesses performance annually or biannually on the basis of information/data available in the relevant areas (key responsibility areas), job related behaviour of subordinates, perceptible manifestation of change in attitudes, behaviour, service of employees etc.

Objectives of Performance Appraisal

Performance appraisal facilitates growth and development of organization and the employees as well. Effective performance appraisal system creates a committed, talented and dynamic workforce that helps to achieve organizational goals. So, performance appraisal contribute a lot for smooth and effective functioning of organizations. Today, most organizations have introduced performance appraisal for different objectives. Some of the important objectives of performance appraisal are discussed below:

1. Promotion decision

Performance appraisal identifies the employees who are achievers, excellent performers. It also indicates the employees who have potential to grow, develop and to take up higher responsibilities. It makes easy for the higher management to take decisions relating to promotion of the employee as information, data concerning performance, behaviour, attitude, aptitude, potentiality are readily available to them.

2. Salary decision

Decision regarding salary raise, increase/sanction of annual increment and monetary incentives are taken on the basis of performance of employees. Performance appraisal helps top management to take decision on such areas as all relevant information, data are available from this system.

3. Identification of training needs

Training need can be ascertained from the performance appraisal as :

- employees express in self-appraisal form about their desire, intention to undertake training on the areas which they think they require improvement
- reviewing officers give their opinions, observation regarding training subordinates need

- weak areas requiring improvement become clear from the performance level of employees.

So, one of the objectives of performance appraisal is to let the top management know the people who need training.

4. *Assignment of Specific Tasks*

Companies may require to assign specific task to employees who have aptitude, liking, expertise, specialised knowledge, skill (e.g. dealer's job in foreign exchange department of a bank's branch or credit officer's job in cash credit department of bank) for performance of job in those specific areas. Performance appraisal helps the top management to identify people for assignment of specific tasks to them.

5. *Competency development*

One of the objectives of performance appraisal is to develop competencies of the employees. It ascertains/identifies areas of activity where employees need improvement so that they can give standard performance. Some employees may have potential to take up higher assignments. This also, is identified through the appraisal system. In all such cases development of competency is made for performance of present job / future job.

6. *Preparing a reservoir of talented, committed work force*

Through performance appraisal higher management may come to know about the employees who are talented, committed and also those who are non-performers, non-achievers and lack requisite knowledge, skill, ability for standard performance. Company arranges for improving competencies of such employees through training and development programmes, in order to prepare a reservoir of achievers, performers and also of committed work force.

7. *Effective running of the organisation*

Performance appraisal lets the management know who are dead woods, incompetent and useless employees of organisation. Company introduces downsizing approach through sabbaticals, voluntary retirement, retrenchment etc. so that organization can run effectively.

8. *Self-development*

When the employees are aware of the importance of performance appraisal for their growth, development, elevation, and satisfaction of psychological needs, they give their best efforts to improve their skill through 'self-development' measure. Such situation, generally, occurs when poorly rated employees come to know their miserable performance through 'feed-back' system.

9. *Use of control activities*

When job-related behaviour of employees is far below the standard behaviour as revealed from the performance rating organization uses control measures (viz. punitive action, demotion etc.) to check behavioural activities.

10. *Preparation of succession planning*

Performance appraisal system exhibits strengths and weaknesses of executive, lets the company know about the employees who are competent, effective and dynamic so that succession planning can be prepared for filling up subsequent vacancies of senior executives.

11. *Helping to design training and development programmes*

Through performance appraisal employees' 'skill-vacuum' (i.e. the gap between 'skill needed' for a job and 'skills possessed' by employees) is ascertained that helps to design suitable training and development programmes to improve skills, abilities of employees so that, they can have requisite skill to excel performance in their present jobs.

12. *Promoting boss-subordinate relations*

Performance appraisal needs a lot of interaction between boss and subordinates during the process of goal setting, action planning, reviewing, evaluating, counselling, reinforcing etc. Thus, it helps to develop mutual understanding between boss and subordinates.

13. *Ascertaining effectiveness of procurement mechanisms*

Procurement activities which include human resource planning, recruitment, selection, placement, induction and orientation relate to hiring/employing of people for organization. Performance of such employees is reflected in the appraisal. So, effectiveness of procurement mechanism could be ascertained from the performance appraisal.

14. *Evaluating training and development programmes*

Employees' job-related behaviours are assessed/appraised by their bosses and recorded in performance appraisal. If, no improvement in performance rating of employees is noticed after receiving training/development programme, the concerned programmes need to be reevaluated.

15. *Developing a 'sense of belongingness', 'we-ness', 'togetherness' amongst employees*

Effective performance appraisal system develops a 'sense of belongingness', 'we-ness', 'togetherness', amongst employees as it,

- ensures unbiased activities of management
- develops faith and confidence on management
- creates an open communication channel
- prepares employees to accept changes
- promotes team building to achieve team-goals
- makes the employees feel that they are part and parcel of organization

Performance Appraisal Methods

Employees' performance is measured by various techniques, the use of which arises from different approaches. No one single approach is best; each approach has strengths and limitations. The approaches that evaluate performance are :

- Independent Approach
- Comparative Approach
- Results Approach
- Contribution-Cost Approach

The classification of techniques on the basis of approaches is shown in figure 8.2

Performance Appraisal Methods/Techniques

Independent Approach	Comparative Approach	Result Approach	Contribution-Cost Approach
1. Essay Appraisal	1. Ranking	Management By Objectives	Human Resource Accounting
2. Checklist Appraisal	2. Forced Distribution		
3. Critical	3. Paired Comparison		
4. Forced-Choice Appraisal			
5. Confidential Report			
6. Graphic Rating Scale			
7. Behaviourally Anchored Rating Scales			
8. Assessment Centre			
9. 360° Feed back			
10. Field Review			

Figure 8.2 : Performance Appraisal Methods

Independent Approach

Under this approach evaluation of employee's performance is independent of any other employee in a work team. Employees are not compared against other employees but they are compared to a standard.

Some of the techniques under independent approach are discussed:

Essay appraisal

It is one of the techniques used by some organizations for evaluating performance of employees. Under this method, appraiser is required to rate employee's performance in essay form to describe strength and weakness, training needed, suggestion for improvement etc. Generally, evaluation is made on the following areas:

- Knowledge in technical areas e.g. operative knowledge, knowledge in company's rules, regulations, policies, procedures.
- Skill and ability to perform present job.
- Ability to work in a team.
- Attitudes towards peers, boss, subordinates, higher management.
- Human skill.
- Potential.
- Ability to perform whole activity independently.

Merits

1. It is easy to carry out in organizations.
2. Rater may not need training for evaluation of employee's performance.
3. It is less expensive.
4. Subordinates may have faith on this method because of its simplicity.
5. It gives complete idea on the areas on which rating is made.

Demerits

1. It is a subjective evaluation method.
2. Since quantitative appraisement is not made, employee's exact performance level can not be known.

3. Preparing essay on employees' performance needs rater's ability to express in writing. The rater who lacks such ability may not be able to express ratees' actual performance. Hence, this method becomes ineffective to measure employee's ability to perform.
4. Areas on which appraisement is made do not adequately represent employee's job activities. Hence, actual performance of employees can not be known.
5. Since writing essay on employees is time consuming performance evaluation may not be perfect if it is done in a short time.

Checklist Appraisal

Checklist appraisal is used to evaluate performance of employees in organizations. The terminology 'checklist appraisal' denotes a technique of performance evaluation made through testing/verification of a list of behavioural descriptions about an employee.

Features:

1. Performance evaluation of employees is not made by rater, it is done by some officer in the Personnel Department/HRM Department.
2. The boss under whom employees work checks the behavioural statement/description about them and indicates 'Yes' or 'No' against each statement already set.
3. All questions or statements may have equal value or some questions may have much more value than others.
4. The officer in the Personnel Department/HRM Department scores the checklist, prepares the list of ratees who need counselling, feedback and sends such list along with final evaluation to the boss/rater for discussion with the concerned employees and for giving them feed back, guidance to improve their behaviour.

Example of a simple checklist:

1. Is the employee prompt in rendering service to customers?

2. Does he take interest to solve customers' problem?
3. Does he help his co-worker in providing service to customers?
4. Does he behave well with customers?
5. Does he keep customers standing/waiting for a long period in front of his counter without giving service?
6. Does he serve customers with smiling face, helping attitude?
7. Is he liked by customers?
8. Does he carry out instructions of his superior?

Merits

1. It is a simple method to evaluate performance of employee.
2. Rater does not have any idea regarding final evaluation of employees' performance. Hence, the possibility of his being biased is less.

Demerits

1. It is time consuming as completion of the process needs two authorities-checking authority and evaluation authority (Personnel Department or Human Resource Management Department) who evaluates performance.
2. Though rater is not evaluator, he can have an idea regarding performance evaluation of employees from the checking of statements he makes and his judgement of statement checking that influences evaluation. Hence, such (cumber-some) process does not yield any result.
3. It is difficult to appraise quantitative performance of employees.
4. It may not be easy to use such method in those organizations where job categories are many that necessitates preparation of separate behavioural statements for each category of employees.
5. It is an expensive method.

Critical Incident

It is one of the methods used by organizations to evaluate performance of employees. Under this technique, boss/supervisor keeps records of key or crucial job related behaviours of employees for the whole review/appraisal period on a day to day basis. After stipulated period, may be, after six months from the commencement of the review period supervisor calls his subordinates for discussion and points out both positive and negative job behaviours with suggestion, advice and guidelines for improvement of negative areas and also for attaining excellence in positive areas.

Merits

1. Performance evaluation of employees is accurate and perfect as supervisor evaluates on the basis of day to day performance records/job behaviour information (both positive and negative behaviour)
2. Rectification of negative behaviour is easy as exact behaviour is recorded with detailed particulars on daily basis that may help to find out measures for rectification.
3. It may create confidence amongst subordinates about evaluation when they find that rater takes it seriously to record all crucial behaviour-negative and positive behaviour on daily basis.
4. Effect of recent behaviour is minimum.
5. It appraises job-related behaviour of employees.

Demerits

1. It is difficult to use such method in big organizations particularly, in those organizations where span of supervision of officers is much more.
2. Executives may not find this method suitable for them looking to the time needed and time available to keep day to day records of key incidents (both positive and negative) of their subordinates.

3. The method is time consuming.
4. It may happen that recent incidents/behaviour activities of subordinates just prior to close of the review period influence evaluation of their performance.
5. Supervisors/raters may take this method casually.
6. Quantification of performance behaviour is not possible. So, comparative performance analysis may not be accurate.

Forced-Choice Appraisal

It occurs in organizations that some raters are very much biased when they appraise performance of their subordinates. To avoid such situation, an appraisal method has been designed and introduced in organizations where raters are required to choose statement, which, according to them, suits ratees' activities, behaviour and performance. This appraisal technique is Forced-Choice appraisal method.

Features

1. Two or more statements relating to subordinates' behaviour, activities are mentioned in appraisal format. Each statement may express positive or negative aspects of behaviour/ activity of the individual being evaluated.
2. Raters tick the statement which is most descriptive or in some cases least descriptive of the concerned subordinate.
3. Rating scores are given by officers in HRM/Personnel Department.
4. 'Answer key' is prepared and kept it with Human Resource Manager/Personnel Manager in strict confidence.
5. Raters remain unware of subordinate scoring.

Example

The following are the examples of statements relating to customer service rendered by a bank employee and the rater is required to choose the statement that describes most of his behaviour. List of statements :

1. He provides service to customers with smiling face.
2. He develops a good rapport with customers.
3. He attends customers' problems immediately after he gets/comes to know the problems and sorts out problems promptly.
4. Most customers express satisfaction about service rendered by him.
5. Customer-complaint after his reporting in the department is almost nil.

Merits

1. This rating method is free from biased rating as the rater himself does not know scoring.
2. It gives accurate rating.
3. Rater needs thorough observation, study and application of his mind to choose the right statement. So, he takes the method seriously that may yield perfect and wise judgement about subordinate's behavioural activities.
4. Ratees may feel happy about performance rating, as rater can not make any favour to any employee by way of giving under/high rating to him.

Demerits

1. It is time consuming as rating process goes through the stages like preparation of statements, choosing statement by rater, scoring/evaluation made by officer of HRM/Personnel Department which need much time to complete.
2. It is expensive as designing format to prepare statement, selecting answer key, and ascertaining correctness/efficacy of answer key involves a lot of money.
3. Rater may not like this method as the system does not permit him to evaluate performance of subordinates who work under him. This job is performed by some officer of the Personnel Department/Human Resource Management Department.

4. Rater is required to choose statements which may not reveal the exact picture/manifestation of ratees' performance, behaviour and activities.

Confidential Report

It is one of the traditional methods of evaluating performances, behaviour, activities of subordinates. Under this method subordinates' strength, weakness, effectiveness, initiative, attendance, punctuality, commitment, loyalty, knowledge, competencies, honesty, integrity, team performance etc. are mentioned in the report. This method is used in government organizations / offices as also in some private organizations. Evaluation is made by immediate boss of subordinates on the basis of the information gathered by him about behaviour, activities of his subordinates through observation, and perception, impression developed in the process of interactions between them for accomplishment of job assigned to them.

Merits

1. It is easy to implement.
2. Rater does not need training to appraise performance. He records overall impression on ratees in the report.
3. Ratee can improve his weak areas as he is informed about his negative behaviour.
4. It is not expensive to use in organizations.

Demerits

1. It is a subjective evaluation process.
2. There is no system of counselling subordinates in situations when they perform miserably low.
3. Evaluation may not be accurate as possibility of rater's biasness exists.
4. It is an old method that needs modification.

Graphic Rating Scale

This is one of the methods used in organizations to ascertain performance level of employees. Under this method, emphasis is given on traits/characteristic of individuals. The concept emerges from the understanding that qualitative traits/attributes of employees contribute a lot to the achievement of organizational goals. Hence, the necessity of getting to know the traits scale/level of employees arises through the use of this appraisal technique.

Features

- Evaluation is made on traits viz. quality of work, initiative, dependability, leadership, job knowledge, punctuality and the likes but some organizations appraise important areas of work/duties of employees instead of assessing trait factors.
- Each trait of subordinate is rated by the supervisor by circling the score in the rating scale.
- Rater gives his comment in the space provided on the form in support of his having assigned rating/points.
- Total assigned value indicates the performance of employee

Example of a typical graphic rating scale is shown in Figure 8.3

Performance Appraisal

Employee's Name : ....

Designation : ....

Deptartment.:..

Employee Code No.:............... Review Period :...................

Name of Reviewing Authority :...

Since when employee is working in the Department :..............

Traits	Rating Scale			Comments
1. Initiative	O	o	100-90	Points
	VG	o	89-80	
	G	o	79-70	
	S	o	69-60	
	US	o	below 60	
2. Dependability	O	o	100-90	Points
	VG	o	89-80	
	G	o	79-70	
	S	o	69-60	
	US	o	below 60	
3. Quantity of work	O	o	100-90	Points
	VG	o	89-80	
	G	o	79-70	
	S	o	69-60	
	US	o	below 60	
4. Job Knowledge	O	o	100-90	Points
	VG	o	89-80	
	G	o	79-70	
	S	o	69-60	
	US	o	below 60	
5. Quality of work	O	o	100-90	Points
	VG	o	89-80	
	G	o	79-70	
	S	o	69-60	
	US	o	below 60	

Rating abbreviation : O- Outstanding VG – Very good, G – Good, S – Satisfactory, US – Unsatisfactory

Figure 8.3 : Typical Graphic Rating Scale

Merits

1. It is a simple method to assess performance of employees.
2. It is easy technique that does not need training to use by raters.
3. Since, rater is required to give comment on rating of each trait, his arbitrary action to evaluate is checked.
4. Under this method emphasis is given on objective assessment. Hence, performance evaluation may be relied upon.

Demerits

1. Rating is made on the traits of the individuals. If, trait selection is not properly made, this method may not reflect true job behaviour of the individuals.
2. Designing rating scale needs high expertise and knowledge.
3. Biased rating in performance evaluation can not be ruled out.

Behaviourally Anchored Rating Scale (BARS)

This is a technique of appraising employee's performance level that considers actual behaviour on job. It is based on critical incident approach that looks into effective behaviour for a particular performance dimension.

Steps to develop a BARS

Step-1. Gathering information regarding critical incidents

Individual employees and supervisors are asked to describe the critical incidents of effective and ineffective performance on the job. Collection of information through such measure is direct.

Step-2. Classifying incidents into performance dimensions.

The same group is advised to classify these incidents into performance dimensions. Incidents may be hundred or more but performance dimensions may be much less (between five and ten)

Step-3. Reassigning incidents.

The second group who has also thorough knowledge in such area of performance is briefed about critical incidents and classification dimensions and is asked to reallocate each incident to the classification/cluster. Reassigning of incidents to a particular cluster / dimension is made on the basis of majority choice/ decision. If majority personnel of this group (say more than 70%) considers that an incident belong to a particular cluster as made by the group in step-2, the same is retained.

Step-4. Scaling incident

The second group is asked to rate each incident in 5 point or 7 point scale to describe as to how effectively or ineffectively it represents performance dimension.

Step-5. Preparing final instrument

Generally, six or seven incidents per cluster / performance dimension are used as behaviour anchors to guide rater.

Behaviourally Anchored Rating Scale is illustrated in Figure 8.4

Extremely good Performance	Could be expected to receive fees from all the persons who remain in the queue during stipulated period to enter into respective registers, to verify records to return counterfoil to them and control the atmosphere.
Good performance	Could be expected to receive fees from all those who remain present and to complete all the formalities but fails to maintain peaceful and congenial atmosphere.
Neither poor nor Good Performance	Could be expected to receive fees and to complete formalities at a slow speed and as a result all persons who remain on the queue may not have chance to deposit fees during specified period.
Slightly poor Performance	Could be expected to receive fees and to complete formalities with the help of co-worker.
Poor performance	Could be expected that the receiving cashier asks the persons in the queue about the amount of different fees and remains busy in conversations with them.
Extremely poor Performance	Could be expected to be unable to receive fees and to enter them in different registers.

Figure 8.4 : Behaviourally Anchored Rating Scale

Example

Example of a Behaviourally Anchored Rating Scale for the dimension 'ability to receive school fees for a receiving clerk in a school'.

Merits

- Critical incidents are taken from the employees and the supervisor who are directly involved in work performance. So, the method developed with such information could be effective to appraise performance of the employees.
- Under this method, performance dimensions/clusters and also critical incidents falling under cluster are chosen by experts/groups of experts. Hence, this is a reliable technique that gives actual information in respect of effective/ineffective employees of the company.
- Detailed expression is made about different scale value (viz. poor performance, outstanding performance etc.) So, rater does not feel any difficulty to use this method as it is easy to comprehend.
- It is easy to implement as it does not need any training for raters and ratees.
- In counselling/feedback session appraisee gets clear idea in respect of his performance/job behaviour as critical incidents specify scale value to determine his performance level of the job.
- Much variation in performance evaluation by different raters is not found in this technique because of thorough and systematic selection of critical incidents, performance dimensions and scale value of incidents.

Demerits

- It is expensive and time consuming.
- Raters find difficult to choose the scale values for evaluating performance as interpretation of the words/factors representing scale values make them confused.

- Wrong selection of employees, supervisors and other people involved in this process can make this technique ineffective.
- As a tool to evaluate performance it has no special identity because it is more or less similar to critical incident method and graphic rating scale method.
- Perfect/accurate rating may not be possible as the method provides scope to raters to rate in a biased manner.

Assessment Centre

(This topic has been discussed in 'Recruitment and Selection Chapter')

Comparative Approach

Under this approach, comparative evaluation of employee performance is made. Each individual employee's performance is compared to other employees. Three methods: viz. Ranking Method, Forced Distribution Method, and Paired Comparison Method are discussed to appraise employee performance.

Ranking Method

Two ranking methods are in great use in organizations. They are Simple Ranking Method and Alternation Ranking Method

A. Simple Ranking Method

This is a technique used in organization to appraise employees' performance through comparative analysis of employees' traits, characteristics and assigning position / place with regard to such traits / characteristics. Under this method employees are ranked / assigned numerical score (like, 1,2,3 and so on) on the basis of their place / position in respect of each trait, characteristic / behaviour. Overall assessment / ranking is made on compiling individual ranking. So, ranking requires executives / managers to rank employees within their departments from best to worst or from highest to lowest.

B. Alternation Ranking Methods

Under this ranking method best and worst employees are ranked / chosen in an alternative manner. That means, after deciding best employee from the lot, worst employee from the remaining employees is ranked.

Process

- A list of employees working in a department is prepared for evaluation of their performance.
- Best employee is chosen from the list in terms of characteristic/trait and his name is crossed off the list.
- On a separate form best employee's name is indicated on the top.
- Worst employee is chosen from the remaining employees of the list and his name is crossed off this list. His name is shown on the bottom of the separate form.
- Next highest employee is identified / assessed and is placed second position on the form after having crossed his name off the list. Next lowest is chosen and placed position on the form accordingly. Choosing the next highest and the next lowest in an alternating manner and placing them in proper place continues until all employees of the department as mentioned in the list for evaluation are ranked.

Merits

1. This is simple and easy method that does not need training for raters and ratees.
2. It is less expensive as it does not involve extra cost towards designing format, training of raters to learn the system for evaluating performance etc.
3. Since, performers and non-performers are identified/ known, company can initiate separate projection / measures for developing skill, knowledge, competencies, attitudes of both groups of employees.

4. Low performers put in best efforts to confront challenges and improve their working.
5. Each employee knows his limitations, weakness and accepts his position / place as compared to others.

Demerits

1. It demoralizes, frustrates employees who are ranked low.
2. It is difficult to use in a big organization especially, a big department where a large number of employees are working under an executive/manager who requires appraising their performance under this method.
3. Chances of biased judgement are not ruled out.
4. Immediate boss / supervisor of non-performers, less performers may not give much importance for growth and development of such employees. He may think that they are lost cases and improvement of their competencies is difficult. He may therefore, initiate measure for their removal from the company services.
5. Accurate ranking may not be possible when a good number of employees have equal level of performance.
6. It indicates ranking / position amongst employees but does not tell quantity variation between employees.

Forced Distribution Method

This is a method used in organizations to appraise employees' performance by putting certain percentage of employee into different categories, as decided early. It occurs that some raters prefer to rate the employees high or low and they become biased in appraising performance. To overcome this situation forced distribution method is introduced. This method uses the characteristics/traits of job performance and promotability as well.

Process

1. For evaluation of work performance employees are categorized into some groups like high performers, above

performers, average performers, below average performers and low performers.

2. Percentage distribution of ratees to each performance category is made. For example, distribution of percentage of employees may be like the following

   high performers 10%

   above average performers 15%

   average performers 40%

   below average performers 15%

   low performers 20%

3. Employees are rated by the managers/executives and are placed in performance categories.

Merits

1. It is very easy to use this method.
2. Rater's bias to evaluate performance either as high performers or as low performers is checked. Rater is required to place the rated employees in different performance categories.
3. Performance evaluation may give accurate rating as raters need to be careful to appraise employees' performance for placing them in different categories.
4. It helps to design and develop training programmes/courses for low performers and below average performers.
5. It helps to change, modify selection tools, techniques so that organization can procure quality and dynamic people as per requirement.
6. It helps to initiate programme for potential development, executive development to prepare a reservoir of talented and competent workforce of the company.

Demerits

1. Raters are forced to maintain percentage distribution as

the percentage quota for high performers or low performers is already earmarked. So, they can not rate some employees as high performers or low performers which they deserve.

2. Since, gradation of employees is made as per distribution system, low performers and below average performers become demoralized.
3. It affects team building, team spirit, interpersonal relations between employees and all this creates unhealthy, in-conducive atmosphere in the organization.
4. Performance categories of employees affect production, productivity, absenteeism and turnover of the employees.
5. It needs extra care, talent, and visionary approach for choosing performance categories and determining distribution of percentage to such categories.

Paired Comparison Method

This is one of the methods to appraise performance of employees by making pairs and comparing to every employee in respect of performance characteristic / trait of such employees. For every trait / characteristic, each employee is paired with and compared to every other employees and the better one is indicated with a '+' mark. After comparison is made, the employee who has obtained maximum number of '+' marks is ascertained and ranked highest for the particular trait.

For calculating total number of comparisons the following formula is applied:

$\frac{N(N-1)}{2}$ where N means number of employees to be rated.

For example, in a group of 5 persons (say, A, B, C, D and E) total number of comparison is $\frac{5(5-1)}{2}$ i.e., 10. So pair is like

AB, AC, AD, AE, BC, BD, BE, CD, CE, DE.

This method is explained in Figure 8.5

For the trait 'job knowledge'

Employee Rated					
As compared to	Mr. A. Dutta	Mr. B Bose	Mr. C. Chandra	Mr. D. Dan	Mr.E. Pal
Mr. A Dutta		–	–	–	–
Mr. B. Bose	+		+	–	–
Mr. C. Chandra	+	–	–	–	+
Mr. D. Dan	+	+	+		–
Mr. E. Pal	+	+	–	+	

Mr. A. Dutta ranks highest ↑

Figure 8.5 : Ranking Employees by the Paired Comparison Method.

Merits

1. It is very easy for the rater to compare and find out the better employee in respect of performance characteristics, traits.
2. It ensures that every employee is compared to every other employee in the work group.
3. Performance evaluation may be accurate as rater needs to be careful to compare each employee with other employees in the department, work team.

Demerits

1. It is very time consuming as comparison is made on a one-on-one basis.
2. If span of supervision is very large, it is difficult to use for appraisal of performance of employees in organization.

Results Approach

This approach to performance appraisal relates to objectives, results of a job. The concept arises from the philosophy that, achievement of results strengthens organizational effectiveness, generates strength and power of the organization to sustain, to face challenges.

The performance management system that uses results is management by objectives, which is discussed below.

Management by Objectives (MBO) : Concept

This is a method of appraising performance of employees through setting of goals jointly by managers and subordinates in terms of company goals. This is objective oriented appraisal system which converts company objectives / goals into individual objectives / goals. The concept is based on participation of each and every individual employee for achievement of the company goals. So, all employees are involved in the goal setting exercise. Individual objectives/ goals are jointly set by subordinates and supervisors/ managers looking to company goals and such individual goals are considered as standard on the basis of which employees' performance is assessed. An example of objectives / goals for a branch manager of a bank, under MBO programme is given in Table 8.1

Table 8.1: Objectives for a Branch Manager of a Bank

Amount of Deposit
Amount of Advance (excluding House Building)
Loan & Agriculture loan
Recovery of Non-Performing Assets
Amount and Number of Accounts of House
Building Loan
Amount and Number of Accounts under different Savings Schemes
Number of customers complaints
Amount of Profit
Amount and Number of Accounts of Agriculture Loan
The numerical goals are decided jointly by Branch Manager and Regional/Zonal Manager.

Management by Objectives (MBO) Process

MBO is a result-oriented appraisal method which is concerned with company objectives/goals. Individual goals are set in terms of company goals. Individual performance is measured periodically, feedback/necessary support is provided to achieve goals and performance evaluation is made at the end of review period. For its effective implementation in the organization as a tool to measure employee performance, it passes through the following stages:

1. Setting individual goal

Corporate plan is established first and then goals are decided on the basis of such plan. At the time of goal setting organization's objectives are taken into account in its entirety.

After organization's goals are fixed, message is transmitted to the senior executives for settings goals of the respective departments. Such executives discuss with their subordinates who are department heads of the organization, in respect of the targets of the departments and set goals jointly. After department goals are set, department head discusses this issue with all department members and make them aware of the situation that necessitate to achieve department goals jointly and in cooperative efforts. Then each individual employee's goals are set jointly on mutual understanding between boss/department head and subordinates. Such individual goals become the performance targets of the concerned individuals.

2. Preparing action Plans

After goals/objectives are decided next step is to prepare action plan so that, the targets / standard fixed for the review period can be attained. Under this phase the activities include:

- splitting of the target / KRAs over some fixed period for review
- exploring and identification of supporting areas that may facilitate achievement of goals

- activities to be undertaken to accomplish the assigned tasks
- determining the resources / infrastructure required to perform the tasks
- finding out the measures to be adopted to overcome the hurdles / trouble to be faced in the process of performing activities

3. Monitoring and Self-directing

The ratee, monitors the whole activities to ensure that the target fixed for the review period is attained, if not surpassed. He exercises self-direction to move on a right track so that stipulated activities are performed.

4. Conducting periodic review meeting

The rater / manager makes periodic review meeting with subordinates to know the periodic achievement. He compares individual employee's performance with standard performance set jointly by him and the concerned subordinate.

5. Providing feedback to the subordinates

Subordinates may sometime find difficulty to achieve targets in usual situations and it is felt necessity by the rater to provide support to reinforce weak areas. So, the manager / reviewer provides feedback / support to the subordinates during the review period to monitor progress towards individual goals.

6. Evaluating performance

The rater evaluates performance immediately on the expiry of review period in terms of standard / goals set jointly at the beginning of the review period.

Advantages

1. It is acceptable to both managers/raters and ratees/ subordinates, as it minimizes subjectivity and relies on verifiable, objective and quantifiable indicators of performance.

2. It is easy to measure performance as performance target is already set. The manager needs to compare individual performance with standard performance so fixed.

3. It increases productivity of the subordinates as performance target is mutually set looking into aspects like capability of subordinates to achieve targets, necessary support/ feedback given by managers to enable subordinates to increase production.

4. It motivates subordinates to achieve goals as
   - objectives / goals are set through involvement of subordinates
   - constant monitoring of progress towards goals is made by managers
   - feedback / support is provided by managers

5. It has a positive effect on organizational effectiveness. MBO programme makes a link between individual performance/ results and organization's goals.

6. It develops a sense of accomplishment among individual employees.

Disadvantages

1. It is time consuming as the whole process (viz. setting goals,conducting periodic review meeting, providing feedback/ support to subordinates) needs much time to be spent.

2. MBO programme focuses on increasing production, achieving targets but neglects the areas like team building, developing cooperation and establishing team spirit amongst peers.

3. This method may not work effectively where superior-subordinate relation is not healthy.

4. The target / standard set under this method may not be perfect, reasonable if, the reviewer lacks sound knowledge in job and does not have requisite skill, competencies to judge subordinates' abilities.

5. The individual goals are set for a short period, may be, for six months' period or for twelve months' term; and this is made at the cost of long range growth. So, it is not effective in the long-term planning of the organization.

360° Feedback

This is a new method used for assessing performance of employees particularly managers, officers in organization. Under this method, managers' behaviours, skills are evaluated by all people who are in someway connected or related to them. They are subordinates, peers, bosses, team members and customers. Managers themselves appraise their own job behaviours through self-appraisal system. This method is also called multi-source assessment as assessment is made by different people, and such technique collects feedback from these sources / persons with regard to ratees / reviewees. P. Ward (1995) has expressed that 360° feedback is 'the systematic collection and feedback of performance data on an individual or group derived from a number of the stakeholders on their performance. So, it is a process of gathering perceptions about a person's behaviour and the act of the behaviour from the different persons who are directly / indirectly related to the activities performed by him. Performance assessment under this method is made by the stakeholders as shown in the Figure 8.6

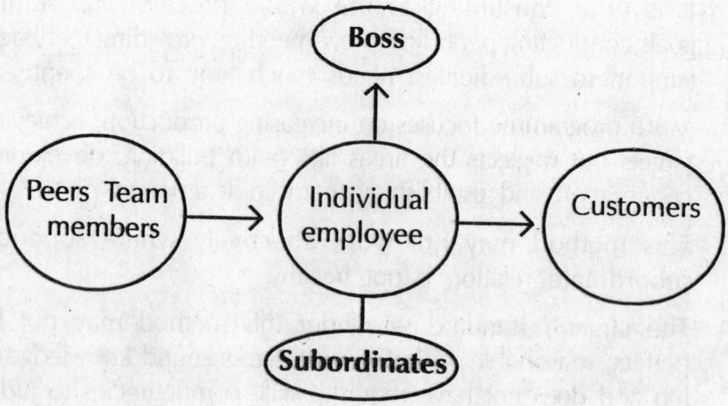

Figure 8.6 : Performance assessment under 360° feedback

The 360^{0} appraisal which was coined in the U.S. in 1998 has been very popular there as a tool to measure employees' performance and also to provide feedback for development. Most of the U.S. Companies are now using this technique. In India, it is emerging as HR tool for development at Wipro, ITC, Motorola, Nokia, Seagram and a few others.

This method has different uses viz. designing scheme for personal development of employees and team members, preparation of succession planning, assessment of training and development needs, decision for pay increase, ascertainment of leadership traits, establishment of interpersonal relationship.

This assessment technique works in a system activity like:

- Selecting raters (viz. peers, subordinates, boss, customers)
- Conducting survey to know opinions, perceptions about ratee's performance, qualities etc.
- Compilation of opinions and analysis of reports
- Preparation of a concise report containing ratings of different raters.
- Presentation of report to the ratee
- Action taken to change/modify ratee's behaviour

Benefits

The 360^{0} Feedback (Multi-source Assessment) has the following benefits if, used in organizations.

1. Rating is unbiased as raters are many and give separate rating about ratee's performance, job behaviour etc.
2. Ratees can compare their own evaluation with those evaluation made by others and accordingly can take measure for improvement.
3. Ratees can estimate their strength and weaknesses from the information/data they get from different sources.
4. Ratees can prepare/develop action plan on the basis of feedback they have received and can strengthen/modify self-improvement efforts.

5. This method encourages more open feedback.
6. Organization can come to know executives' abilities, skill, potentialities and accordingly can initiate executive development programme.
7. It removes ratees' feelings, impression about their qualitative traits, performance level and gives a true view on these aspects. All this helps ratees rectify their poor areas and get elevation to the higher positions.
8. This method develops a feeling of self-awareness amongst ratees.
9. It creates a climate of continuous improvement as ratees take corrective steps throughout the period of review.

Limitations

1. Managers may take revenge against the raters who have rated badly on the performance behaviour of ratees.
2. It affects interpersonal relationship between raters and ratees especially, in situations where raters evaluation is not well accepted by ratees.
3. It is time consuming. During a specific period of time raters may find it difficult to complete evaluation exercise. Hence, ratings made hurriedly by raters may not be perfect/accurate.
4. Free and frank ratings may not be possible in some cases specially when subordinates evaluate bosses' performance.

Field Review Method

This is a method of appraising performance of employees through field survey/review by the officer of the personnel/HR department of the organizations. This technique is generally used in such cases where raters' biasness is noticed or where disagreement between raters is found.

This method involves the following activities:

- Initiation of performance review of employees by HR

executive/officer or personnel officer at the workplace (field review).

- Presenting questions to employees' supervisor about each employee's performance level, promotability, qualitative traits, knowledge, skill, ability, attitudes' aptitude, weak areas, training need and recording reply of concerned supervisor.
- Obtaining information by asking questions to peers, employees about their work performance, deficit of skill if felt, support if needed etc.
- Studying/analyzing points of agreements, disagreement / differences in respect of information given by the concerned persons.
- Performance review by appraiser (HR/Personnel staff)

Merits

1. Rater's biasness is eliminated.
2. Since, third party intervention (specially intervention from Personnel/HR department) is involved information/replies are given by the concerned persons very cautiously. Hence, rating on the basis of such information may tend to be accurate.

Demerits

1. It is time consuming as third party activity is involved.
2. Supervisor may not take this technique in good spirit.
3. It may adversely affect working climate in department.

Contribution-Cost Approach

Measuring performance of employees in the context of contribution over employees' cost is a new concept. Under this approach, human resource accounting method is used to appraise employees' performance.

Human Resource Accounting Method

Under this method, employee's performance is evaluated on the basis of contribution made by him in the organization as compared to cost. The concept of this technique arises from the philosophy that employees are assets / resource. Like any other resource, human resource has a great value in the organization for its survival, growth and development. Human resource is, therefore, needed to be focussed as assets in company's records. Some organizations have introduced Human Resource Accounting as a tool to measure employees' performance in context of contribution made by them (i.e. value added by employees) over cost of recruitment, selection, development of such employees. Hence, employees' contribution to the organization may be in excess of employees' cost (that is surplus contribution or positive performance) or may be in short of cost (that is deficit contribution or negative performance). Such performance level is measured in percentage, that means deficit/surplus contribution is shown in percentage. Percentage of contributions and its corresponding ratings are decided. Ratings may be 'excellent' 'very good', 'good', 'satisfactory', 'unsatisfactory' against the percentage of contribution to cost of employee.

Application of this technique for measuring employee performance in Indian organizations is still in its infant stage.

Problems with Performance Appraisal

The main objective of performance appraisal system is to accurately measure job behaviours of employees to take decision in vital aspects like pay rise, promotion and development of employees. It is, therefore, of urgent necessity to ensure that employees' performance is rightly measured. But, in reality it happens that because of some problems appraisal system can not measure actual performance of employees. Such problems arise out of

- Rater characteristics
- Appraisal system
- Corporate appraisal policy

1. Rater Characteristics

Rater is the key factor in evaluating performance of employees. He should be neutral, reasonable, rationale, knowledgeable personality to judge employees' job behaviours. But, his judgement may get biased as is observed from the following errors he makes at the time of appraising of employee performance.

(a) Central Tendency Error

Some raters do not want to rate employees' performance very high or very low, they rate employees as average. This tendency of raters in respect of rating of employees' performance is central tendency. That means, such raters make their ratings in the middle of the rating scale. For example, if the rating scale ranges from 1 to 7, the raters rate their employees as 4. They make no differences among employees with regard to job performance.

(b) Halo Error

Halo error is the tendency of a rater to rate positively on all factors due to the impression of one positive factor. That means, halo error occurs when rater is influenced by some positive performance factor and rates other factors in the same positive way. For example, if an employee is honest rater becomes biased and rates other factors positively. So, the employee in the instant case is rated as outstanding. The rater is contaminated by the particular factor and can not judge other factors rationally, accurately. It creates inter-personal problems as rater does not make distinction between poor performance and excellent performance.

(c) Horns Error

Horns error is the opposite direction of rating by the rater. It is the tendency of a rater to rate negatively on all factors due to the impression of one negative factor. For example, if an employee is uncooperative, rater rates on all other factors negatively. Rater's rating negatively on judging on a factor creates a lot of problems in organizations. The employees who are negatively rated become demoralized, de-motivated, frustrated and find it difficult to be performers.

(d) Leniency Error

Leniency error is the tendency of a rater to rate the employee performance very high or very low. That means, rater is positively lenient in appraisal or negatively lenient in appraisal. Such positively lenient or negatively lenient raters rate all subordinates performance consistently high or low.

Lenient rating by a rater creates a problem in organization as undeserved employees get unexpected/undue rating while performers get less rating. So, the rater understates/overstates performance of the employees. Such rater does not make any difference between employees about their work performance. All employees' work performance, job behaviour, qualitative traits are considered to be the same. The performers who are underrated become confused, get demoralized while highly rated non-performers do not go for improvement of their skill, abilities that makes them more ineffective.

The situation becomes much more problematic when subordinates' performance is rated by different raters who have different value system/mind set to fix standard for appraising performance of employees.

(e) Resemblance Error

People possess different qualitative traits and thus form different dispositional/temperamental state like aggressive, cool, quite, calm, hot etc. Raters rate those subordinates more highly who resemble them than those who do not. For example, if the rater perceives himself as a cool temperamental person he rates the subordinates excessively high who are cool in temperament. So, the subordinates who do not have such similar quality are rated low. Because of such error, raters can not make accurate, actual evaluation of employees' performance.

(f) Contrast Error

It happens in organizations that some raters rate the

employees' performance not on the basis of standard of performance but on the basis of performance of colleagues/ peers in the department and in the process raters make some error in appraising performance. This sort of error is contrast error. Such raters do not look to standard performance of subordinates; they look to each employee's performance as compared to performance of other employees / peers in the department. Hence, a good performance may not have high rating if, other colleagues are excellent in performance.

(g) Error arising out of prejudice

It may occur that some raters have liking or disliking of persons' age, sex, race, religion, caste, appearance etc. and they rate their subordinates positively or negatively, as per their liking or disliking. So, raters become biased while evaluating performance of employees. Employees are rated high if their characteristic/s is / are liked by raters. For example, if the rater does not like senior employees he may rate such employees low. Thus, the actual performers may not get proper judgement of their performance and subsequently they become frustrated.

(h) Recent Behaviour

Some raters evaluate subordinates' performance on the basis of their recent activities. They do not take cognizance of past performance of employees. It may happen that some employees have shown excellent performance / job behaviour mostly all through the review period except in one or two occasions in recent period. Such rater rates the employees badly as they have not fared well recently.

(i) Pretentious activities

Some employees pretend to be knowledgeable, smart, effective workers and give false promise, commitment to the supervisor to put in efforts to achieve goals with the intention to remain in the good book of the supervisor. This type of employees do less and talk more and subsequently win over the situation. Rater rates such subordinates excessively high which they do not deserve.

2. Appraisal System

To know accurate level of performance of employees it is necessary to modify, reinforce appraisal system as performance evaluation is affected due to the following:

(i) Unclear standard

Different raters interpret standard differently. Standard of performance may be excellent, very good, satisfactory and unsatisfactory. If the standards for excellent performance and others are not clearly defined raters get confused and may rate differently.

(ii) Voluminous performance review format

If, the review format is voluminous that contains information not relevant to employee performance, raters may need much time to fill in forms and to process the whole activity. Raters may, therefore, take such task casually and evaluate performance haphazardly.

(iii) Single rater

Possibility of bias rating can not be ruled out in case of single rater. Rater may not give much importance on rating as he knows whatever rating he gives that becomes final and stands. So, quality rating is affected.

(iv) Subjective assessment

Assessment on the basis of subjectivity may not be accurate. Hence, rating may vary from rater to rater.

3. Corporate Appraisal Policy

Corporate appraisal policy affects evaluation of employee performance. The following aspects of appraisal policy may create problems/impact on employee rating.

(i) Top management attitude

Top management's apathetic attitude may send the message to the raters regarding employee performance evaluation system. It may happen that supervisors do not take it seriously to make rating of employee performance accurately when they feel that higher management do not give much emphasis on effective implementation of such system.

(ii) Training to supervisor

If corporate policy remains silent for imparting training to supervisors to make them acquaint with performance appraisal system supervisors may not be able to evaluate performance of employees perfectly. For effective functioning of appraisal task raters should have thorough idea for evaluating performance and using system through training and development measure.

(iii) Appeal in case of unfair evaluation

If policy decision is taken to consider appeals of employees in respect of unfair evaluation rater may evaluate performance consciously and chances of making error in rating will be less.

Potential Appraisal

Potential appraisal is an assessment / appraisal of a person's capability to perform job with higher responsibilities. In other words, ascertainment of a person's latent / inherent capacity to handle higher job is potential appraisal. So, level of competency, capability of a person to perform higher cadre / grade job is measured through potential appraisal system.

Concept

Every company needs officers/executives in different grades/ cadres for its effective functioning in a desired manner. So, when vacancies arise due to superannuation, resignation, dismissal, discharge of employees, diversification expansion of business business process reengineering initiation etc. necessity is felt to fill up those vacant posts basically through promotion. Now the questions arise : (a) Who are the people to be promoted? (b) How are the people identified for promotion?

The answer to question number (a) is those persons having capability to handle higher level jobs are to be promoted and answer for question (b) is those persons having capability of performing higher jobs are to be identified through potential appraisal.

So, potential appraisal is measurement/assessment of persons' capabilities to work in higher level jobs. People may not have potential of equal degree. Potentiality differs from persons to persons. Some people may have high potential, some may have less. It is the potential appraisal that assesses degree of potential people do have.

In industrial settings performance appraisal mechanism is used to assess past performance of employees and through this system employees' effectiveness or ineffectiveness in the present job can be assessed. This mechanism can identify employees who are excellent, average, poor in present job. But, the excellent employees in the present job role may not be effective/successful if, they are promoted to perform the higher level job in different roles. The reason behind this is, that an employee may be effective in the present job role but may not be effective in the different job roles as the latter may need employees with different level of capability/competency. So, in such case performance appraisal that provides performance rating in the present job may not help organization to take decision in respect of promotion of employees. It needs a mechanism that can provide data, information in respect of employees' capabilities to handle higher level jobs. This mechanism is potential appraisal.

Objectives of Potential Appraisal

Potential appraisal relates to assessment of employee potential for growth and development of organization and the employee as well. It plays a key role in the development of human resources and also in the achievement of organization goals. Potential appraisal has a lot of objectives. The important objectives are given below:

1. Identification of employees having capabilities to perform higher level jobs

It identifies people who have potential to take over higher jobs. This task is difficult to accomplish in industrial settings. It may take the help of assessment centre/development centres to find out suitable/capable employees for promotion.

2. Assessment of general potential

It assesses whether the employees have abilities to perform some types of work. Employees' aptitudes, level of competency, skill are appraised for better utilization in the organization activities.

3. Identification of training needs of employees

For growth and development of organization employees' development of skill, knowledge, abilities is needed. This is possible through training. Potential appraisal identifies the area which requires training for reinforcement/improvement.

4. Implementing succession planning activities

It helps organization to effectively carry out succession planning activities by way of providing data / information in respect of employees who are suitable for filling in vacant posts.

5. Assisting employees in personal development process

It makes the employees aware of their strengths and weaknesses through feedback / counselling, discussion programmes so that they can prepare their personal development plan effectively.

6. Helping organization to decide its strategy

It makes organization know its competent, effective, potential workforce as also non-achievers, dead woods, non-performers. Looking into strength of human resources, organization can decide its strategy. For example, the organization can decide whether it can go for business process reengineering, diversification of activities, reduction of employees through VRS etc.

7. Helping organization to survive, grow and develop

In the changing scenario, every organization has to face tough competition against MNCs and other organizations. For confrontation against such challenges and for sustenance, growth, development of organization, it needs dynamic workforce. Potential appraisal helps organization to develop the employees and to create a reservoir of committed, competent workforce who can give befitting challenges through production of quality goods and service at low rate.

Requirements for an Effective Potential Appraisal System

Potential appraisal contributes a lot to the development of organization and employees as well. So, it needs to be effective to help organization achieve its goals. Effective potential appraisal system can work well in following situations/conditions.

1. Top management active support

If, the Chairman/Executive Director of organization takes personal interests and gives active support for implementation of the potential appraisal system, this system can work effectively. The senior, middle and junior executives become prompt and serious to make the review process smooth, regular as they know top management keeps records of functioning of this activity, and lapse/neglect of any officer in this regard is communicated to the higher management.

2. Corporate policy

Organization should have detailed, clear policy with regard to introducing a system for reviewing potential of employees. Absence of incorporating such system in organization's policy most executives take it casually and do not attach importance for its effective working.

3.Existence of congenial and conducive work atmosphere

If, good working situation exists where mutual understanding, faith and confidence are established between boss and subordinates, potential review may be meaningful and may make assessment proper and accurate. So, this is an essential requisite for effective potential appraisal system.

4. Healthy organizational culture

Effective potential review requires a healthy culture in the organization where climate of openness, collaboration, trust, autonomy, proaction exists. Such culture promotes values and develops a 'sense of we-feeling', 'togetherness' and 'belongingness'. All this helps to make unbiased assessment of employee potential.

5. Detailed job descriptions

Organization should have thorough and detailed job descriptions for each job and the functions involved in performing the jobs. If, each job has clear job descriptions, the functions to be performed can be identified, and through potential appraisal mechanism it can be ascertained whether employees are available to perform.

6. Qualitative traits for each job role

For effective potential appraisal system organization should ensure that each job role has clear specification as to the nature, extent and type of qualitative traits required to perform function of such job. Qualitative traits may be

- managerial skill and abilities
- technical knowledge, skill, capabilities
- human skill
- conceptual skill

If, it is clearly listed out the type of skill, level of competence etc. required for each function potential appraisal may make accurate assessment.

7. Rational and effective methods used for ascertaining qualitative traits

For implementing potential review system organization should have rational and effective methods in practice to measure qualitative traits of an employee in a particular job. Such methods may be assessment centres, development centres, performance review records, simulation exercises etc.

8. Existence of practice to conduct feedback programme

To make potential appraisal system effective, organization should have a programme for giving feedback to the employees in respect of their strengths and weaknesses and to help them develop weak areas. If, employees can come to know about the level of potential through feedback, they can develop perception about themselves and prepare their career planning and development programme accordingly.

Books Recommended

1. M. Armstrong and A. Baron : Performance Management: The new realities (Institute of Personnel and Development, London, 1998)

2. H.K. Bernadin, J.S. Kane, S. Ross, J.D. Spina D.L. Johnson: Performance appraisal design, development and implementation in Handbook of Human Resource Management ed. (G.R. Ferris, S.D. Rosen and D.J. Barnum, Blackwell,Cambridge MA, 1995)

3. P. Ward : A 360-degree turn for the better, People Management.

4. P. Lawson (ed) : Performance Management : An overview (M. Walters, The Performance Handbook, Institute of Personnel and Development, London, 1995)

5. C.H. Englemann and CH Roesch : Managing Individual Performance (American Compensation Association, Scottsdale, AZ, 1996)

6. L. Handy, M. Devine and L. Health : 360-degree Feedback :Unguided missile or powerful weapon? (Berkhamsted, Ashridge Management Group, 1996)

7. M. Bolar : Performance Appraisal (Vikas, New Delhi, 1978)

8. T.V. Rao : Performance Appraisal (Vikas, New Delhi, 1985)

9. B. Pattanayak : Human Resource Management (Prentice - Hall of India Private Ltd., New Delhi, 2001)

10. F. Hartle : Transforming the Performance Management Process (Kogan Page, Lodon, 1995)

11. S. Fletecher : Competence-Based Assessment Techniques (Kogan Page, London, 1992)

12. Richard Henderson : Compensation Management : Rewarding Performance (6th ed. Englewood Cliffs, N. J. Prentice-Hall, 1990)

13. Udai Pareek and T.V. Rao : Designing and Managing Human Resource Systems (Oxford & IBH Publishing Co Pvt. Ltd., New Delhi, 1992)

14. Michael Haris : Human Resource Management (McGraw-Hill, New York, 1995)

15. Gary Dessler : Human Resource Management (Prentice-Hall Inc. Upper Saddle River, New Jersey, 2000)

16. D. A. Decenzo and S. P. Robbins : Human Resource Management (6th ed. John Wiley & Sons Inc. NY, 1999)

Questions

1. What is performance appraisal? Discuss the importance of performance appraisal.
2. 'Employees' performance is measured by various techniques use of which arises from different approaches'? What are those approaches? Discuss in brief the approaches.
3. What is critical incident? What are its merits and demerits?
4. Do you think any one method is sufficient to measure performance of employees? Give your justification in support of your view.
5. What is Graphic Rating Scale? What are its salient features?

Draw up a specimen of a graphic rating scale. Discuss merits and demerits of this performance appraisal method.

6. What is BARS? Discuss the steps to develop a BARS.
7. How would you prepare a BARS for a receiving clerk in a school? Discuss merits and demerits of BARS.
8. What do you mean by Forced Distribution Method? Discuss the disadvantages of this method.
9. What is MBO? State the MBO process. Draw up a sample objectives for a MBO programme.
10. Discuss why do some organizations use MBO as a method for appraising performance of their employees?
11. 'It happens that because of some problems appraisal system can not measure actual performance of employees'. Discuss in brief those problems.
12. What is potential appraisal? How does it differ from performance appraisal?
13. State the objectives of potential appraisal.
14. What are the prerequisites for an effective potential appraisal system?

Case Study

About the Company : XYZ Cotton Textile Mills Limited is situated at Belur, West Bengal. It is not very old factory. In 1986, this Mills started its production activities. The company had installed sophisticated and latest machineries. In 2001, the company completed the modernization work. The basic activities of this company include: Spinning, Weaving, Dyeing, Printing. The company has three marketing branch offices one each in Mumbai, Kolkata and Delhi. The Head office of the Textile Mills is in Kolkata. The Belur Factory runs three shifts except Printing, Stores, Finance, Quality control, HR Administration and Warehouse.

The Chairman and Managing Director Dr. A.K. Palkiwala

specialized in weaving has joined this organization in the month of February, 2000. In February 2001, Mr. P.R. Bakshi has been appointed as Factory Manager of the Mills.

About Human Resources

The company accepts employees as assets that contribute to the achievement of organizational goals. The Belur factory has 1200 employees on permanent roll.

Dr. A.K. Palkiwala, CMD of the Company takes personal interest to implement HR oriented policies smoothly. He is considered a dynamic personality, who makes new changes in the whole system of production and functioning to create a world class workforce in order to obtain competitive advantage in the market.

It is due to persistent efforts of Mr Palkiwala the company has been able to introduce HRD system that inter alia looks to the following activities :

- Training and development
- Performance appraisal
- Potential appraisal
- Creativity reward
- Career planning & development
- TQM
- Employee participation
- Quality circle
- Compensation
- Counselling programme
- Attitudinal survey and correctional programme
- Excellent deliverer reward
- Employee involvement and empowerment

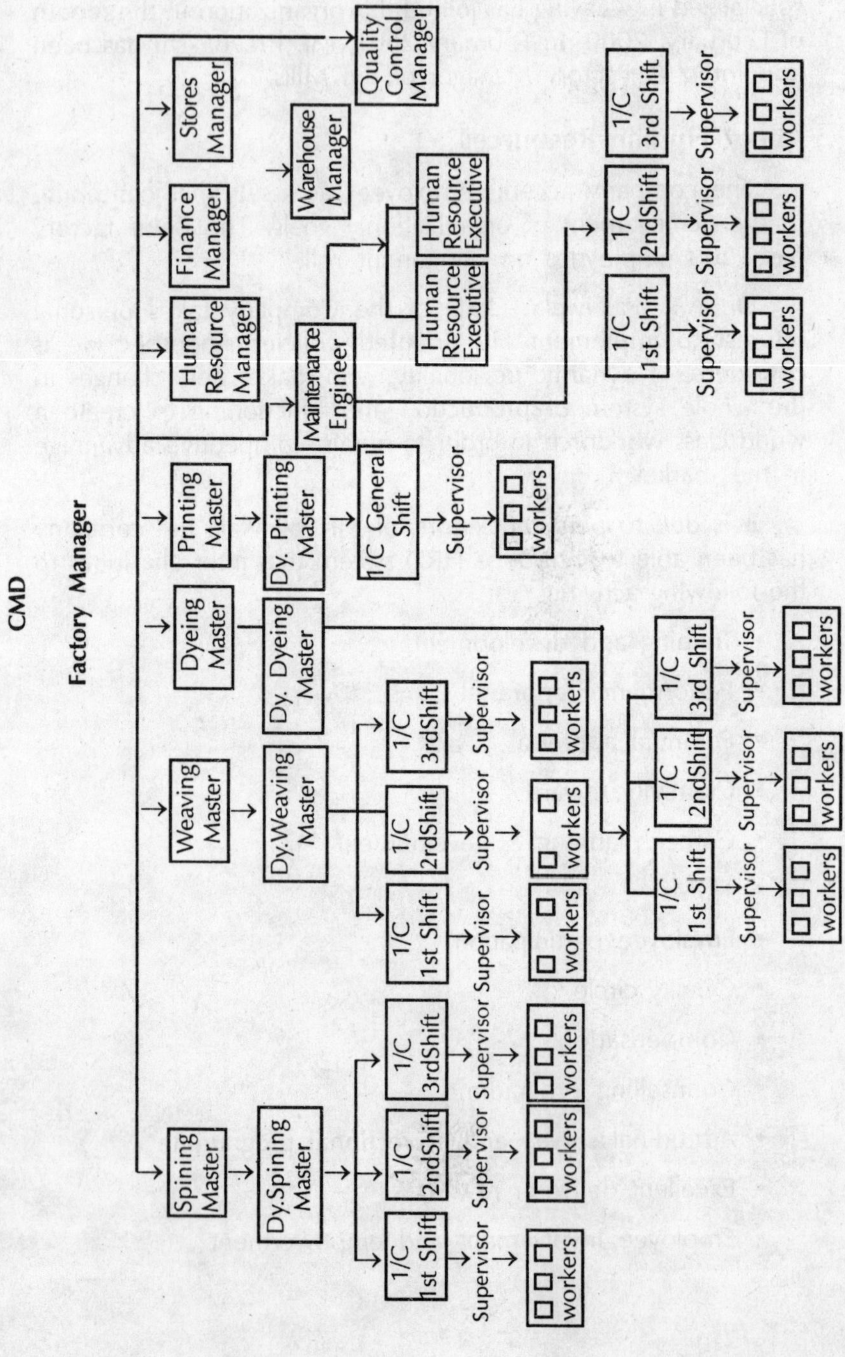
CMD
Factory Manager
Spining Master
Dy.Spining Master
1/C 1st Shift
1/C 2ndShift
1/C 3rdShift
Supervisor
workers
Weaving Master
Dy.Weaving Master
1/C 1st Shift
1/C 2ndShift
1/C 3rdShift
Supervisor
workers
Dyeing Master
Dy. Dyeing Master
1/C 1st Shift
1/C 2ndShift
1/C 3rd Shift
Supervisor
workers
Printing Master
Dy. Printing Master
1/C General Shift
Supervisor
workers
Maintenance Engineer
1/C 1st Shift
1/C 2ndShift
1/C 3rd Shift
Supervisor
workers
Human Resource Manager
Human Resource Executive
Human Resource Executive
Finance Manager
Stores Manager
Warehouse Manager
Quality Control Manager

Achievements

- The company has secured ISO9000 certificate in 2001 for quality production and marketing activities
- It has received Award for Excellent Performance and Quality Product from the Ministry of HRD in 2002 and 2003.
- The market share of the company has increased considerably from 15% in 2000 to 75% in 2003.
- The company's profit shows an increasing trend (30% in 2000, 50% in 2001, 75% in 2002 and 100% in 2003)

Mr. P.R. Bakshi Factory Manager

Mr. Bakshi is a cool, soft spoken and well mannered person. He is a workaholic, busy, hard working personality. He keeps every aspect of the entire factory activities under his grip. He works 14 to 16 hours daily in the factory and at home he remains busy with official work, he makes telephone calls, attends phone calls of different persons discussing business work. On Sunday he works for 5 to 6 hours in the factory. He keeps his managers and officers busy on work on Sunday. He pays visits to Marketing Branch offices to study the market and sales potential. He also visits to valued clients' offices to know their opinion about quality of the products, their requirements and to sort out problems, if any. He remains 6/7 days a month away from head quarters. He has no time to look to family matter. He can not spare time to attend ritual performance. He never visits Darjeeling Missionary School where his only son studies in standard V; one of his relatives take care of his son in Darjeeling.

The job role of Mr. Bakshi includes :

- Overall administration of the factory
- Supervision of the activities of functional heads
- Smooth and effective running of factory
- Coordinating and supervision of the activities of Marketing Managers.

- Developing liaison with Factory Inspectors, Government Labour Department officials, Inspectors, Tax officials
- Ensuring growth and development of the company

In January, 2004 the Chairman and Managing Director received an anonymous complaint against Mr. Bakshi with regard to his behavioural activities. In the said complaint it was alleged that his whimsical, autocrat and stubborn activities have demoralized the whole working community of the company. Earlier, CMD got to know from some line managers about the style of functioning and undesirable act of behaviour of Mr. Bakshi in some specific cases. Then Mr. Bakshi was directed to rectify and improve his behaviour.

In March, 2004 the company engaged XYZ Consultants of Delhi to study factory working and employee morale and submit their observations and findings to the management to improve employee morale and to change factory operations to produce quality goods at low cost.

The consultancy team had a detailed study/observations of factory operations for 3 months, made attitudinal survey and held discussions/interactions with some employees of different cadres of the company.

Some of the findings of the study are given below :

1. 90% of the experimental group are unhappy on the activities of Mr. Bakshi
2. Performance Appraisal System does not function smoothly as Mr. Bakshi who is reviewing authority / final reviewing authority fails to maintain time schedule for review of performance of subordinates. HR Manager reminds Mr. Bakshi for timely rating/submission of EPR. but, Mr. Bakshi does not give much importance to such activity, as he thinks this sort of job is secondary; the primary one is to increase production, to achieve targets and to increase profit.
3. Mr. Bakshi does not believe on delegation of authority to the subordinates. For sanctioning leave of workers the department supervisors are not authorized. The leave

applications are forwarded to department heads. TA bills, leave applications and all other matters that could be handled/dealt by respective department heads need sanction/approval of the Factory Manager.

4. In most cases, Mr. Bakshi can not attend to committee meetings like Executive Committee Meeting of QCs, Purchase Committee Meeting as he remains away from headquarters. Since, he is the key member of such committees, meetings are adjourned and as a result vital issues are left undecided.
5. Need-based training is not given. The persons who are identified for training through a system developed by HRM Department with active support and consent of Mr. Bakshi are not sent for training. Those employees who are liked by Mr. Bakshi are nominated for training. It is not considered whether such training helps concerned employees to excel present performance or future/identified assignment. Thus, transfer of learning to workplace which is an important tool to measure effectiveness of training is absolutely absent.
6. Mr. Bakshi rates the subordinates' performance not exclusively on the parameters fixed for such purpose, he looks to their qualitative traits/characteristics and also some other negative/positive factors. All this influences him in evaluating performance.
7. The employees of the factory belong to any of the three unions namely INTUC, AITUC and CITU. All leaders of such unions are happy with the functioning of the factory manager.

   Mr. Bakshi has developed a rapport with union leaders. He gives them time to discuss their problems. He holds structured meetings twice a year with all the unions and implements agreed issues. After Mr. Bakshi's joining there is not a single instance of work stoppage, slowing-down of performance, work-to-rule or any form of industrial conflict.

8. Customers are very happy with Mr. Bakshi. Volume of sales has increased. There is no significant complaint from customers. He gets along very well with the customers.

Group Activity

- Make some groups with 5 to 6 members in each group.
- Select a leader of each group.
- Discuss the following problems/questions among group members.
- Prepare group views to present before the members ofall groups.
- Present the group views by leaders one by one.

1. (a) What type of errors Mr. Bakshi makes while evaluating subordinates' performance? Discuss.

   (b) What does Mr. Bakshi perceive about performance appraisal system?

2. What are the strengths and weaknesses of Mr. Bakshi's style of functioning?

3. What are the reasons for not delegating the authority by Mr. Bakshi to his subordinates? What according to you could be the areas/items for delegation?

4. What do you think could be the feeling of employees about the style of functioning of Mr. Bakshi?

5. Why does Mr. Bakshi select the employees who may not need training? Do you think Mr. Bakshi is ignorant about the importance of need identification for training and evaluation of training programme?

6. Do you have any suggestion regarding organization structure of the company?

7. List the items what Mr. Bakshi should do and should not do?

8. Discuss the role of Human Resource Manager in such situation.

9. Do you support the culture of long working hours and also working on Sundays? Does it affect family life?

10. (a) Do you think the style of functioning of Mr. Bakshi affects employee morale, quality of product and industrial relations?

    (b) What is your suggestion to improve morale?

    (c) What is the future of the cotton Textile Mills if, Mr. Bakshi continues with the same paradigm and style of functioning?

9

Morale, Productivity and Employee Participation

Definition of Morale

Dictionary meaning of morale is a state of mind with reference to confidence, courage, hope, zeal, etc. So, it is a feeling, emotion of the individual that develops his self-concept / personality. Morale, in this sense, refers to individual morale. But, morale does not imply individual only. It is also a group morale. Individual person's personality / morale affects others in the group. When every individual in the group affects each other a new personality develops. This personality is group morale.

Jack Halloran (1978) talks about individual morale and group morale. Whereas an individual's morale is a single person's attitude towards life, group morale reflects the general tone or esprit de corps of a collective group of personalities. Each person either heightens the prospect of the esprit de corps or lowers the concept of a cooperative effort. Group morale is everyone's concern, and it must be practised continually, for it is ultimately achieved and is constantly changing. Group morale demands mutual respect for one another.

In organization, morale refers to group morale as people

work in group, team and each person has an influence over other's morale in the team/group. In other words, morale is the summation of feelings, emotions of employees working in a team towards job, supervisors, company, working conditions, peers, pay, promotion and so on. Morale may be high or low. Similarly, attitudes (i.e. feeling, emotions etc.) of the people in the group may be positive or negative. If, the positive attitudes are more than the negative attitudes, morale is high, and morale is low when positive attitudes are less than the negative attitudes of the people.

Morale can be measured in an organization through attitude surveys, interviews with individual employees and ascertaining critical incidents of employees. Morale of employees is also reflected in wastes, spoilage, absenteeism, employee turnover, tardiness, grievances, exits, accidents and sickness. In case of high morale, magnitude of such factors is less and magnitude increases when morale is low.

Factors affecting morale

Morale is the state of feeling, emotions of the employees about the company, job, supervisors and so on. It is influenced by some factors which are described herein below:

1. Company policies, practices especially HR, IR policies and practices affect employees to a great extent. Good policies and practices make the people happy and committed which help in morale building process.
2. Compensation given to employees in exchange for services rendered by them influences much in forming attitudes towards the company in which they work.
3. First line workers work directly under supervisors. Hence, supervisors' attitude, style of functioning, behaviour, techniques used to dispose of grievances affect a lot in building morale of the workers.
4. Employees are human beings. They have desire, needs, aspirations, expectations. They want to grow, develop and satisfy their psychological needs through well-designed

career planning and development. Hence, good promotional scope/opportunities develop positive attitudes amongst employees which increase their level of morale.

5. In organizational settings employees work in team/group with co-workers. Each worker's attitude/personality influences the activities of other workers. So, morale is formed through influences of co-workers. If, co-workers possess positive attitudes, morale is likely to be high and reverse is the case when co-workers have negative attitude.
6. Working conditions of the workplace affect employee morale. Good and comfortable working place make the employees happy and develop positive attitudes towards organization.
7. If, the job itself is challenging and employees find pleasure in working with such assignment, they develop positive attitude and high morale. Thus, job influences in building morale of the employees.

Importance of Morale

Morale is important in achieving individual goals, team goals and oganizational goals. High morale is a symptom of prosperity whereas low morale brings discontentment, unhappiness, dissatisfaction amongst employees which creates a situation of conflict, aggresiveness, nowork, less work, uncongenial and unconducive atmosphere.

Importance of morale can be measured from the following.

1. High morale improves quality of work as the people at work take much interest in work and give much efforts in improving quality of products.
2. High morale reduces absenteeism rate as the employees feel bored to remain at home without work. Besides, employees find their workplace comfortable, pleasant and conducive to work.
3. Wastes are less when workers sincerely and attentively do their job. Seriousness, sincerity, commitment of workers

come when they develop positive attitudes towards their job, company, promotion, supervision and so on.

4. Accident rate tends to be less when employees operate machines with great zeal, enthusiasm and interest. This is possible when their morale is high.
5. Industrial disputes are less in numbers as the employees are happy with the organization. Contented workfoce develop high morale and do not create any situation that disrupts production.
6. Employees with high morale establish mutual understanding, mutual faith and confidence between them and their bosses. So, healthy climate of industrial relations exists in organization.
7. Industrial peace is prevalent in a situation where employees possess positive attitudes towards the company, company policies, attitudes, style of functioning of management personnel and others. That means, employees with high morale bring peace in industry.
8. Employees with high morale stay with the company. Hence, labour turnover rate is less in such company.

Morale and Productivity

There is a general assumption that morale and productivity have complementary relation. The situation is like this - if morale of employees is high, productivity is high and if morale is low, productivity is low. But, this assumption does not hold good in all situations. Various research studies confirm that there is no direct causal relationship between morale and productivity. Keith Davis (1980) expressed that there is not always positive co-relation between the two. Workers with high morale may be high producers or low producers or only average producers. D. Katz (1949) observed that morale has four dimensions viz, job satisfaction, satisfaction with wages and promotional opportunities, identification with company and pride in work group. It was found that the dimensions 'pride in work group' was significantly co-related with productivity. Miller and Form found four combination of relationship between productivity and morale (i) high productivity, high morale (ii) low productivity, low morale (iii) high productivity, low morale and (iv) low productivity, high morale. However, the relationship between morale and production is illustrated in Figure 9.1

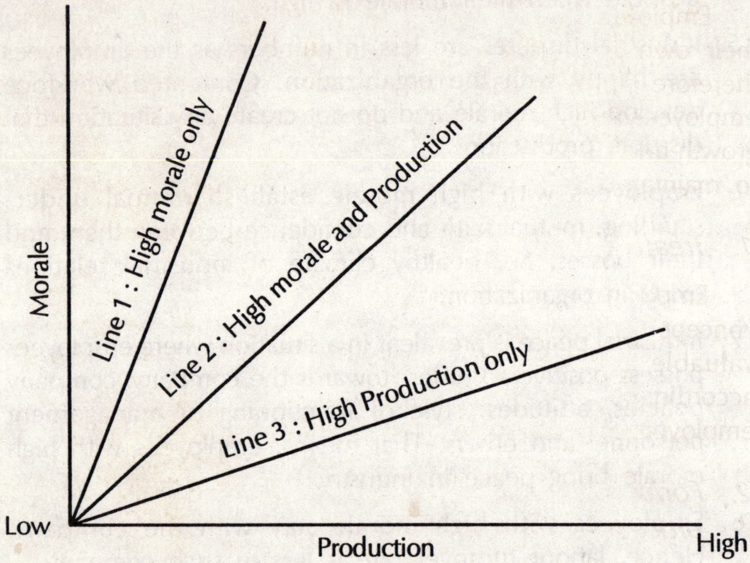

Figure 9.1 : Showing the relationship between morale and production

High production and low morale situation is revealed from line 3 of the Figure. A supervisor can increase productivity through introduction of scientific management, time studies, motion studies and strict supervision, and can have high production but low morale. But, it is very much doubtful about its long lasting effect. The opposite can also be true. The supervisor can make the people happy by creating an atmosphere under which they may not require to work hard. So, this employee appeasement situation is depicted by line - 1. There is high morale but little production is made. The most desirable condition is shown in Line -2 which reveals a situation of high morale and high production.

However, the evidences so far available, do not evince the general assumption that high morale has direct relation with high productivity.

Maintenance and Improvement of Morale

Employees should have high degree of morale to achieve their own goals and also organizational goals. Organizations, therefore, need to ensure maintenance of minimum level of employee morale and also improvement of morale for its survival, growth and development. The following measures may be taken to maintain and improve morale.

1. Treating employees as assets not tools of the machines

Employers' mind-set and thought pattern about employee concept needs change. They should think their employees as valuable assets of the companies and should treat them accordingly. When employees get human treatment from their employers / management, their morale level is increased.

2. Formulating and implementing positive HR/IR policies, procedures and practices

Positive HR policies and practices in the area of recruitment, promotion, welfare, health benefits, IR policies and practices for expeditious settlement of disputes, grievances, discipline management, collective bargaining etc. help the management to improve morale of the employees.

3. Providing attractive compensation package

If, the workers can not satisfy their physiological needs through wages / salaries, incentives, fringe benefits they get from organization, they remain unhappy, discontented. Under such condition, it is futile to expect higher degree of morale. Workers' community can be happy when they get attractive compensation package in exchange of their labour to meet their physiological requirement. Hence, attractive wages/salary, incentive, perquisites may help to maintain and raise morale of employees in the company.

4. Satisfying psychological needs of the employees

Most employees desire challenging job, responsibility, recognition, status, authority and above all higher assignment to satiate their psychological needs. All these are possible through job enrichment and smooth, well-defined career planning and development which act as morale-booster of the employees.

In addition to above, following measures may facilitate to maintain and improve employee morale:

(i) Introducing collective bargaining as a method of settlement of disputes.

(ii) Creating a climate of co-operation, mutuality and openness in organization.

(iii) Designing grievance redressal procedures.

(iv) Promoting harmonious industrial relations in the company.

Definition of Workers' Participation in Management

Participation is a sort of involvement of individual in group activities to contribute to group goals. In organizational context, participation refers to involvement of employees as representatives of the employees' community in the decision making process of the management. Stevens (1990) believes that 'participation is about employees playing a greater part in the decision making process'.

The concept of workers' participation in management is a sort of industrial democracy which gives the rights to the employees' representatives to participate in decision making process. The term 'participation' is also extended to forms of financial participation such as profit sharing.

V.G. Mhetras (1966) has suggested five levels of participation in decision making viz.

(i) Information participation that refers to sharing information in respect of sales programme, balance sheet, production, economic conditions of the firm etc. Here the workers have no right to scrutinize the information provided.

(ii) Consultative participation that refers to sharing of views on such matters as working conditions, welfare programme, work and safety methods etc. Here, the joint council works as an advisory body. Management may or may not accept suggestions and final decision is taken by the management.

(iii) Associative participation. In such case, management accepts and implements the unanimous decision of the council.

(iv) Administrative participation. Here, the degree of sharing authority and responsibility of administrative work is much more than in other cases.

(v) Decisive participation. Here, decisions are taken jointly on matters relating to production, safety, welfare etc. This is the highest form of participative activities.

Objectives of Workers Participation in Management

The objectives of workers participation in management include:

1. Developing a sense of belongingness

It develops a sense of 'belongingness', 'we-feeling' 'togetherness' amongst employees in organization which is pre-requisite for achieving organizational goals.

2. Creating an atmosphere of mutuality

It creates an atmosphere of mutual understanding, mutual faith and mutual confidence between employees and management.

3. Reducing industrial conflict

It reduces industrial conflicts as most of the issues are settled through joint participation, discussion and negotiation.

4. Ensuring increased production

It ensures increased production through cooperative efforts as workers think themselves as part and parcel of the company.

5. Generating commitment of employees

It generates loyalty, commitment of employees to the success of the company.

6. Bringing changes to produce quality goods

It can bring changes in operation, methods, techniques of production to produce quality goods as per requirement, in view of changing scenario.

7. Improving satisfaction level of employees

It improves level of satisfaction of employees as through participation they can satisfy their psychological needs.

8. Promoting industrial relations

It helps to bring harmony and peace in industry, and thereby develops healthy industrial relations in organization.

9. Improving QWL

It improves the quality of working life (QWL) of employees.

Forms of Workers' Participation in Management

There are different forms of workers' participation in management. Forms of participation vary from industry to industry. Some of the forms of workers' participation in management in our country are discussed herein below:

(i) Works Committee (1947)

This committee is constituted in industrial establishment where 100 or more workers are employed. This is a statutory committee set up under the Industrial Disputes Act 1947, with the equal number of workers' and employers' representatives. Though, the setting up of this committee is statutory obligation, recommendations of the committee are not legally binding. The aim of setting up of such committees, is to promote measures for securing and preserving amity and good relations between the employers and workmen and, to that end, to comment upon matters of their common interest or concern and endeavour to compose any material difference of opinion in respect of such matters.

(ii) Joint Management Council (1958)

It is a joint consultative/deliberative body constituted with the equal representatives of workers and management with the objectives of maintaining peace and harmony in industry through disposal of grievances/issues of the workers at the earliest possible time. The Second Five year Plan recommended the setting up of joint management councils at those units having more than 500 or more employees.

(iii) Worker-Director (1970)

The Government of India accepted the recommendations of the administration reforms commission to appoint workers' representatives on the Board of Directors of public sector undertakings. The Nationalized Bank (Management and Miscellaneous Provisions) Scheme 1970, was also passed which required, each nationalized bank to have employee directors on its Board-one representing employees and the other representing officers having tenure of 3 years. The practice of appointing Worker-Directors to the Boards is in force in Hindustan Antibiotics Ltd., NTC, Public Sector Banks, BHEL and so on.

(iv) Worker Participation Scheme (1975, 1977)

The Central Government adopted through a resolution a new scheme of workers' participation in management, on October 30, 1975. This is a voluntary scheme covering all manufacturing and mining industries whether in public, private or co-operative sector which employ 500 or more persons. The scheme provides for the setting up of shop councils at the shop and floor level and joint councils at the plant level.

Shop Councils

The salient features of shop councils are discussed below:

- There shall be one shop council for each department or

shop, or one council for more than one department or shop considering the number of employees in the department or shop.

- Each shop council shall consist of an equal number of representatives of employers and workers.
- The total number of members may not generally, exceed 12. However, the number of members of each council may be determined by the employer in consultation with the recognized union or registered unions of workers.
- The employer's representatives to be nominated by the management shall be from the unit concerned, and the representatives of workmen shall be from among workers of the department or shop concerned.
- The chairman of council is nominated by the management and vice-chairman is elected by the worker-members of the council.
- The council shall function for a period of 2 years.
- The council shall have regular meeting to discuss matters like welfare, social security measures, working conditions, production, and safety measures, smooth functioning of the department/shop, discipline, attendance aspects etc.
- The decisions of the council are taken on the basis of consensus.

Joint Council

The worker participation scheme 1975, provides for setting up a joint council for the whole unit where 500 or more persons are employed. The main features of the joint council are given herein below:

- The joint council shall function for a period of 2 years.
- The chief executive of the unit is its chairman and vice-chairman is nominated by workers' members of the council.

- The members of the joint council shall be from the unit.
- The secretary is appointed by the joint council from amongst the members of the council. He is responsible for smooth functioning of the council.
- The joint council meets once in a quarter to discuss:
- matters remaining unresolved by shop council
- matters relating to fixation of productivity norms, training and development of employees, preparation of working hours and holiday schedules, optimum utilization of raw materials, quality of products, health, welfare, safety measures for the unit/plant and so on.

In 1977, workers' participation scheme was extended and commercial and service organizations in the public sector having 100 or more employees were also covered.

The New Scheme of Workers' Participation in Management (1984)

After thorough overhauling the functions of participative activities and progress of various schemes in organizations a new scheme was prepared and notified by the Government in 1984. The important features of this scheme are briefly mentioned.

- The scheme is applicable to all public sector organizations irrespective of number of workers employed in the organizations.
- Participation under this scheme is at the shop floor level, plant level and also at the board level.
- In both levels-shop floor level and plant level there shall have equal representation from both the parties. The size/extent of representation and also the mode of representation of workers are determined through consultation by the management with the unions.
- Shop-floor level forum discusses the matters relating to storage facilities, production, wastage control, welfare measures, health and safety measures, cleanliness etc.

The plant level forum discusses

- the matters not resolved at the shop level or concerning more than one shop
- the matter relating to housekeeping, quality improvement, material supply, review of monthly targets of production, storage, productivity, economic and financial aspects, welfare, personnel matters and so on.
- decisions at shop level and plant level are taken on the basis of consensus.

Board level forum reviews the work activities of shop and plant level forums in addition to other functions.

In the matter of evaluation of functioning of the scheme, the Ministry of Labour constituted a tripartite committee for submission of report and suggestions for corrective measures to the Government.

The Participation of Workers in Management Bill, 1990

The Central Government introduced Participation of Workers in Management Bill in the Parliament on 25th May, 1990. The salient features of the Bill are as follows:

- The Bill provides for setting up of Shop Floor Councils, Establishment Councils and Board of Management at shop floor level, establishment level and board level respectively.
- The Bill suggests for three-tier participation of workers in management at shop floor level, organization level and board level.
- The shop floor council and establishment council will consist of equal number of representatives of employer and workmen.
- The Bill provides for the principle for electing the workers' representatives through secret ballot.
- The council shall function for a period of 3 years from the date of constitution of the council.

- The Bill provides that in the Board of Management the representation of workers and other workers shall be 13% and 12% of the Board strength respectively, with minimum of one workers' representative in the Board.
- The Bill provides for choosing of chairperson of shop floor council and establishment council by and from amongst the member thereof.
- The powers of shop floor council and establishment council have been extended to have a wide coverage of activities.
- The Bill provides for constitution of a monitoring committee to review and advise upon matters arising out of the scheme.
- The Bill extends the coverage of the scheme to all corporate establishments.

Effective Workers' Participation in Management

Workers' participation in management is a process of involvement and participation of workers' representatives in the decision making of the management. The principal activities of participative management include effective involvement, sharing views, meaningful participation and contributing to management decision making of the organization. To perform such activities and to make participation effective, some conditions are required to exist. They are:

(i) Culture of mutuality

Organization, should have a culture of mutuality where people feel free, open to perform their job, develop a team spirit for cohesive working, establish healthy human relation, find a congenial place to show their worth and develop a sense of belongingness, we-ness and togetherness. Such climate helps to make the participation effective.

(ii) Top management thinking and desire

It is very much important to know as to what top management desires/thinks about permitting workers' representatives to participate in the company's vital decision making process. If top management sincerely wants workers' involvement and participation in the system workers feel the seriousness of such process. Under such situation it is possible to carry on effective decision making in the organization.

(iii) Level of morale and job satisfaction of workers

The high level of morale and job satisfaction of workers indicates a favourable situation for effective workers' participation in management.

(iv) Workers' perception, thought pattern about management

Workers', high thinking, image, impression about management approach, style of functioning, method of dealing with problems create a soothing, congenial climate for successful workers' participation in management.

(v) Workers' attitudes, values, beliefs

Positive attitudes, values and beliefs of workers prepare a ground for effective participation in management decision making. Such workers develop confidence, faith on the efficacy of participative system.

In addition to the above, the following conditions contribute to make the participation successful.

- If, the company develops a training system and the workers are given training, education to make them acquainted with company's mission, philosophy, strategy participation may be meaningful. Under such situation, workers can actively participate and effectively contribute to the discussion.
- If, the management recognizes the role of workers for growth and development of the organization, it satisfies the psychological need of the workers that contribute to effective participation in management decision making process.
- If, the organization introduces a system to mould the mind set of the trade union leaders they can accept

changes. Such trade union leaders can make active participation.

- If the organization develops a climate of openness, trust, collaboration, autonomy, proacting, the workers may contribute to worthy participation.
- Well defined participation programme removes ambiguity of the workers in respect of topics / issues to be discussed in the decision making meeting. They can do some homework for effective interactions with the participative team and in the process can make the participation meaningful.
- The top management through action and treatment can make the employees realize that participation is for 'real participation' and not for 'ritual participation'.

Empowerment

Empowerment is the process of shifting authority and responsibility to other in the organizational setting. Empowerment takes place when higher management transfers the power, authority, and responsibility to lower level employees. Shifting of authority and responsibility to the workers is made to take over the charge of the work they do. The concept of shifting of power, authority is very simple in the sense that the person who has been doing some job for years together develops thorough idea, knowledge, competence over the job and keeps everything under his grip. Now, if such person is given overall charge of the work he does, with adequate authority and responsibility he can take decision on his own for accomplishment of the job. He performs quality work and at the same time he gets motivated and develops a sense of commitment and a 'feeling to reciprocate in consideration of the power shifted.' It generally occurs that most human beings desire recognition, power, status, authority, and responsibility and when they achieve they exert drives to utilize their full energy, abilities, and competencies to excel their performance. Such people prepare their mind set to achieve, to perform, to win, to succeed and to strive their best to go ahead in that direction as projected. Empowerment is such a mechanism that helps to achieve individual goals, team goals and organizational goals through handing over the charge of the job to the jobbers to perform the job with authority to take decision on their own. So empowerment relates to individual development and the development of organization as well. Empowerment as a process of passing authority and responsibility to lower level employees is introduced in organizations like GE. Medical Systems, Tata Information System, Asea Brown Broveri and others.

Importance of Empowerment

Importance of employee empowerment can be ascertained from the following:

(i) Employee empowerment improves quality of goods produced by employees.

(ii) In changing scenario, workers need acceptance of changes in operation, methods, techniques, quality of products and this is possible if organizations practice employee empowerment.

(iii) It brings congenial and conducive atmosphere in the organization to achieve organizational goals.

(iv) A culture of openness and trust is developed which establishes healthy relations between supervisors and employees.

(v) It helps to create motivated and committed work force in organization.

(vi) It satiates the need of workers for recognition, status, challenging work, responsibility (that means workers' esteem need is satisfied through empowerment).

Quality Circle (QC)

Quality circle is one of participative methods used in industrial settings. The concept of QC first originated in USA but implementation was made in Japan afterwards. Now let us explain the concept and meaning of Quality Circle. The term 'Quality Circle' means a small group formed with employees working in the same department, on voluntary basis, to identify, discuss and analyse problems and suggest solutions in the quality related issues in the regularly held meeting on company time. It is some sort of improvement group which solves problems of the workplace / work areas to produce quality goods and to deliver the same to the satisfaction of customers.

The main features of QC are as follows:

(i) It is a small group. The total number of group members is generally 4 to 12 depending upon the size of the department / work area.

(ii) It consists of volunteers.

(iii) It holds regular meeting once in a week/fortnight or month for a specific period, during working hours.

(iv) The leader of the group is elected by the group members.

(v) It is an employee-talent search process for effective and smooth running of departmental activities.

(vi) It identifies problems, analyses problems, recommends solution, implements accepted proposals, reviews results and takes follow up action.

From the above it is clear that quality circle is a small group of volunteers usually 4 to 12 depending upon the size of the work areas, who are engaged in work related problems and who hold meeting regularly to identify, analyse and resolve such problems for improving quality and total performance of the organization. In our country many organizations are practising Qcs. Some of such organizations are BHEL, SKF, Godrej and Boyce.

Structure of Quality Circle

The structure of quality circle in Indian organizations consists of several levels viz. non-members, members, leader, facilitator, steering committee and executive committee or top management committee. The organizational structure is shown in Figure 9.2.

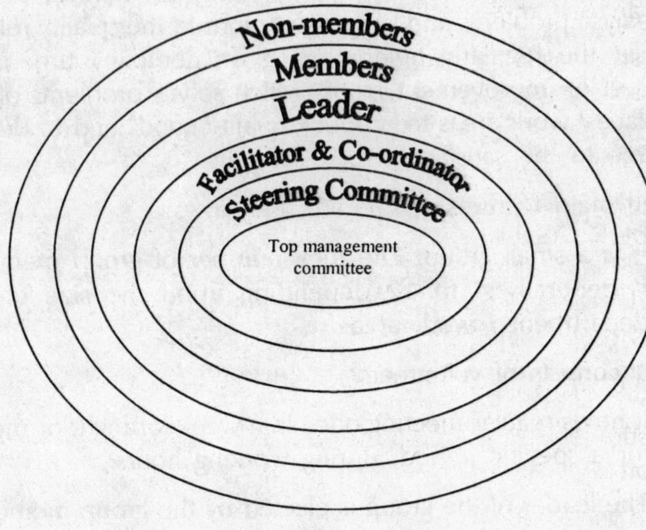

Figure 9.2 : Organizational Structure of QC

Non-members

Non-members are those employees of the concerned department who are not directly involved in circle activities but play important role to implement approved suggestions/ recommendations of the circle members. It is well-nigh impossible to implement members' suggestions if, non-members do not extend cooperation.

Circle Members

Members are those workers of work area/department who volunteer to form circle to discuss and propose ways of improving quality and solving other work related problems in their areas. Total number of circle members may vary from 4 to 12 depending upon the size of the work area. Membership to Qc is not compulsion or binding on the workers, it is totally a voluntary form of participation. The main activities of circle members include

- regular attendance of meeting,
- active participation in the discussion,

- identification of issues deterring improvement,
- analysis of issues/problems
- submission of suggestions for improving quality and solving problems arising in work related areas.

Circle Leader

Quality circle is headed by the leader who is elected by the members of the circle. Generally, it happens that line management takes the charge of the circle. The main function of the leader is to conduct meeting where members threadbarely discuss problems creating barrier for smooth functioning of the departmental work and also for improving quality of the product. Leader motivates the members to contribute their views/ suggestions for digging out the inhibiting areas and for offering solution to overcome the problematic situation. The leader may have such assignment for a particular project and after the concerned project work is over, members may elect any other member as leader.

Facilitator

The facilitator is generally management personnel having a good position in the organization. He is selected by the top management to facilitate smooth and effective functioning of circle activities. He is guide, friend, adviser, coach, teacher to the circle members. He is a link personality between leader and steering committee. He helps in preparation of report, presentation and submission of report to the next hierarchy of the circle. He takes the stock of operational activities, helps in smooth functioning. He lets the steering committee know the latest development of Qc activities.He looks to the training needs of the members and coordinates training activities. He develops healthy relations amongst the members. He is a dynamic personality and possesses the qualities to make the things happen in quality circle.

Steering Committee

This committee is formed with the top management

personnel of core departments and departmental heads of the unit/plant. It formulates guidelines for smooth working of Qcs and also review the functioning of Qc activities.

Steering committee provides infrastructure, resources to strengthen Qcs, designs/formulates objectives, goals, strategy of Qcs.

Steering committee nominates leader for training to improve human skill and also leadership skill. The committee presents the suggestions/recommendation of the Qc before the top management for approval.

The meeting of the steering committee is convened by the facilitator who is also the member of the steering committee. Such meetings are usually presided over by the Chief Executive officer of the plant.

Top Management Committee or Executive Committee

This committee is constituted with CMD and 2-3 top level management personnel to formulate company policies and procedures with regard to quality circles of organization.

Top management support is very much needed to operate any scheme. So, for effective functioning of Qc activities, role of executive committee (EC) is important. The more the EC takes interest in Qc, the higher will be the degree of successful performance of Qcs.

Objectives of Quality Circles

S. Ingle (1985) has identified objectives of quality circles which are related to people and task. The principle objective of Qc is to ensure delivery of the quality goods and services to confront challenges against competitors so that organization can survive, grow and develop. So the objectives of Qc include:

- Self development
- Mutual development
- Satisfaction of psychological needs
- Improvement in communication and attitude

- Problem prevention
- Team building
- Linkage among people
- People improvement
- Participation
- Reduction of absenteeism and grievances
- Improvement in quality
- Reduction of wastes, scraps
- Reduction of cost
- Improvement in productivity
- Safety improvement
- Problem solving
- Promoting human relation
- Reduction of error
- Creation of a reservoir of committed workforce
- Promoting sense of belongingness

Books Recommended

1. S. R. Udpa: Quality Circles – progress through participation. (Tata McGraw Hill, New Delhi, 1992)
2. B. R. Dey: Quality Circles. (Macmillan, New Delhi, 1988)
3. B. R. Virmani: Workers Participation in Management (Macmillan, New Delhi, 1978)
4. D. Dewar and J. F. Beardsley: Quality Circles (International Association of Quality Circles, U.S.A. 1980)
5. K. C. Alexander: Participation Management : The Indian Experience (Sri Ram Centre, New Delhi, 1972)
6. S. W. Gellerman: Motivation and Productivity, (D. B. Taraporevala Sons & Co. Pvt Ltd., Mumbai 1970)

7. Michael Armstrong: A Hand book of Human Resource Management Practice (Kogan Page Limited London, 1999)

8. Jack Halloran : Applied Human Relations—An Organizational Approach (Prentice-Hall of India Private Ltd., New Delhi, 1978)

9. D. Katz : Morale and Motivation in Industry in Current Trends in Industrial Psychology (Pittsburgh, University of Pittsburgh Press, 1949. Pp 159-60)

10. V. G. Mhetras : Labour Participation in Management (Mumbai, Manaktalas, 1966)

11. S. Ingle : Quality Circles Master Guide (New Delhi, Prentice Hall of India, 1985)

12. Keith Davis: Human Behaviour at Work Organizational Behaviour (Tata MCGrawaHill Publishing Company Ltd. New Delhi, 1980

Questions

1. What is 'morale'? Discuss the factors affecting morale.
2. "Morale is the state of feeling, emotions of the employees about the company, job, and supervisors and so on". – Discuss in this context concept of morale and the factors influencing morale".
3. What do you mean by the term 'morale'? Why is morale important?
4. "Various research studies confirm that there is no direct causal relationship between morale and productivity" Discuss.

   Discuss in this context the relationship between morale and productivity.
5. Define 'morale'. Suggest the measures to improve morale of employees.
6. What do you mean by the term 'workers' participation

in management'? Discuss the objectives of workers' participation in management.

7. Discuss in brief different forms of workers' participation in management.
8. Define the term 'workers' participation in management'. – Discuss the main features of shop council and joint council.
9. Explain the term 'empowerment'. Discuss importance of employee empowerment in organization.
10. What is Quality Circle? Discuss organizational structure of quality circles.
11. Explain the term 'Quality Circle'. Discuss the objectives of quality circles.
12. State briefly the prerequisites for effective workers' participation in management.
13. Write notes on
    (a) Morale
    (b) Wokers' participation in management
    (c) Works committee
    (d) Empowerment
    (e) Quality Circles
    (f) Steering Committee
    (g) Executive Committee

Case Study

Mr. S. P. Bhatia is an executive of a big organization. He is Area Manager of the North Eastern States and posted at Guwahati. He is a biased personality. He does not like people nor does he accept them as human beings. He is not acceptable to the people at work. People do not pay him respect. He is afraid of Mr. R. K. Chatterjee happened to be union leader, now head of one department working under him. Mr Chatterjee is also a biased person. His acceptability by his colleagues is negligible. He is hard in his heart. He is vindictive like Mr Bhatia. Both personalities are more or less the same in regard to their activities, their role character, ego pattern and behavioural manifestation.

Mr Bhatia discusses problems with Mr Chatterjee pertaining to other department and seeks suggestions from him in presence of the concerned department head. It also happens that Mr Bhatia sometimes considers the issues of other departments raised by Mr Chatterjee with an intention to apparently strengthen his understanding with Mr Bhatia.

Mr Bhatia expresses his feeling to Mr S. P. Gupta Head of HRM Department, in the matter of interference of Mr Chatterjee on the issues and problems pertaining to his department. Mr Bhatia emphasizes that Mr Chatterjee's entry to his department should be minimized and no information which is confidential in nature be supplied to Mr Chatterjee if requested.

Mr Bhatia elaborates the dubious character of Mr Chatterjee and advises Mr Gupta to refrain from discussing or seeking suggestions on any matter relating to his department.

Mr Gupta gets surprised and tries to find out the reality as he observes that his boss, Mr Bhatia gives much more importance on Mr Chatterjee and on vital aspects including those of confidential in nature the boss discussed with him. The interactions between Mr Gupta and the boss Mr Bhatia which often take place are given here under:

Mr Bhatia: Mr Gupta, does Mr Chatterjee come to your department frequently?

Mr Gupta: Not frequently, Sir. Occasionally, and that too on urgent work.

Mr Bhaita: How is the important and confidential information divulged? Mr Chatterjee gets all information and supplies to the right person/s before rofficial communication reaches.

Mr Gupta: Sir, I confirm that no information, whether confidential or unimportant in nature, is leaked through our department staff.

Mr. Bhatia: I have information that staff members of your department have established a good rapport and understanding with Mr Chatterjee. Is it true?

Mr Gupta: Sir, it is quite usual that staff members build up good human relations and understanding amongst all the staff members of the office. But, in no way does this relation affect department secrecy and privacy. Sir, I have a small appeal to you

Mr Bhatia: Yes, Mr Gupta, come on, tell me.

Mr Gupta: Sir, you attach undue importance on Mr Chatterjee. In my presence you ask for suggestions on vital and confidential issues pertaining to our department and you act upon his suggestions.

Mr Bhatia: Mr Gupta, it is not that. I do not want his intervention on matters not connected with his department.

Mr Gupta: It is fine. Sir, then why do you discuss with Mr Chatterjee those issues pertaining to our department?

Mr Bhatia: I discuss those with him just to study his mind set on the matter and sometime I also consider his suggestions to appease his sentiment. You know, all these are outward shows. I make him understand that he is an important person which he is not and I take decision on vital issues after consultation with him.

Mr Gupta: That's right. I assure you Sir, no information pertaining to our department be given to Mr Chatterjee without your permission.

[***Source:*** *A. K. Ghosh: Managing Human Resource – Strategic Approach to win, Manas Publications, New Delhi, 2002. Pp120-22*]

Read the above case thoroughly and discuss the following points/issues:

1. a) What sort of relationship between Area Manager and other officers exists in the organization?

   b) If such situation / relationship continues what will happen in future?

2. a) Do you think as HR Manager of the company, such work environment will affect employee morale?

   b) What do you feel could be the consequences of low morale?

3. Under such situation how Mr Gupta will deal with the problems as pointed out by Mr Bhatia?

4. If, you were HR Manager of that factory what would be your suggestion to improve employee morale and promote healthy industrial relations?

5. Do you think under such environment participative management would be effective?

10

Introduction to Industrial Relations

Meaning of Industrial Relations

In narrow sense, the term 'industrial relations' means relations between parties in industrial establishments. That means, nature of relationship established amongst the parties in the industry. Dictionary meaning of industrial relations is the relations between management and employees in industrial concerns. In short, the term, 'industrial relations' means the relations between employees and management arising out of day to day work in industry.

Different authors and experts have expressed their views on the concept of industrial relations. Dale Yoder views industrial relations, 'as a whole field of relationship that exists because of the necessary collaboration of men and women in the employment process of an industry'. From the analysis of Dale Yoder's opinion it is revealed that, the employees work in industry as per terms and conditions of employment and in the process of working in collaborative system both, management and employees develop relations with each other and this relationship as a whole is industrial relations.

International Labour Organization has stressed upon the relations between state, employers' organizations and workers' organization or the relationship between occupational organizations. John T Dunlop (1958) has expressed his views on the concept of industrial relations as the relations between three actors-employer, employees and government.

We may have clear idea about industrial relations from the following :

- Industrial relations is the relation between management and employees.
- The relationship may be positive, negative or mixed.
- Pattern of IRs is influenced by people's value, belief, perception, aptitude, personality, attitudes, ethical value etc.
- State acts as regulator, facilitator in shaping IRs pattern in industry.
- The relationship is based on economic, non-economic issues arising out of terms and conditions of employment as also practices not covered under the terms.
- Means of IRs are HR/IR polices, procedures, rules, regulations, legislations etc.
- Collective bargaining is the effective mechanism of shaping the pattern of industrial relations.
- Changing economic scenario, technological advances, organization mission, strategic approach, trade unions' role contribute a lot to influence IRs pattern.

Industrial relations activities are shown in Figure 10.2

Characteristics of Industrial Relations

The salient characteristics of industrial relations are discussed herein below :

1. Parties in the industrial relations activities : Basically, two parties-workers and management are involved in the process of establishing relations. However, the government agencies regulate /maintain industrial relations.

2. Interactive Process : Industrial relations arise out of

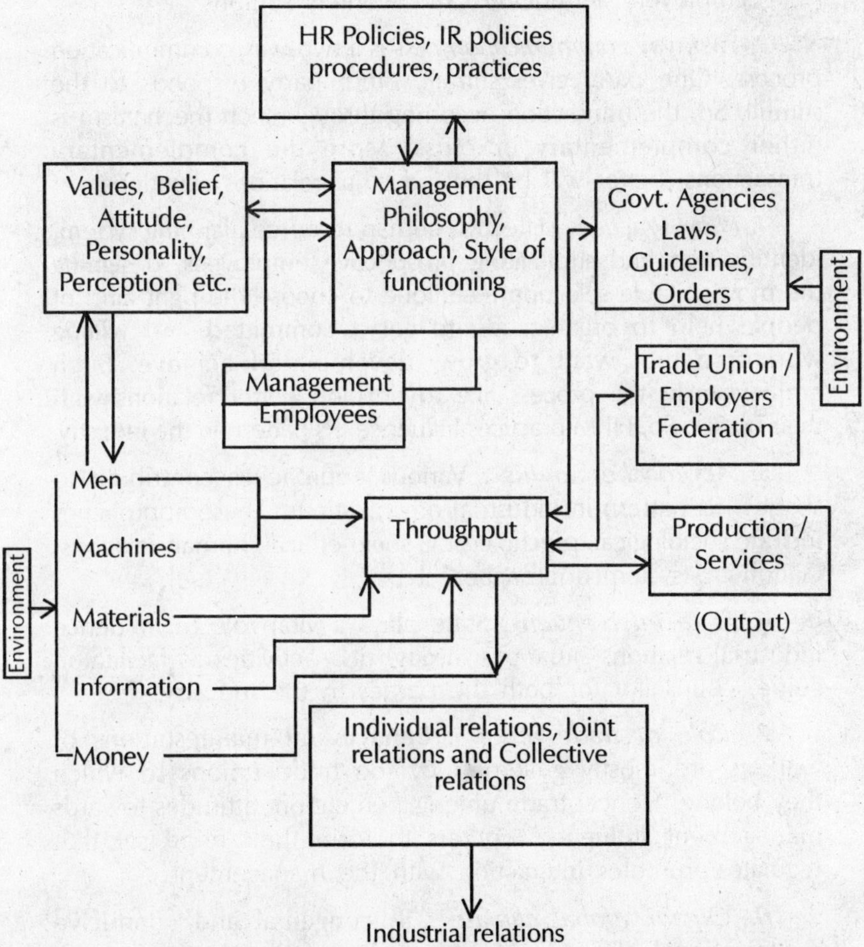

Figure 10.1 : Industrial relations activities

interactions between different persons/parties. They are supervisors, workers trade unions, employers' associations. So, interactive process takes place between

- Supervisors and industrial workers
- Supervisors and group/team members
- Management and trade union leaders

• Employers' federations and workers' unions

3. Two-way communication : IRs is a two-way communication process. One party gives stimuli, other party responds to the stimuli. So, the transaction occurring through such mechanism is either complementary or cross. More the complementary transactions, better will be the industrial relations situations.

4. HRM Practices : Effective human resource planning system, identification and stimulating prospective employees, designing the most suitable selection technique to choose the right kind of people help to organization to get a committed and willing workforce that want to grow, develop and achieve. Such employees in the process like to develop better relations with their bosses. So, HRM practices influence IRs pattern in the industry.

5. Approaches to IRs : Various approaches contribute to shape IRs pattern in industrial organizations. These approaches include sociological, psychological, socio-ethical, human relations, Gandhian, system approaches etc.

6. State Intervention : State plays a vital role to influence industrial relations situations through its activities as facilitator, guide, counsellor for both the parties in the industry.

7. Role of trade union : Behavioural manifestations of workers are mostly governed by the trade unions to which they belong. Hence, trade union's perception, attitudes towards management influence workers to form their mind set that regulates/promotes interaction with the management.

8. Organizational climate : If, congenial and conducive organizational climate prevails, workers feel homely, interact spontaneously, communicate boss about their problems, difficulties directly and come close to him to exchange/share the views each other in respect of work, change of job design, introduction of any operative system, process etc. Under such situation, possibility of establishing healthy human relations develops and these relations influence industrial relations pattern of organization.

9. Dispute Settlement Process : If, the management personnel belive on the philosophy of settling workers' grievances/

disputes through bi-lateral negotiation process, They give much more emphasis on mutual talk, sharing responsibility, collaboration, partnership dealing and mutual trust. In the process changes in workers' atitudes, behaviour and thought pattern are likely to occur which effect industrial relations.

10. Outcomes of IRs : Outcomes of IRs are reflected in production both in quantity and quality, services, mandays lost, wastes, accident rate, productivity, labour turnover rate, absenteeism rate, number of bipartite negotiations, company's image, growth, development etc.

11. Competency Development : Healthy industrial relations help to develop workers' skill, knowledge, ability, aptitude and change their attitudes, perception to enable them to participate in collaborative activities / collective bargaining process effectively.

12. Issues in IRs : Industrial relations climate / situation is greatly influenced by the issues-economic, non-economic governed by service contract / terms and conditions of employment. Besides, the issues not covered under service rules viz. behavioural, and attitudinal issues influence IRs pattern.

Objectives of IRs

The main objective of industrial relations is to create congenial, conducive climate, healthy environment, enabling organizational culture so that individual goals, team goals and organizational goals are achieved. The other objectives of IRs are discussed herein below :

1. Uninterrupted production and increased productivity

The objective of IRs is to keep the production process/ services running so that target of production / services set by organization is attained and also to increase productivity to enable the organization to grow and develop.

2. Less / Zero conflict

If, better industrial relation is established both management and workers develop mutual understanding and put in best efforts to resolve disputes through bilateral discussion, negotiation. So, conflicts are minimized if, not reduced to zero.

3. Industrial peace and harmony

The sound industrial relations bring industrial peace and harmony while unsound industrial relations create situation/ climate of disharmony, industrial unrest, conflict.

4. Contented and committed workforce

The objective of industrial relations is to create a contented and committed workforce by way of increasing their wages, providing fringe benefits, social security measures, opportunities to develop, grow etc. This is done through establishment of healthy industrial relations.

5. Dynamic workforce

Sound industrial relations create a dynamic workforce to get acquainted with the changing scenario, to know the organization needs, demands, place in the competitive race and to help the organization to survive, grow and develop. IR policies, procedures are framed to give emphasis on workers' involvement, participation in decision making process, to develop competencies through training, education, counselling.

6. Management of organizational complexity

In view of liberalization, privatization and globalization (LPG) organization has to face a tough competition as multinational companies (MNCs), transnational companies (TNCs) occupy a place in the market. For producing quality product and also variety of products different sophisticated machines, devices with complicated operation processes are installed, which need workforce to accept changes, update knowledge, skill. Sound industrial relations through developing human relations, understanding, mutual confidence and enriching knowledge, imparting training to enhance the level of competence and skill, manage the organizational complexities.

7. Developing Trade Unions

If union leaders, active members are educated, aware of changing environment, position of the organization where rank and file work and also rights, duties and responsibilities of the workers, most of the workers' problems are solved by themselves. So, it is one of the objectives of IRs is to educate trade union people and to support and develop them to act as real trade unions for the right cause of the workers and for growth and development of the workers and the organization as well.

8. Cordial human relations

One of the objectives of IRs is to promote employer employee relations i.e. human relations through effective interaction and communication process. Organization philosophy, climate, management approach, style of functioning facilitate to develop mutual understanding, mutual faith between boss and subordinates.

9. Educating workers

Because of illiteracy, ignorance workers are unable to judge the specific situation, issues and give consent or agree to take recourse to action which is unjustified, unwaranted and uncalled for. IRs' objective is to educate the workforce, to develop their skill, ability to perceive the situation rightly, to make them aware of their strength and weaknesses so that they can negotiate their grievances, issues, problems with their boss and can resolve them.

10. Promoting trust, creativity, cooperativeness

Sound industrial relations create a conducive and congenial climate in organization which promotes trust, creativity, cooperativeness amongst the workers.

Under such organizational milieu, workers develop a feeling of 'belongingness', 'we-ness', 'together-ness' which drive them to undertake any job for making things happen. Workers become loyal, committed, particular about their job role, and make no/less wastes, accident. Labour turnover rate, absenteeism rate are reduced.

Factors of Industrial Relations

The term 'industrial relations' means the relationship between labour and management which arises through interactive processes. Both labour and management interact each other on different issues-may be the issues relating to employement terms and conditions as specified in the standing orders/bipartite settlement, HR practices or the issues concerning court judgement, legal implications, government orders, instructions. Origin/development, representation, settlement of the issues depend on various factors which indicate/influence the pattern of industrial relations. These factors are socio-ethical and cultural, ideological, technological, psychological, political, governmental, international, economic/financial, market conditions and enterprise related factors. Details of these factor are discussed. Factors influencing industrial relations are shown in Figure 10.2

Socio-ethical and cultural factor

Interaction between workers and management personnel becomes effective and complementary when both the parties possess positive thought process, values, beliefs that facilitate to develop a state of collaborative approach, willingness to help, desire for accepting risk, responsibilities to function in a joint venture and application of rational, judicious approach on the issues. All these traits and attributes develop mostly from social, ethical and cultural activities. So, the positive social, ethical and cultural values influence interaction between labour and management in a positive way. In such situation, human relations will be cordial and industrial relations will be better.

Technological Advancement

In case of advancement of technology production is increased, quality of the product is improved, extent of defective product is minimised, cost of production is reduced, producitivity is increased. All this increases the wages of the workers and makes them happy. The contented and happy

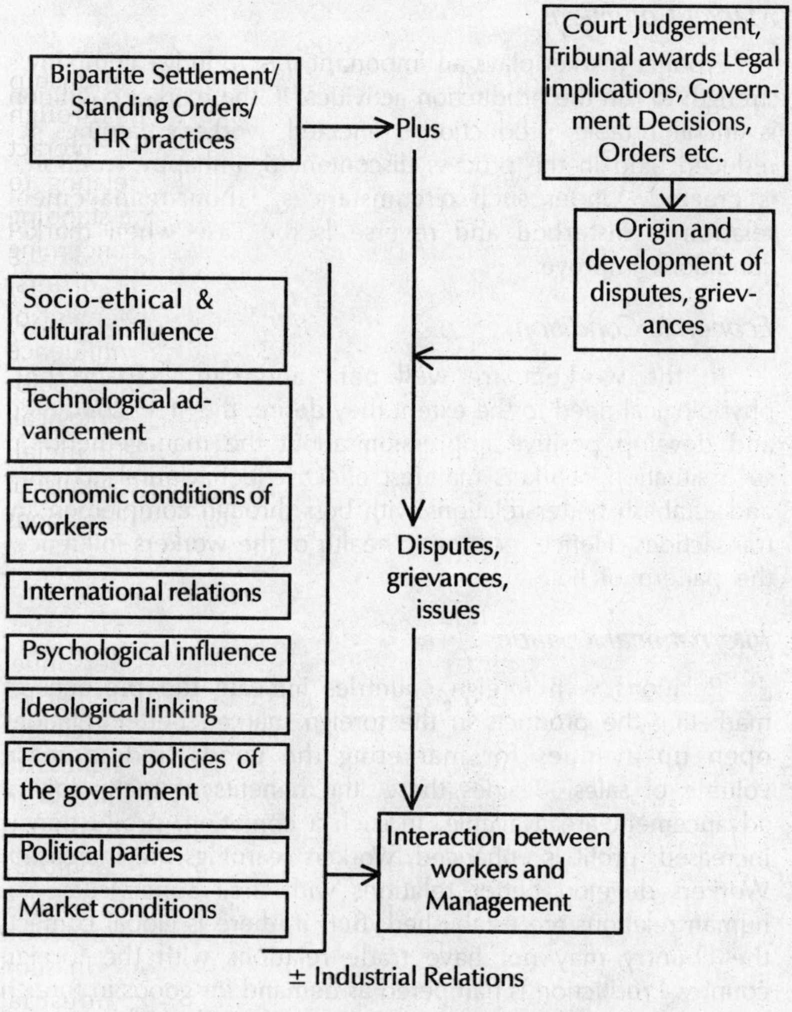

Fig - 10. 2 : Factors influencing Industrial Relations Pattern.

workers are much more willing to keep the production activities running than to disturb the system, and for this, they establish good relations with their boss. So, advance in technology influences the industrial relations pattern of the industry.

Market Conditions

Product market plays an important role to judge company's strength to run the production activities. If, the market condition is uncomfortable, production is affected, worker's earnings get reduced, and in the process discontented, unhappy workforce is created. Under such circumstances, labour-management relation is disturbed and reverse is the case when market conditions improve.

Economic Conditions

If, the workers are well paid and can satisfy their physiological need to the extent they desire, they feel contented and develop positive impression about the management. In such situation, workers mainfest effective behavioural activities and establish better relations with boss through complementary transactions. Hence, economic health of the workers influences the pattern of IRs.

International Relations

Relations with foreign countries indicate the prospect of marketing the products in the foreign market. Better relations open up avenues for marketing the goods and increase volume of sales. Besides these, the benefits of technological advancement are available. In such a condition, production is increased, profit is enhanced, workers' earnings are increased. Workers develop better relations with their supervisors. So, human relations are established. But, if, there is global conflict, the country may not have trade relations with the foreign country. Production is hampered as demand for goods in foreign market is reduced. Workers' earnings are affected, industrial relations is disturbed.

Psychological Factor

Mind-set, perception, attitudes of both workers and management, determine outcome of their interaction. Conflict arises when perception level differs, attitudes vary, mind-set is dissimilar and all this disturbs the labour management relations.

Better human relation occurs, when positivities in all these psychological areas prevail.

Ideological factor

Since labour-management relation arises out of interaction between labour and management the influence / guidelines of the government or governmental machineries / agencies, the ideological similarities, dissimilarities amongst workers, trade union leaders, government also affect interactive processes. So, more the similar ideology the concerned parties possess, better is the industrial relations.

Economic Policy

Economic policies of the government manifest its philosophy, approach towards workers, employers and affect employer employee relations. Economic policies concerning liberalization, privatization and globalization (LPG) accept the concept of 'global village' where MNCs, TNCs have free access to carry on business/ industrial activities. Under such situations, small, weak and medium-size organizations are unable to face competition and find difficulty to survive. Hence, labour management relation is affected. Even the workers in MNCs, TNCs feel unhappy, discontented as they remain under the threat of losing their jobs.

Political Parties

Political parties influence government to formulate labour policies, to enact laws, to issue instructions, orders to industrial organizations on different aspects. They also dominate trade union people and rank and file to behave and manifest activities in a way they desire. In the process, labour-management interaction is controlled by political parties and whole industrial pattern is influenced.

Conditions for congenial industrial relations

Sound industrial relations are essential to achieve individual goals, team goals and organizational goals. Absence of congenial labour-management relations creates an atmosphere of disharmony, labour unrest, conflict, disturbance in production activities, piling up of workers' grievances, higher rate of labour absenteeism, fall in productivity, and profit. This situation tends towards virtual collapse of the functional activities of the organization. Hence, healthy / congenial industrial relations is a must for survival, growth, development of the people and the organization as well. For promoting congenial industrial relations the following conditions are required to exist in industrial setting.

(i) Management attitudes

Management personnel must think the workers as part and parcel of organization. Better industrial relation is established when workers realize that the attitudes of the management are supportive, helping, positive and consider them as members of organization.

(ii) Organization culture

Organization should have the culture to generate and develop enabling and proacting capability of the people at work, so that number of disputes becomes less and the disputes / grievances which crop-up are settled mutually at the shortest possible time.

(iii) Management philosophy, approaches and style of functioning

Sound industrial relations are established when top management personnel are liberal, participative, facilitative, enlightened and are concerned for people and work. They practice both theory 'X' and theory 'Y' at the time of necessities.Their philosophy, style of functioning, approaches are for growth and development of the people and the organization as well.

(iv) Collective bargaining, grievance procedures as methods for settlement of disputes

Congenial industrial relation is possible if, the management people accept, encourage collective bargaining process, grievance procedure as methods for settlement of disputes and do not force / compel the workers for adjudication of the issues. In such organization, it occurs that practice is already in vogue to dispose of grievances / issues through mutual discussions/negotiations. Regular structured meetings with union representatives are held at different levels to discuss and sort out the agenda issues bilaterally. Day-to-day issues which require immediate solutions are dealt with promptly and in case of need workers'/unions' suggestions are sought. These sorts of organizational functioning help in promoting industrial relations.

(v) *Collaborative / cooperative organization climate*

Existence of collaborative / cooperative climate helps to develop human relations. Under such conditions, both management and workers come close to each other and establish mutual understanding, mutual trust and mutual faith. So, in an organization, where conducive climate exists for establishment of mutuality of relationships, it is possible to develop better industrial relations.

(vi) *Existence of educated, conscious and positive trade union*

Existence of educated, conscious and positive trade unions help the management to increase production, to improve quality, to reduce labour turnover rate through making workers aware of their rights, duties, responsibilities and their role as individuals, members of the team and members of organization, and this way they achieve organizational goals. Educated, conscious and positive leaders show their convincing, compromising activities in the collective bargaining process / negotiation as they develop impression that they grow with the growth of organization and they lose everything when organization loses. They do not resort to unfair, restrictive practices and expect fair, unbiased treatment from the management. Prevalence of such condition in the organization facilitates establishment of healthy industrial relations.

(vii) *Initiative by top management*

If, the top management of organization takes initiative or expresses encouraging activities for introduction and implementation of workers' welfare / benefit schemes, these come into force uninterruptedly. This stimulates the workers to develop positive mind-set, impression about top management and the organization as well. This situation helps to nurture a comfortable climate to establish sound industrial relations.

(viii) *Attitudinal, job satisfaction survey*

If, organization develops practice / system to study employees' needs satisfaction, morale, aspiration, expectations, demands in a planned and continuous manner through attitudinal, job satisfaction survey and takes appropriate measures to satiate their needs, workers feel involved, contented, committed and intended to reciprocate. In such condition, workers develop sense of 'we-feeling', 'togetherness', 'being in the family' which facilitate congenial climate for the improvement of industrial relations.

(ix) *Fair and rational management*

If, the management is fair, rational, and gives honour to implement court order, governement directions, orders, guidelines, regulations, bipartite settlements, tribunal awards, agreements, a climate of mutual trust, confidenceand faith is established which is one of the prerequisites for sound industrial relations.

(x) *Positive, stimulating HR policies, procedures and practices*

If, positive and stimulating policies, procedures are formulated and practised in organization in the area of wage and salary administration, human resource planning, recruitment, selection, reward management, training, career planning and development, performance appraisal, potential appraisal, counselling, quality circles, workers' involvement, TQM, QWL, welfare, social security measures, discipline management etc., workers feel proud of being the members of organization. This feeling indicates expression of maintaining healthy human relations and conveys the message of performing all kinds of activities for achieving goals.

(xi) Use of HRD mechanisms

If, organization introduces HRD techniques for development of skill, knowledge, abilities of workers for performing present job, future job through training and education, workers get acquainted with the operative processes, work methods etc. and thus, enrich knowledge, upgrade skills and competencies. These training and education mechanisms are also applied for development of knowledge, ability and skills of supervisors that help to develop trust, understanding and confidence between management and employees.

Importance of harmonious industrial relations

Industrial relations is the creation of an atmosphere of relationship between labour and management. Such relationship arises out of interaction between two parties. If, the interaction makes fruitful outcome which pleases both labour and management, it brings harmony and peace in the industry and reverse is the case when interaction makes difference and creates a state of disagreement. Harmonious industrial relation bring prosperity while disharmonious industrial relations stand in the way to progress. Hence, harmonious industrial relations is very important for growth and development of organization. Importance of harmonious industrial relations can be judged from the following:

Benefits to Workers

Sound industrial relations may provide a lot of benefits to workers in an organization. Some important benefits to workers include :

- It makes the functioning of the industrial activities of organization smooth and effective and keeps workers' deployment process uninterrupted / unaffected.
- It increases production and productivity as workers find congenial atmosphere to work.
- It creates a climate of cooperation where both labour and management come close, develop understanding, solve disputes and grievances mutually.

- It enhances workers' wages and allowances, provides welfare amenities, introduces reward system and satiates the need, aspiration and expectation of workers.
- It makes the employees contented, happy, committed, loyal through formulation of employee-oriented IR/HR policies, procedures and practices.
- Satisfaction of workers' physiological and psychological needs is possible, as both workers and management personnel work for growth and development.
- It develops a sense of 'we-feeling' 'togetherness', 'involvement' amongst the employees which drive them to ensure perfection, completeness, accuracy in all sorts of functional activities and delivery of world class quality of products and services to customers.
- Level of job satisfaction and morale of employees is increased in a climate of harmonious industrial relations.
- Collective bargaining mechanism is accepted as a tool of settling disputes and grievances of the employees. Day to day grievances, problems are sorted out through direct negotiation, discussion and also through grievance procedure machinery. All this is possible when harmonious industrial relations exist.
- In an atmosphere of sound industrial relations workers may find improvement in quality of work life (QWL), participative system in decision-making, introduction of quality circles, interest of management to solve their problems, design of career planning and development, unbiased evaluation of performance and action orientation by management.

Benefits to management

Management personnel may have an ample benefits from a healthy industrial relations system. *Benefits are discussed below:*

- Industrial conflict becomes less/zero.
- Production and productivity tend to be on the higher

side as workers participate in organizational activities as members of the team and intend to grow with the growth of the company.

- Since, workers co-operate spontaneously organization can compete with the competitors and can grow and develop.
- Customers' delightment is possible through delivery of quality goods and personalised services.
- Industrial peace prevails as mutual understanding, faith and confidence between labour and management is established and both the parties avoid confict.
- Management can make the people dynamic through creation of change environment and application of OD mechanism to improve / develop core areas of human resources-skill, knowledge, competencies, talent, attitude, aptitudes, values, beliefs, perception etc. Such organizational environment creates a ground for workers to accept changes to show their worth, values in a state of dynamism.
- Organization can have a reservoir of talented, committed human resources.

Benefits to society

- Instances of lay off, retrenchment of workers are remote.
- No adverse behavioural activities are manifested by the employees in the society as they feel high degree of QWL.
- Production and distribution system remain uninterrupted. Supply of goods is ensured. Price is not increased, rather shows declining trend.
- Climate of lawlessness that arises out of industrial disputes viz. strike, dharna, closure, lockout does not prevail in the society.
- Societal peace prevails.

From the above discussion it is observed that harmonious

industrial relations benefit workers, employers (management) and society. Hence, importance of sound industrial relations can not be exaggerated, particularly in the present changing scenario (i.e., change in economic policies, change in technology, change in job requirement, change in markets and the like.) which needs dynamic HR and dynamic organization to face competition against MNCs, TNCs, and this is possible if, a state of harmonious relations between labour and management exists.

Books Recommended

1. John T. Dunlop : Industrial Relations Systems (Henry Holt & Company, New Yourk, 1958)
2. Keith Davis : Human Relations at Work : The Dynamic of Organizational Behaviour (Mumbai, Tata McGraw Hill, 1967)
3. Dale Yoder : Personnel Management and Industrial Relations (New York, 1948)
4. F.H.Harbison and R. Dubin : Patterns of Union-Management Relations (Science Research Associates, Chicago, 1947)
5. N.P. Dufty: Industrial Relations in India (Allied Publishers, Mumbai, 1964)
6. R.D. Aggarwal (ed): Dynamics of Labour Relations in India : A Book of Readings (Tata McGraw Hill, Mumbai, 1972)
7. P. Verma : Management of Industrial Relations. (Oxford IBH, New Delhi 1981)
8. V.B. Singh : Climate for Industrial Relations : A Study of Kanpur Cotton Mills (Allied Publishers Mumbai, 1968)
9. C.B. Mamoria and S. Mamoria : Dynamics of Industrial Relations in India (Himalaya Publishing House, New Delhi, 1995)
10. E. A. Ramaswamy : Industrial Relations in India (Macmillan, New Delhi 1981)

Questions

1. Define the term 'industrial relations'. State the salient characteristics of industrial relations.
2. The term 'industrial relations' has been expressed 'as a whole field of relationship that exists because of the necessary collaboration of men and women in the employment process of an industry'. How would you justify this ?
3. Do you think an organization can achieve its goals even when unhealthy industrial relations climate exists? Discuss in support of your views.
4. Explain the objectives of industrial relations?
5. 'For promoting congenial industrial relations some conditions require to exist in industrial setting' - Discuss in this context the pre-requisites for healthy industrial relations.
6. 'Some factors influence the industrial relations of an organization' - What are these factors? - Discuss
7. Explain the importance of harmonious industrial relations.

Case Study

Mrs Sulochana is a clerk attached to Regional office of a nationalised Bank in Bangalore. She is intelligent and particular about her assigned task. She completes her allotted job much earlier than the usual time. Her output is more than average. She is smart, obedient and polished. She excels in communication. Normally, she commits no mistake in her work. She enjoys positive strokes from her immediate boss, Mr Naresh Kumar for perfection and accuracy in her work. She can grasp her assigned job in no time and renders service to the utmost satisfaction of her boss. She never says no to her superior whenever any additional task is given.

Mrs Sulochana has some shortcomings. She likes leisure period. She can not work for long at a stretch. After doing some work, she feels bored, uneasy and fatigued. She can not remain in her seat after the assigned task is finished and she moves to other colleagues who remain engaged at their job. She starts gossiping and disturbs their work.

She has the habit of remaining absent frequently without taking prior permission. She sends messages to her boss about her not coming to office. On resumption of duties she submits application for sanction of leave. She frequently leaves office with permission from her boss before the scheduled time of departure on flimsy pretexts.

She keeps her immediate boss happy who appreciates her and gives her recognition for quality work. Since, she does not keep allotted jobs pending, her boss gives her some relaxation for attending/departing office. She has developed a good understanding with the boss and has earned confidence in her work.

She is responsible and accountable to her immediate boss, Mr. Naresh Kumar for her work performance but her attendance, punctuality, salary and leave administration are controlled by Mr Chanakya Bhat, Senior Manager (office administration). Mr Bhat keeps a close watch on her mobility and attendance activities at the office.

Mr. Bhat is a non-acceptable person. He is a negative personality. He never helps people. He does not believe in the motivational approach. He does not treat people as human beings. He perceives people as non-performers and leisure seekers. He is an autocrat in his behaviour and activities.

In the instant case, Mrs. Sulochana resumed her duties after three days of absence. All these three days she informed office about her absence. Mr Bhat was away from headquarters during those three days. The day Mrs. Sulochana came to report for duties, Mr Kumar was present. On seeing Mrs Sulochana, Mr Bhat started firing her. The following transactions / exchange of stimuli and responses occurred between them.

Mr. Bhat : Why have you not submitted your leave application?

Mrs. Sulochana :	Sir, our office hour starts from 10 a.m. It is now 5 minutes to 10 a.m. I have just come to attend office after my illness
Mr. Bhat :	On earlier occasions also you delayed submission of your applications for sanction of leave of absence.
Mrs. Sulochana :	Sir, it had not happened in my case. Everytime I got my leave sanctioned before I proceeded for privilege leave or I sent a communication to office about my inability to attend office when it was a casual or sick leave.
Mr. Bhat :	No, no, you are not correct. You are in the habit of not submitting leave applications on time. This time also you have repeated the same thing. You did not bother to inform us about your not coming to office.
Mrs. Sulochana :	Sir, I telephoned at the office. I wanted to talk to you but you were out of Headquarters three days ago. I gave the information to Mr. Kumar, my boss about my indisposition. I also told him that I would not be able to join duty for three or four days. I never delayed submitting my application for sanction of leave of absence. I know the rules as I have rendered 20 years of sevice with organization.
Mr. Bhat :	Don't talk about 20 years' service. I know how to set the thing right. You have no casual leave to your credit. As forsanctioning privilege leave, one has to apply 30 days ahead of the date of availing of privilege leave.
Mrs. Sulochana :	Since, I have no casual leave credit balance, you will have to sanction privilege leave.

Mr. Bhat : You have become over smart. You do not know how to talk? Are you commanding me to sanction privilege leave? I will teach you a lesson.

Mrs. Sulochana : Sir, I did not mean that. I simply wanted to say that if my casual leave was exhausted, it is you, my superior boss, to see how my absence period would be adjusted, may be by debiting privilege leave. (Then she started crying.)

Read the above case thoroughly and answer the following questions.

1. What sort of relationship is established between Mrs. Sulochana and Mr. Kumar?
2. Do you think the relationship between Sulochana and Mr. Bhat arises out of interpersonal conflict?
3. If you were the Head of HRM Department at Bangalore Regional office of the bank
   (i) how would you tackle such problems?
   (ii) if the relationship between supervisors and subordinates in the organization is almost the same as that of relationship between Mrs. Sulochana and Mr. Bhat, do you think
      (a) it will have an adverse effect on building harmonious industrial relations?
      (b) the concerned bank will have no problem to achieve organizational goals?
   (iii) what prerequisites you will prescribe for healthy industrial relations in the bank?

11

Industrial Disputes

Industrial Conflicts – Concept

In narrow sense industrial conflict means conflict between parties in industrial establishments. Dictionary meaning of 'conflict' is 'disagreement', 'mutual antagonism as of ideas, interests etc.' So, industrial conflict is disagreement/mutual antagonism as of ideas, interests etc. between parties in industry. In industrial setting parties are invariably workers and management. In the process of working, workers express their need, expectation, desire for fulfilment and satisfaction. They want more money i.e., attractive wages, allowances, monetary incentive which the management may not be agreeable to pay. Workers demand of better fringe benefits, health benefits but management may provide less than that of their requirement. They want recognition, status, power, advancement, higher quality of work life but management may be reluctant to give. Under such situation, a state of disagreement/mutual antagonism between workers and management develops which gives birth to industrial conflict. So, industrial conflict is a general concept, and this conflict gets the shape of industrial dispute in a specific dimensional situation. Basically, there is no difference between 'industrial conflict' and 'industrial dispute', variation lies only in scope and coverage.

According to section 2(k) of Industrial Disputes Act 1947, 'industrial dispute' means any dispute or difference between employees and employers or between employers and workmen, or between workmen and workmen, which is connected with the employment or non-employment or the terms of employment or with the conditions of labour, of any person."

Analysis of the provision of the Act reveals the following:-

- *Industrial dispute is a dispute or difference*
  - *(i)* between employeers and employers, or
  - *(ii)* between employers and workmen or
  - *(iii)* between workmen and workmen
- *Industrial dispute is connected with*
  - *(i)* employment or
  - *(ii)* non-employment or
  - *(iii)* terms of employment or
  - *(iv)* conditions of labour of any person

Some of the issues which are held by different courts as industrial disputes are mentioned below:

- Re-instatement of a dismissed workman [Western India Automobile Association V Industrial Tribunal, M'bai, A.I.R. (1949) F.C.iii]
- Employer's failure to reply to a letter of demand sent by the workmen [Triangular Motors Ltd.; M'bai V Their workmen, 1949) L.L.J. 79]
- Profit bonus [F.W.Heiglers & Co. Ltd. V.N.C. Chakravarty, A.I.R. (1949) F.C. 142]
- Rejecting a polite request of the employees by an employer [Sree Minakshi Mills V. State of Madras, A.I.R. (1954) Mad. 143]
- Declaration of lockout by an employer and workers' entitlement to wages or compensation for the lock out period [Shamnugger Jute Factory Co. Ltd. V.S.M. Modak, A.I.R. (1949) F.C. 150]

- Dispute in respect of two workmen's designation espoused by the Delhi Union of Journalists having 25% of the working journalists of the newspapers establishment as members [Workmen of Indian Express Newspapers (Pvt.) Ltd. V Indian Express (Pvt.) Ltd. (1970) 2 L.L.J. 132]

Forms of Industrial Conflicts

Industrial conflict may take different forms starting from the phase of showing protest, demonstration, deputation during recess period to the culminating phase of cessation of work, gherao etc. These forms of industrial conflicts / disputes are the reflection / manifestation of group / concerted action of the employees. Employers use lockout weapon as a form of industrial dispute when magnitude of the conflict is very serious. Sometime political parties call bandh, industrial strike in support of employees.

The different phases of workers' activities for redressal of their grievances / settlement of industrial disputes are shown in Fig. 11.1. It may happen that workers in some organizations do not follow the forms of disputes / phases of activities in seriatim, they may resort to some form of dispute superseding other. It depends on the type of leadership, nature of dispute, issues involved, management attitude, environmental situations etc.

Different forms of industrial conflicts are briefly discussed herein below:

Demonstration / Deputation during recess period / duty hours

Workers or some executive members of trade union show their unhappiness over some issues which remain unsettled or are disposed of irrationally, whimsically through demonstration, deputation during recess period before head of the department or head of the personnel / human resource management department, factory manager or in front of their office.

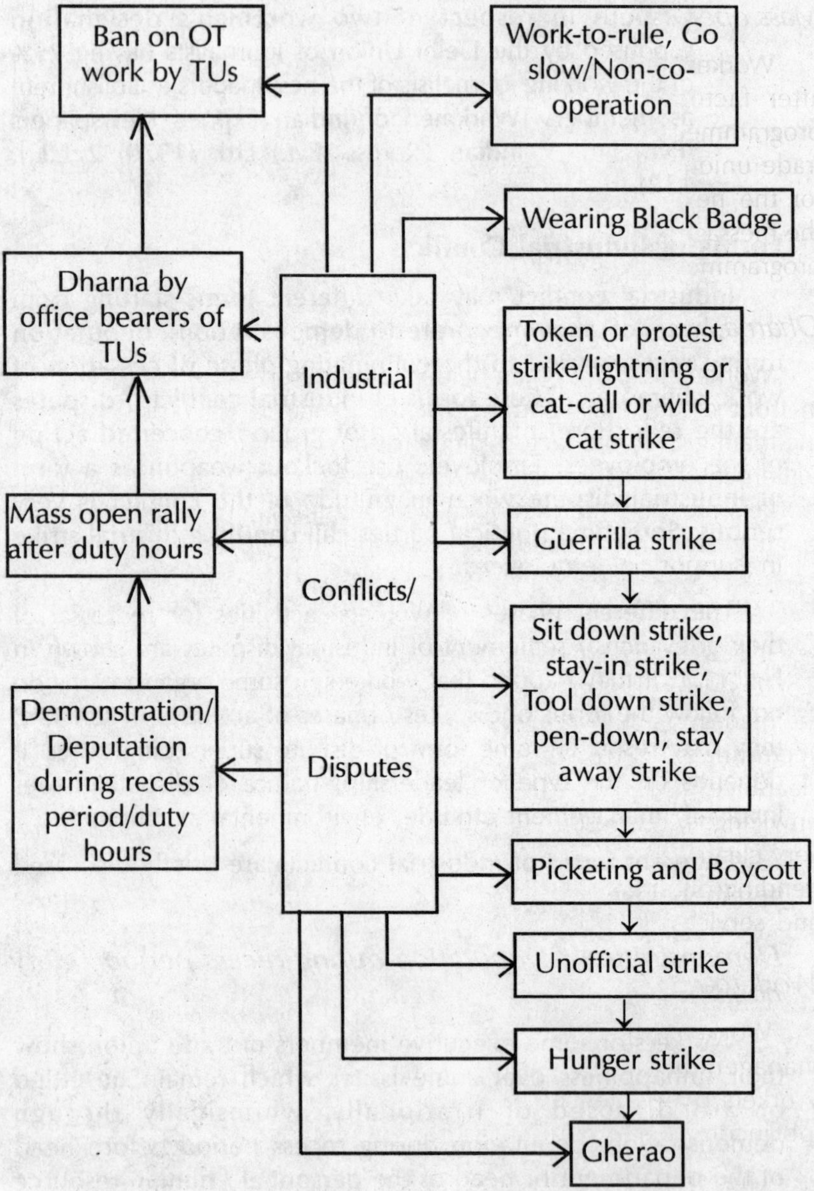

Figure 11.1 : Forms of industrial conflicts/disputes : Phases of workers' activities for redressal of grievances/disputes

Mass open rally during holiday/after office/factory hours.

Workers participate in the open rally during holiday or after factory/office hours where next course of agitational programme is decided. This rally is arranged and conducted by trade union to appraise extent of workers' support and consent for the next phase of agitational programme as also to send the message to the management about their solidarity and action programmes decided by them.

Dharna by office bearers of trade union

Workers who are office bearers of trade union stage dharna in front of the main entrance of the executive chamber or in the main gate of the factory/office to show protest for immediate settlement of their issues. In some cases, during dharna some workers manifest their emotional feeling and use abusive, filthy languages against executive/s while shouting.

Ban on OT work by trade union

It is decided by trade union to which workers belong that workers will not perform overtime work if, they are directed by the management to do so. When the workers find that excessive/accumulated work requires overtime work for immediate clearance, they resort to such action to express their reluctance/unwillingness to work beyond scheduled hours. The intention is very clear. Workers create pressure on management to clear the pending order of goods/ pending job in order to deliver goods and services to customers.

Work-to-rule, go-slow, non-cooperation

Work-to-rule is resorted to by the workers when the management does not pay heed to their problems/issues. Workers perform their work strictly as per rule. They keep the job incomplete and pile up till their demands are settled.

The intention of the workers is to exert upon the management to agree to their demands and to solve the issues. Work-to-rule is a misconduct as per Standing Orders/Bipartite Settlement of the company.

Go-slow is a device used by the workers to slow down their rate of production/service with the intention to make the management agree to solve their problems / issues. This is a concerted action of the workers to give less production / service than scheduled/usually performed. Apparently, this is not a strike, but in reality this is more than a strike as this keeps the production and all sorts of activities running for which company bears establishment and running expenses but produce much less than targeted / scheduled.

Go-slow is a misconduct under Bipartite Settlement / Standing Orders of the company and punishment is imposed on the delinquent workers.

Non-cooperation is a tool adopted by the workers to protest against management decision. They want immediate settlement/ disposal of their issues and for redressal, they start non-cooperation with the management by not agreeing to their request for doing overtime work, or other specific job beyond stipulation of their job role, by slowing down performance, by doing work strictly as per rules.

Wearing black badge

This step is taken by the workers to condemn / not to agree management decision / activities and exert upon management to settle / dispose of their issues immediately. Workers wear black badge to convey message to the management about their solidarity and unity over the issues.

Token or Protest Strike, Lightning Strike, CatCall Strike or Wild Cat Strike.

To understand token / protest strike, it is desirable to know what is strike? According to section 2(q) of the Industrial Disputes Act, 1947 strike means -

(i) a cessation of work by a body of persons

(ii) a concerted refusal of any number of persons who are or have been so employed in any industry to continue to work or to accept employment, or

(iii) a refusal under common understanding of any number of such persons to continue to work or to accept employment.

So, strike has the following characteristics

(a) It is a cessation of work by a group of persons

(b) It is a concerted refusal to continue to work or to accept employment.

(c) It is a refusal under a common understanding to continue to work or to accept employment.

Token strike is a short duration strike and has all the characteristics of strike. Through token strike workers convey the message to the management to ventilate grievances / settle issues immediately. This token strike is first stage for indefinite strike / long duration strike. It is also called protest strike.

Lightning strike is like a lightning in the sky which appears all on a sudden without giving any intimation or giving some indication to occur immediate before its occurrence and disappears quickly. This form of strike is of short duration. It contains all the characteristics of strike. This strike is also called cat-call strike or wild cat strike.

Guerrilla Strike

It is the lightning strike which comes suddenly without warning/communication. It may last for a few hours, a day, or an indefinite period. The difference between lightning strike and guerrilla strike is in the matter of communication. In case of guerrilla strike no indication / communication is given for resorting to strike but, in case of lightning strike a short notice may be given.

Sit down strike, stay-in strike, tool-down strike, stay away strike:

All these are forms of strike. In such forms of strike, all characteristics of strike under section 2(q) of the Industrial Disputes Act, 1947 are present. Sit down strike is called stay-in strike, or tool down strike. This sort of strike is called pen-down strike when employees working in the offices down their pen and refrain from doing work. Workers resorting to such form of strike do not allow other workers to enter into the premises for work. Executives also are not allowed to come inside the factory premises. Strikers remain in the factory till settlement of their issues.

Stay away strike is a form of strike when workers do not enter into premises but cease work and protest against the management through organizing / participating rally, conference.

Picketing and Boycott

Picketing is a form of strike, which is used by workers during industrial conflict situation. Some workers remain posted in front of the premises of the employer and request the others not to enter into the work place for work during strike. Some workers march and patrol the area with banners / placards mentioning their demands, reasons for their going for strike, employer's attitude and inaction etc. The main objective of picketing is to draw attention of the public about their grievances and to obtain public support / sympathy and also to urge upon the management to accede to their demands. Picketing may be peaceful or violent.

Boycott is a form of industrial conflict. Trade unions, use this weapon against the management for settlement of disputes. The process may start from non-co-operation activities but it may culminate with refusal of work.

Unofficial Strike

This is a form of strike resorted to by some workers in the organization without approval of their trade union leaders. The decision to cease work is taken by striking workers themselves. In such situation, workers have no confidence on their leaders and also on the management personnel. It occurs that workers resort to such form of strike when procedure for grievance settling is not exhausted.

Hunger Strike

This is a manifestation process for showing anger, unhappiness, displeasure by the workers on remaining on fast during duty hours/beyond stipulated hours of work in front of management chamber/premises or main entrance of the premises. Workers resort to such strike weapon in batches or sometime it happens that only trade union leaders go for hunger strike. The main objective is to put pressure on management to come to their terms by way of creating public sympathy/support. This measure is adopted by the workers in very serious situation when some workers are at peril or may be, that their genuine demands remain unsolved/unsettled for a long period.

Hunger strike is, strike within the definition of strike under section 2(q) of the Industrial Disputes Act. In Katkona Colliery Western Coal fields Ltd. V. Central Government Industrial Tribunal (CGIT) cum Labour Court, the Hon'ble High court of Madhya Pradesh held that if, hunger strike is not simply refraining from taking food but is also accompanied by cessation of work by a body of persons employed in any industry, the same word obviously come within the definition of strike.

Gherao

Workers use this technique in extreme situation when they feel to achieve their gain through keeping the management personnel in a state of physical discomfort, inconvenience and hardship for some period, may be for some hours, days. Gherao is an encirclement/confinement of management by some workers for settlement of disputes/grievances. In most cases blockade is created by 'ghearao makers', so that nobody can have an access to the place of gherao or can move from the 'gherao-place'. Gherao is illegal and is a grave/serious misconduct. The National Commission on Labour deprecated the technique of gherao instrument of coercion and expressed that if, such means are to be adopted by labour for realization of its claims, trade unions may come into disrepute. It is the duty of all trade union leaders, therefore, to condemn this form of labour protest as harmful to the interest of the working class itself.

Lockout

Lockout is one of the forms of industrial conflict. Employer uses this device when production suffers due to industrial unrest, workers' agitation, strike, go-slow, work to rule etc. Employer keeps the industrial activities suspended for some period and so closes temporarily the place of employment. Section 2(Q) of the Industrial Disputes Act. 1947 defines lockout as the 'temporary closing of a place of employment, or the suspension of work, or the refusal by an employer to continue to employ any number of persons employed by him.'

Causes of Industrial Disputes / Conflicts

Industrial dispute is dispute or difference between employer and workers. Such dispute arises when workers want to satisfy their physiological and psychological needs and management fails to satiate such needs. In other words, workers want more wages, allowances, incentive, housing accommodation, medical benefits, transport facilities, canteen facilities, good working conditions, better welfare amenities, fringe benefits, social security measures, challenging job, authority, responsibilities, promotion, status, recognition, good treatment etc. but management fails or shows unwillingness to meet up their requirements. In such situation, interactions between management and workers create difference / dispute between them which, in turn, takes the shape of industrial dispute.

Pocket Book of Labour Statistics indicates the following factors responsible for work stoppages:

(i) Wages and allowances

(ii) Indiscipline

(iii) Personnel

(iv) Charter of demands

(v) Standing Orders / Rules / Service Conditions / Safety measures

(vi) Bonus

(vii) Non-implementation of agreements

(viii) Better amenities

(ix) Leave, hours of work and shift

(x) Inter / intra union rivalry

(xi) Retrenchment and lay off

(xii) Violence

(xiii) Work load

(xiv) Suspension/change of manufacturing process

(xv) Other factors

Industrial Disputes Act 1947, prescribe the causes of industrial disputes. In terms of section 2(k) of the Act, causes of industrial disputes are:

(i) Employment causes

(ii) Non-employment causes

(iii) Terms of employment causes

(iv) Causes concerning conditions of labour of any person.

From the survey conducted by the author in the sampled collieries in West Bengal during 1970-72 it is revealed that the following factors contribute to the causes of strike as expressed/ opined by the workers, union leaders and management personnel of those sampled collieries:

(i) Economic factor

(ii) Employment conditions

(iii) Promotion

(iv) Working condition

(v) Welfare measures

(vi) Living condition

(vii) Unionism

(viii) Management / supervisor's attitude

(ix) Social Security

(x) Others viz. political causes, individual interest, instigation by management.

The survey conducted by the author indicates that the following factors contribute to the causes of lockouts in sampled collieries of West Bengal

(i) Counter measure

(ii) Union attitude

(iii) Management attitude

(iv) Contingent factor

(v) Economic factor

(vi) Others viz. conflict between partners, investment of capital from one venture to other, employers' arbitrary decision to close down mines etc.

In the present changing scenario, tough competition for survival, growth and development amongst indigenous companies and MNCs/TNCs is evident in the market. Hence, expectations, demands, needs, requirements of workers, trade unions and management change considerably. In such situation, industrial disputes/conflicts arise out of the following:

1. Wages and allowances (higher wages and allowance to meet up physiological needs.)
2. Monetary reward, incentives
3. Promoting quality of work life (QWL)
4. Designing and implementation of unambiguous career planning and development
5. Welfare benefits-both statutory and non-statutory (i.e. subsidised canteen facilities, creches, drinking water, housing accommodation, transport facilities, supply of articles through cooperative societies at a reasonable price, medical benefits, hospitalization facilities)
6. Fringe benefits-leave encashment, leave travel concession, paid holidays, scholarship to employees' children,

education allowance, canteen allowance, concessionary benefits.

7. Bonus, gratuity, retiral benefits, additional retirement benefits.
8. Lay off, retrenchment, dismissal, discharge
9. Disciplinary issues-issuance of show cause, charge sheet, suspension, orders of punishment.
10. Disposal of grievances, pending issues.
11. Implementation of agreed issues, provisions of bi-partite settlement, standing orders.
12. Implementation of the court orders, tribunal awards.
13. Employment of casuals, temporary workers, badlis
14. Management attitude, treatment, behaviour, style of functioning, approaches.
15. Trade union attitude, response to organizational requirements, demands, attitudes towards company policies, procedures, practices.
16. Introduction of new machines, computers.
17. Down sizing/right sizing of employees, voluntary retirement, sabbatical
18. Hiring of employees, promotion, transfer.
19. Diversification of business, closing of sections/ departments, acquisition, merger.
20. OD intervention, change management.
21. Financial health of the company, apprehension of violence, unusual situation, retaliation
22. Intra-union rivalry, inter union rivalry, violent attitude, physical assault.
23. Working conditions
24. Recognition of unions

25. Unfair labour practices
26. Settlement through collective bargaining process, participation in decision making.
27. Expression of sympathy towards other workers, workforce solidarity, political causes

Methods for prevention and settlement of industrial disputes/ conflicts

Industrial dispute arises from a situation of disagreement, difference between labour and management in an organization. Both employer and employees become unhappy, feel discomfortable, develop misunderstanding, mistrust. Human relation is disturbed. Industrial scenario manifests different forms of conflicts/industrial disputes like go-slow work to rule, gherao, dharna, strikes, lockouts etc. resulting in decrease in production, profit, non-supply or less supply of goods and services, loss in business, market, creation of unemployment, pathetic economic conditions of workers, lawlessness, disorderly behaviour of workers, loss in national income and the like. Such situation affects employers, employees and society. Country's development is disturbed. So, all these are manifestations of unhealthy and unsound industrial relations, that deter achievement of organizational goals. Hence, for establishing harmonious industrial relations and for the growth and development of employees vis-à-vis organization, some preventive and curative/remedial measures are required to be taken, so that industrial disputes do not crop up, and in the event of raising some disputes arrangement is made to settle those disputes immediately.

Methods for prevention of industrial disputes

Industrial disputes do not occur in an organization when both employer and employees are happy, contented and develop mutual understanding, mutual faith and confidence each other. Workers remain happy and satisfied when they get better wages, allowances, incentives, welfare benefits, fringe benefits, social security, higher quality of work life, lucrative career planning and development, status, recognition, job responsibilities, involvement, participation in decision making, good treatment from the management and the like. Management, in order to make human resources dynamic, to produce world class quality of products and also to face stiff competition needs to create a state of congenial and healthy industrial relations, through formulation and implementation of HR policies, procedures, practices and also changing philosophy, approach and style of functioning concerning employees in organization.

The following are preventive methods of industrial disputes generally adopted by the management in organization.

A. Standing Orders

It is one of the methods used by the management to develop mutual understanding, confidence, faith between them and workers through framing of clearly defined rules and regulations that govern terms and conditions of employment. Workers want just and fair conditions of employment and also their participation in the process of preparing terms and conditions of employment. The rules made in this regard are 'standing orders'. In terms of the provisions of the Industrial Employment (Standing Orders) Act, 1946 the industrial establishments employing 100 or more employees shall have standing orders which covers the matters like hours of work, holidays, pay days, wage rates, shift working, attendance, termination of employment and others as mentioned in the schedule given below.

The Schedule

Matter to be provided in the following Standing Orders

1. Classification of workmen, e.g. whether permanent, temporary, apprentices, probationers or badlis.
2. Manner of intimating to workmen periods and hours of work, holidays, pay-days and wage rates.
3. Shift-working
4. Attendance and late coming

5. Conditions of procedure in applying for, and the authority which may grant leave and holidays.
6. Requirement to enter premises by certain gates and liability to search.
7. Closing or reopening of section of industrial establishment, temporary stoppage of work and the rights and liabilities of the employer and workmen arising therefrom.
8. Termination of employment and the notice thereof to be given by employer and workmen
9. Suspension or dismissal for misconduct and acts or ommission which constitute misconduct.
10. Means of redress for workmen against unfair treatment or wrongful exaction by the employer or his agents or servants.
11. Any other matter which may be prescribed.

The certified standing orders are the terms and conditions of service between the employer and his employees. Before certification of the standing orders, the certifying officer sends a copy of the draft standing orders received from the employer, to the trade union of the workmen along with a notice for submission of objection if any, in the prescribed manner, and gives the opportunity to the trade union of being heard of objection for addition / modifications to the standing orders. After this, certifying officer certifies the draft standing orders with the modifications, if any. The standing orders act as preventive method of industrial disputes for the following:

(i) Most of the issues that generate industrial disputes relate to terms and conditions of service of employees which are incorporated in the standing orders. If, the terms and conditions of service are conducive and favourable to the employees, they heartily accept them. Employees become happy and contented with the standing orders.

(ii) Trade union is given opportunity of being heard of his suggestion / objection for modification, addition before certification is made. So, workers develop a sense of involvement, partnership feeling and participation in the process of formulating rules and regulations by the management.

(iii) Standing orders make the employees committed, loyal to the organization as this manifests employer's positive intention towards employees.

(iv) Workers' level of job satisfaction and morale are enhanced, as they feel satisfied on the matter like job, promotion, working conditions, pay etc. which are incorporated in the standing orders.

(v) Better terms and conditions of service of employees promote quality of work life (QWL), provide scope for advancement, develop systematic / rational evaluation of performance, improve core components of human resources and create changes in attitudinal dimensions of employees. All this makes a dynamic workforce to face, accept and confront challenges for betterment and development of people vis-à-vis organization.

(vi) In a situation, when workers are provided comfort, convenience, amelioration through formulation of excellent standing orders congenial and conducive state of organizational climate prevails. This brings industrial harmony and peace.

(vii) Interactions between employer and employees become positive / comfortable when employees find favourable standing orders. Both the parties come close and develop mutual understanding, faith and confidence. This makes the employer-employees relations / human relations solid and healthy.

B. Code of Discipline

It is a preventive method used to bring harmony and peace in the industry. Simply, code of discipline means a set of regulations or principles that control and promote discipline. This code of discipline is exercised to regulate and promote the conduct of both workers and management. The norms and rules are framed and followed by management and workers to restrict and improve their behaviour in order to develop mutual understanding, mutual confidence and faith between themselves. It is felt that through enactment of labour legislations, labour-management relations can not be improved. The most essential requirement is, therefore, to frame some mutually agreed norms / rules of conduct which both management and workers should follow.

The importance of mutually agreed code was discussed in the Second Five Year Plan and it suggested that voluntary code of discipline be framed and followed by the management and labour in the industry. The matter was raised in the Sixteenth Indian Labour Conference in 1957, to follow the principles by employees and employers for maintaining and improving discipline in industry and so, code of discipline was evolved. The central trade union organizations i.e. Indian National Trade Union Congress (INTUC) All India Trade Union Congress (AITUC), Hind Mazdoor Sabha (HMS), United Trade Union Congress (UTUC) on behalf of workers and the employers' association i.e. Employers' Federation of India (EFI), All India Organization of Industrial Employers (AIOIE) and All India Manufacturers' Organization (AIMO) on behalf of employers accepted the code. The code of discipline came into effect form 1st June 1958.

The code of discipline helps to prevent industrial disputes and brings harmony in industry. This is clear and justified from the following.

- Since the necessity to frame rules/norms to improve behaviour, discipline is felt spontaneously both by employers and employees and code of discipline is accepted by them, they honour the code. This prevents the industrial disputes to crop up.
- The code of discipline is based on mutuality of principles that results in development of mutual understanding,

mutual trust and mutual confidence amongst management and workers in the industry.

- Attitudinal changes amongst workers and management occur. Both the parties feel the importance of continuing uninterrupted production and services. So, industrial unrest and conflict do not crop up.
- Code of discipline facilitates creation of conducive, congenial environment in organization. This brings harmony and peace in the industry.
- A state of co-operation, 'we-feeling' 'togetherness' exists which unites the workers and management to work as members of one family / unit. This situation avoids conflict, disputes, disagreement, and differences.
- Since both the parties agree to abide by the rules, norms of discipline, they honour the code and ensure that the number of workstoppages, cases of go-slow / work to rule, lockouts and other forms of industrial disputes are reduced.
- Cases of intimidation, coercion, threat, gherao, physical assault, unfair labour practice, victimization do not occur.
- Disputes are settled at the earliest. Collective bargaining and grievance procedure mechanism are used to ventilate grievances / issues.

The code of discipline, as evolved by the Ministry of Labour and Employment, has four facets of code which the parties are required to follow in order to maintain discipline and to ensure better discipline in industry. These are given below:

1. To maintain discipline in industry (both in public and private sectors). There has to be

(i) A just recognition by employers and workers of the rights and responsibilities of either party as defined by the laws and agreements (including bi-partite and tri-partite agreement arrived at all levels from time to time) and

(ii) A proper and willing discharge by either party of its obligations consequent on such recognition.

The Central and State Governments, on their part, will arrange to examine and set right any shortcomings in the machinery they constitute for the administration of labour laws.

2. To ensure better discipline in industry Management and Union Agree

(i) that no unilateral action should be taken in connection with any industrial matter and that disputes should besettled at appropriate level.

(ii) that the existing machinery for settlement of disputes should be utilized with the utmost expedition.

(iii) that there should be no strike or lockout without notice.

(iv) that affirming their faith in democratic principles, they bind themselves to settle all future differences, disputes and grievances by mutual negotiations, conciliation and voluntary arbitration, provided that the provision regarding voluntary arbitration as aforesaid shall not apply to cases involving security consideration.

(v) that neither party will have recourse to (a) coercion (b) intimidation (c) victimization or (d) go-slow.

(vi) that they will avoid (a) litigation (b) sit-down and stay in strikes and (c) lockouts.

(vii) that they will promote constructive co-operation between their representatives at all levels.

(viii) that they will establish, upon a mutually agreed basis, a grievance procedure which will ensure a speedy and full investigation leading to settlement.

(ix) that they will abide by various stages in the grievance procedure and take up no arbitrary action which would by pass this procedure and

(x) that they will educate the management personnel and workers regarding their obligations to each other

3. Management agrees

(i) not to increase work-loads unless agreed upon or settled otherwise

(ii) not to support or encourage any unfair labour practice such as (a) interference with the right of employees to enrol or continue as union members (b) discrimination, restraint or coercion against any employee because of recognised activity of trade unons and (c) victimization of any employee and abuse of authority in any form

(iii) to take prompt action for (a) settlement of grievances, and (b) implementation of settlements, awards, decisions and orders

(iv) to display in conspicuous places in the undertaking the provision of this code in the local language,

(v) to distinguish between action justifying immediate discharge and those where discharge must be proceeded by a warning, reprimand, suspension or some other form of disciplinary action should be subject to an appeal through normal grievance procedure,

(vi) to take appropriate disciplinary action against its officers and members in cases where enquiries reveal that they were responsible to precipitate action by workers leading to indiscipline, and

(vii) to recongnise the union in accordance with the criteria evolved at the 16th session of the Indian Labour Conference held in May 1958.

4. Unions agree

(i) not to engage in any form of physical duress

(ii) not to permit demonstrations which are not peaceful and not to permit rowdism in demonstration,

(iii) that their members will not engage or cause other employees to engage in any union activity during working hours, unless as provided for by law agreement or practice,

(iv) to discourage unfair labour practices such as (a) negligence of duty (b) careless operation (c) damage to property (d) interference with or disturbance to normal work and (e) insubordination

(v) to take prompt action to implement awards, agreement, settlements and decisions,

(vi) to display in conspicuous places in the union offices, the provisions of this code in the local language and

(vii) to express disapproval and to take appropriate action against office bearers and members for indulging in action against the spirit of the code.

The code does not have any legal sanction but, the central employers' and workers' organizations take steps against their members who breach the code. Such steps include (a) asking the members to explain infringement of provisions of the code (b) giving notice to set right the infringement (c) warning or censuring the erring member, disaffiliating the member organization, wide publicity for breach of the code by any member.

The National Commission on Labour in its Report (1969) expressed displeasure about acceptance and compliance of the code by the parties. Lack of whole hearted support by the parties to comply with the provisions of the code was also noticed by the Commission. The Commission desired to give legal shape to some provisions of the code like recognition of union, unfair labour practice, grievance procedure, voluntary arbitration and other.

C. Tripartite bodies

Tripartite bodies formed with the representatives of employers' organizations, employees' organizations and Government to study the industrial relations climate of different industries and help to ensure peace and harmony in industries. Such tripartite bodies include Indian Labour Conference (ILC), Standing Labour Committee (SLC), Committee on Conventions, Industrial Committee and other tripartite committees like Steering Committee on Wages, Central Implementation and Evaluation

Machinery, Central Board of Workers' Education, National Productivity Council and others.

(i) Indian Labour Conference

This is the highest tripartite body that deliberates upon the issues relating to labour-management relations jointly and finds solution to advise the central government in the matter referred by the government. The objectives of ILC are-

- to develop mutual understanding between the members of employers' organizations and employees'organizations and to establish rapport with the government.
- to eliminate differences between parties and to work effectively as a team to suggest the government to take measures for bringing healthy industrial relations.
- to consider the issues referred to it by the government from the overall view point of country's economic development that mostly depends on uninterrupted production arising out of a situation of congenial and conducive industrial climate.
- to study the different aspects of industrial relations and to evolve measures in industry.

(ii) Standing Labour Committee

This tripartite body makes discreet study of the issues referred to it and gives suggestion to the government keeping in view the necessities of maintaining and promoting peace and harmony in industry and healthy industrial relations as well. Some of the issues for which it submitted suggestions in the recent past include bonded labour, employment, vocational training, child labour etc.

(iii) Committee on Convention

This committee helps to prevent industrial disputes through different measures like providing various benefits of international standard to the workers. Its main function is to see which ILO conventions remain unratified by the government and to submit suggestion for ratification and implementation.

(*iv*) *Industrial Committee*

This committee is constituted with the representatives of employers' organizations, employees' organizations and government. It has equal number of representatives from the employers' organization and employees' organization. Indian Labour Conference acts as coordinator between industrial committee and the government on the issues referred to this committee. The main objectives of industrial committee include

- to give suggestion on the specific issues to the ILC to make thorough discussion / deliberation and give its view on the proposals for legislation and other policy and administration issues
- to see the aspects that prevent industrial disputes on the issues referred to it and to submit suggestions

(*v*) *Other Tripartite committees*

Some of the tripartite Committees are discussed below:

1. Steering Committee on Wages

This committee is formed with the representatives of employers, workers, State Governments and an economist. Its main function is to study the price structure of different products, production aspects, wage matter etc. It acts as a research body and prepares report through survey work. Different authorities appointed for wage fixation and other bodies, institutions may take the help from the findings of the survey work carried out by this committee. This committee helps to prevent disputes arising out of wage issues by way of giving the real situation / actual information with regard to production, price of goods and the wages paid by the organization. Employers' capacity to pay and also the rationality/ justifiability of workers' demand for wages can be ascertained from the report of this committee.

2. Central Implementation and Evaluation Machinery

The necessity for setting up of Implementation and Evaluation Division in the Centre was felt at the Standing Labour Committee Session in 1958, as industrial harmony and peace was disturbed due to non-implementation of some settlements, awards by some employers in industries. In order to prevent disputes and to establish congenial industrial relations, Implementation and Evaluation Division in the centre was set up under the Ministry of Labour. So, tripartite committee was constituted with equal number of representatives (i.e., 4 representatives from each party) from the employers' organizations and workers' organizations and government.

Area of functioning

The activities of this machinery include

- to see the extent of implementation of awards, code of discipline, settlements etc and ensure implementation
- to find out cause of non-implementation of agreed issues and to take measures for implementation
- to settle the long pending issues
- to find out genesis of strikes, lockouts and other forms of industrial conflicts and to fix up the responsibilities
- to ascertain the efficacy of labour laws, policies, settlements etc. and to suggest measures to remove the weak areas
- to build up harmonious industrial relations through avoidance/prevention of disputes.

Implementation and Evaluation Division and tripartite committees are also set up in the states with the objectives of preventing disputes in state industries.

3. National Productivity Council (NPC)

This council is constituted with the members of workers' organizations, employers' organizations, some independent experts and the government.

The objectives of NPC are given below:

- to study the trend of production and productivity of workers
- to give the information as to the level of production of workers and to suggest measure to improve production
- to encourage workers to increase production and productivity
- to help strengthen collective bargaining process by supplying correct information of production to workers trade unions
- to help increase wages so as to avoid disputes arising out of wage issues.

4. Central Board of Workers' Education

This tripartite body headed by a Chairman (nominated by the government) consists of representatives form central trade unions, employers' organizations, Central Government, State Governments, University Grants Commission, Indian Adult Education Association, and one independent trade unionist nominated by the Ministry of Labour and Employment.

The main objective of the Board is to educate the workers and trade union leaders, so that they can realize their duties, rights and responsibilities and develop understanding between them and their superiors.

The Board's area of activities include

(i) to change the attitudes of worker to accept / adopt the work environment through education and training

(ii) to acquaint them with organization culture, philosophy, policies, procedures, rules, regulations, so that they can perform better

(iii) to make the workers know their job roles, leave rules, standing orders, disciplinary matter etc.

(iv) to develop 'a sense of belongingness', 'we feeling', 'togetherness' amongst the workers through counselling, participation in workshops, interactive processes.

(v) to educate the workers, so that they are not biased to union decision and can judge the real situation.

(vi) to impart training to the trade union leaders to improve their ability, skill to understand their importance as representatives of workers in organization as also as role players to develop the organisation.

(vii) to make the workers/trade unions know the basic things that they grow with the growth of the organization, and they exist if, the organization exists.

(viii) to motivate the workers so that they can feel the importance of trade union and can take part in constructive activities

The Board, thus, plays an important role to prevent industrial disputes.

D. Preventive Method through Industrial Dispute Act

Industrial disputes arise out of interaction between management and trade union / workers and such disputes can be prevented if, their interaction is positive and complementary. Industrial Disputes Act 1947 restricts the arbitrary activities of both trade unions and employers and drives them to develop better relations between them. Violation of the provisions under Industrial Disputes Act is punishable with imprisonment or with fine or with both.

E. Other Preventive Measures

(i) Trade Unions Activities

Trade Unions play the key role in shaping the pattern of industrial relations through its activities. The attitudes of trade union leaders, their belief, value structure, financial position of trade unions, leadership competences, unity and solidarity amongst members, degree and extent of unionism etc. decide the climatic conditions of work culture as also labour-management relations in the industry. Sound and solid trade union, positive mind-set of the union leaders, dynamic leadership, attitude to accept changes, constructive and 'as-the-situations demand' trade unionism help the leaders develop rapport with the management. All this facilitates to establish harmonious industrial relations and to avoid conflicts in industry.

(ii) Employers'/management Activities

Employers' attitude, philosophy, style of functioning perception, value structure, approaches to IRs etc. reflect in dealing with workers' problems, grievances. Dynamism in employers' thinking process and activities, formulating and developing positive HR/IR policies, welfare and social security measures, introduction of HRD mechanism etc. manifest conducive, comfortable climate and activities in the industrial set up.

Under the above situations, both workers and management do not resort to unfair labour practice. Further, cases of strikes, lockouts, lay offs, retrenchment, withdrawal of any concessionary benefits, changing service conditions of workers do not occur. However, workers' / trade unions' and management / employer's activities that tend to occur such above situations are regulated by the provisions of Industrial Disputes Act, 1947. This Act helps the parties to change their behavioural pattern and establish good relations between them

(iii) Works Committees

This committee is constituted in the industrial establishments where 100 or more workers are employed. This is a statutory committee setup under the Industrial Disputes Act 1947, with the equal number or workers' and employer's representatives. Though the setting up of this committee is statutory obligation, recommendations of the committee are not legally binding. The main objectives of the works committee are given below.

(i) to create a climate of mutual understanding, mutual faith and mutual confidence so as to establish harmonious industrial relations

(ii) to see that industrial disputes do not occur

(iii) to remove the differences between management and workers / trade unions in respect of issues / problems

(iv) to develop clear perceptions on the issues, so that no disputes arise out of misperception

(v) to promote better human relations between the representatives

(vi) to introduce a system of industrial democracy where both parties interact/participate

(vii) to settle dispute through joint discussion, open deliberation

This committee discusses / deals with day to day issues and other issues like bonus, welfare and social security, terms of conditions of service, employment conditions, working conditions etc. and develops congenial and conducive atmosphere of work that prevents disputes to crop up.

(iv) Joint Management Council (JMC)

It is one of the methods used to prevent disputes in industry. This is a joint consultative / deliberative body constituted with the equal representatives of workers and management with the objectives of maintaining peace and harmony in industry through disposal of grievances / issues of the workers at the earliest possible time. In this council workers' representatives are taken from recognised union.

The necessity for setting up of joint management council in industry came from the following:

a. strategic vision of the government to move towards socialistic pattern of society where workers' participation/ involvement in industrial management was needed
b. recommendation of Indian Labour Conference (ILC) for workers' participation in 1957
c. Industrial Policy Resolution statement
d. Importance of participation / association of workers given in the Second Five Year Plan
e. Report of the Study Group wherein formation of JMC was recommended
f. ILC's approval for setting up of JMCs in industries in 1957.

First JMC was set up in 1958 with the following objectives.

(i) to consult, discuss and suggest the issues which are not individual issues and also the issues not included in the agenda for collective bargaining

(ii) to help in the administration of standing orders, bi-partite settlements and to discuss in the matter of strikes, closures etc.

(iii) to assist the management for smooth running and non-interrupted production of organization

(iv) to help the management to introduce new techniques, methods, devices in organization so that it can cope with the changing situation

(v) to develop a feeling of being part of management that increases workers' morale and change in attitude

Methods for Settlement of Industrial Disputes

Industrial disputes arise out of difference between labour and management on different issues like employment, terms of conditions, discipline, management and labour attitude related issues and others. If, the issues are not settled expeditiously there will be labour unrest and workers will resort to agitational programmes in the form of strike, gherao, go-slow, dharna and the like resulting in loss of production, loss of market, reduction of profit, tarnishing goodwill, reputation of the company. So, for smooth and effective functioning of the organization and for achieving organizational goals settlement of disputes is a necessity.

For immediate and amicable settlement of disputes the following methods are used in industrial setting.

A. Grievance Procedure

It is the method for disposal of grievance of the employees of organization. It is natural that the employees want to get their grievances redressed by the management at the shortest possible time. They don't like to keep pending their day-to-day issues / grievances like employment conditions welfare, social security, fringe benefits for days together. So, they manifest their feeling of dissatisfaction / resentment in their behavioural activities which make their relations with the management unhealthy, bitter, and unpleasant. This sort of relations stands in the way of achieving individual goals, team goals and organizational goals and deters growth and development of people at work and the organization as well. So, in order to settle / dispose of the issues speedily the need for grievance procedure is felt. That means, there is a need for introduction of a system for redressal of grievances within a reasonable period of time through different authorities / hierarchies.

The necessity for introduction of grievance procedure in Indian industries can be felt from the following:

(i) The Factories Act 1948, provides for employment of welfare officer in factories where 500 or more workers are employed. The state government has framed rules in this respect requiring welfare officers to look after workers' complaints and grievances and also the implementation of different labour legislations.

(ii) Under the Industrial Employment (Standing Orders) Act 1946, every establishment employing 100 or more workers requires to frame standing orders which, inter alia, contains provisions for introduction of method/means for redressal of workers grievances against unfair treatment or wrongful exactions by the employer or his agents or servants.

(iii) The Industrial Dispute (amendment) Act, 1982, provides for setting up of grievance settlement authority for the settlement of industrial disputes connected with an individual workman employed in the establishment, where fifty or more workmen are employed.

(iv) The Code of Discipline lays down for establishment of a grievance procedure on mutually agreed basis to ensure a speedy disposal of issues / grievances to promote sound relations between labour and management.

(v) The Indian Labour Conference, 1958, suggests for a model grievance procedure for disposal of grievances in a phased tier system.

Under the model grievance procedure concerned worker requires to verbally approach the designated officer/immediate boss for disposal of his grievance. If, no solution is made within 48 hours or the concerned worker is unhappy with the decision he represents his case personally or with the help of co-worker, to the head of the department. If, the aggrieved worker does not get reply within 3 days from the date of submission/representation of his case or is dissatisfied with the decision, he or his representative submits before the grievance committee constituted with the nominees of workers and management of the organization for redressal of the grievance. If, the grievance committee fails to send its recommendation within 7 days to the manager, the reason for failure of submission of recommendation is recorded. If, the committee can not have unanimity in decision, the matter requires to be referred to the manager. The manager gives his decision within 3 days. If, the worker is not happy with the manager's decision, he may prefer appeal before the higher authority who works as appellate authority for this purpose. The aggrieved worker may take the help of his unoin representative on the day of hearing of his appeal. The disposal of appeal is expected to make within 7 days from the date of receipt of the appeal. If, the appellate authority's decision is not acceptable to the concerned worker, the management and the union may refer the matter to voluntary arbitration within 7 days from the date of receipt of the order of the appellate authority.

In case of issues relating to discharge, dismissal, the aggrieved worker may prefer appeal before the dismissing authority or any senior officer specified for the purpose, within 7 days from the date of dismissal/discharge.

However, in the organisation grievance procedure is established mutually by the union and management and successful implementation of grievance procedure as a method for settlement of industrial disputes depends mostly on the degree and extent of relationship the management and workers / u nion develop between them. Steps for settlement of grievances under Model Grievance Procedure are shown in Figure 11.2

B. Conciliation

It is one of the statutory methods for settlement of industrial disputes. Settlement of disputes is made by the third party, who is called conciliation officer appointed by the government, through persuasion and establishing mutual understanding between trade union people and management representatives attending the conciliation. Normally, conciliation process starts when either party (management or employee) refers the dispute not settled/discussed in the collective bargaining to the conciliation officer or when industrial disputes are already in existence/ apprehended. Role of conciliation officer is to act as mediator, facilitator, advisor, guide, helper, pathfinder, solution-explorer for amicable settlement of the disputes. The appointment and duties of conciliation officers are provided in the Industrial Disputes Act 1947. The objectives of conciliation include:

- bridging the gap / differences between management representative and worker / worker representative.
- establishing mutual trust, understanding between parties through creation of congenial environment for discussion/ conciliation.
- manifestation of unbiased behavioural activities of the conciliation officer in order to establish confidence amongst the parties.
- putting in efforts to avoid strikes, go-slow, lockout through amicable settlement of disputes.
- bringing harmony and peace in industry.

C. Board of Conciliation

This is a tripartite body constituted by the government for settlement of disputes. The necessity for setting up this board is felt when the disputes referred to conciliation officers are not settled by them. Hence, for disposal of such issues, Chairman is appointed by the government, to head the board consisting of equal number of nominated members of the parties to the disputes. The board endeavours to bring about a settlement of

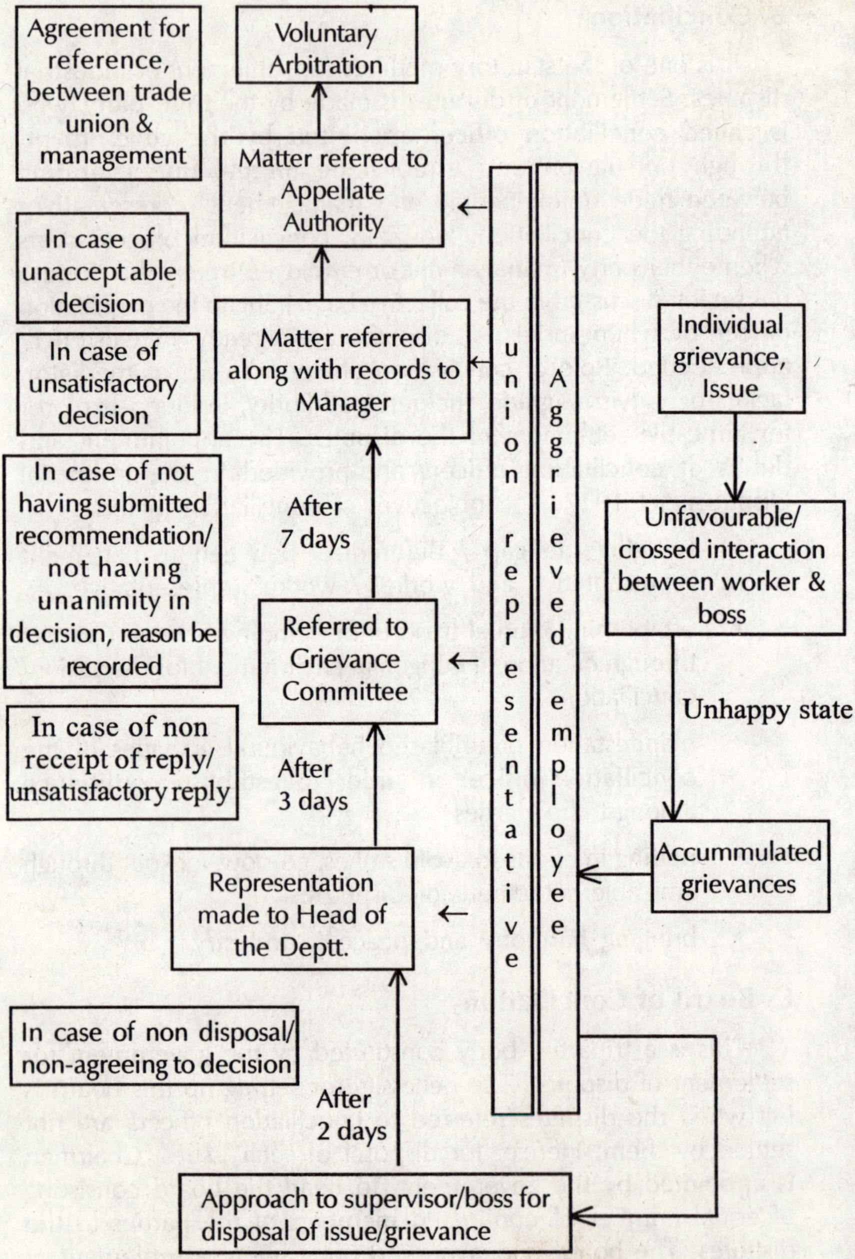

Figure-11.2 : Steps for settlement of grievances under Model Grievance Procedure

the disputes through persuasion. The board sends report to the government in respect of settlement signed by the parties to the dispute. In case of failure to reach an agreement, failure report is sent to the government together with a full statement, recommendation for determination of dispute etc.

D. Voluntary Arbitration

It is one of the methods used for settlement of industrial disputes. The salient features of voluntary arbitration are mentioned below :

(i) Arbitration award is a third party judgement/decision.

(ii) When the conciliation fails, reference to arbitration is made by the parties to the disputes under persuasion of the conciliation officer.

(iii) The arbitrator is appointed by the parties.

(iv) Cost of arbitration (arbitrator's fees) is borne by the parties.

(v) Arbitrator submits his judgement to the government who, inturn, publishes it within 30 days from the date of its submission.

The voluntary arbitration is an effective method for settlement of disputes as:

(a) arbitrator's appointment is made spontaneously by the parties. No compulsion is imposed to accept any person as arbitrator

(b) arbitration award is easily implemented by the parties

(c) it brings both the parties together, removes the area of their differences and helps develop understanding between the parties

(d) it is an acceptable mode for solution of the problems

(e) possibility of biased judgement is remote

(f) award within time frame is possible

(g) it is a process for settlement of disputes amicably through their own person.

E. Adjudication

It is one of the methods of settlement of disputes. It is done through intervention of a third party appointed by the government. This third party is Labour Court or Industrial Tribunal or National Tribunal. The adjudication process starts on reference of industrial disputes by the government in case of failure of conciliation proceeding or on reference by the government when in its opinion industrial dispute exists or is apprehended, or on reference of industrial dispute mutually by the parties.

The adjudication award is binding on all parties to the industrial disputes. The main features of adjudication are as follows:

- It is a method of settlement of dispute by third party intervention
- Parties are under compulsion to contest the case/dispute referred to the adjudication machinery and to accept the award
- It creates a climate of bitter feeling/understanding between the parties
- Settlement by third party is not accepted spontaneously by the parties and they honour the adjudication award as they can not escape.
- The issues or disputes not settled in the collective bargaining/conciliation process but decided/settled by the adjudication machinery creates a climate of win-lose situation in the organization which is not a sign of healthy industrial relations.
- The adjudication machinery under Industrial Disputes Act, 1947 consists of Labour Court, Industrial Tribunal and National Tribunal.

Labour Court

It is one tier under three-tier adjudication machinery constituted for settlement of disputes. It consists of one person appointed by the government. The concerned person is/has been a judge of a High Court or has been a District Judge/Additional District Judge for a period not less than 3 years or has held any judicial office in India for 7 years or more. The Labour Court deals with following matter for settlement of disputes:

(i) the propriety or legality of an order passed by an employer under the standing orders

(ii) the application and interpretation of standing orders

(iii) discharge or dismissal of workmen including reinstatement of, or grant of relief to, workmen wrongfully dismissed

(iv) withdrawal of any customary concession or privilege

(v) illegality or otherwise of a strike or lockout, and

(vi) all matters beyond the jurisdiction of Industrial Tribunal

Industrial Tribunal

This dispute settlement machinery is constituted with one person appointed by the government. This person who acts as presiding officer is or has been a judge of High Court or has for a period of not less than three years been a District Judge or an Additional District Judge. The Tribunal may get the advice of two assessors if, appointed by the government, in the matter of the proceeding before it.

The Industrial Tribunal may adjudicate upon the industrial disputes relating to any matter which are within the jurisdiction of Labour Court as specified in the Second Schedule under the Industrial Disputes Act, 1947 and also the industrial disputes relating to any matter specified in the Third Schedule under the Act as mentioned below:

1. Wages including the period and mode of payment,
2. Compensatory and other allowances
3. Hours of work and rest intervals
4. Leave with wages and holidays

5. Bonus, profit sharing, provident fund and gratuity,
6. Shift working otherwise than in accordance with standing orders
7. Classification by grades
8. Rules of discipline
9. Rationalization
10. Retrenchment of workmen and closure of establishment, and
11. Any matter that may be prescribed

The Tribunal adjudicates upon a dispute when the government refers the dispute by order in writing for adjudication. The government refers the dispute to adjudication under the following situations:

(i) where the parties to the dispute apply in the prescribed manner either jointly or separately for reference to the Tribunal and the government is satisfied that the persons applying represent majority of each party

(ii) where in its opinion industrial dispute exists or is apprehended

(iii) where the dispute relates to a public utility service and a notice of strike or lockout has been given under section 22 of the Industrial Disputes Act and it considers that the notice has not been given frivolously or vexatiously.

As a machinery for settlement of dispute, Industrial Tribunal is useful when trade union is weak and can not have collective bargaining power to settle problems.

National Tribunal

It is constituted to adjudicate in industrial disputes which in the opinion of the Central Government, involve questions of national importance or are of such a nature that industrial establishments situated in more than one state are likely to be interested in or affected by such dispute.

It consists of one person appointed by the Central Government and this person who is or has been a judge of High Court, works as Presiding officer of the National Tribunal. The Central Government may appoint two persons as assessors to advise the National Tribunal in the proceeding before it.

National Tribunal initiates adjudication process on obtaining reference in writing from the Central Government to adjudicate upon the disputes relating to any matter specified in the Second Schedule or Third Schedule under the Industrial Disputes Act. It holds its proceeding expeditiously and submits its award to the Central Government within the period specified in the order of reference. The maximum time limit for submission of award in case of individual dispute is three month.

Books Recommended

1. V. B. Singh : Climate for Industrial Relations : A Study of Kanpur Cotton Mills (Allied Publishers, Mumbai, 1968)
2. Pramod Verma : Management of Industrial Relations (Oxford IBH, New Delhi, 1981)
3. C. B. Mamoria, S. : Dynamics of Industrial Relations Mamoria and S. V. Gankar (Himalaya Publishing House, Mumbai, 2003)
4. E. A. Ramaswamy : Industrial Relations in India (Macmillan, New Delhi, 1981)
5. S. C. Jain : Productivity and Discipline (Allied Publishers, New Delhi, 1988)
6. H. John Bernardin and Joyce E. A. Russel : Human Resource Management (McGraw-Hill, New York, 1993)
7. A. M. Sarma : Industrial Relations – Conceptual and Legal Framework (Himalaya Publishing House, Mumbai, 1989)
8. John B. Miner and Mary Green Miner : Personnel and Industrial Relations (Macmillan, New York, 1985)

9. Dale S. Beach : Personnel – The Management of People at Work (Macmillan, New York, 1980)

10. S. L. Agarwal : Labour Relations Law in India (Macmillan, New Delhi, 1980)

11. C. S. Srivastava : Industrial Relations Machinery (Deep and Deep, New Delhi, 1983)

Question

1. What is industrial dispute? Discuss different forms of industrial disputes.
2. What is industrial dispute as per Industrial Disputes Act, 1947? Are industrial disputes and industrial conflicts the same? Discuss any two forms of industrial conflict.
3. What is strike? Explain different forms of strike.
4. Is there any difference between 'go-slow' and 'work-to-rule'? Can management take any disciplinary action against an employee if, he resorts to go-slow activities?
5. State the differences between 'strike' and 'lock-out'
6. What is 'guerrilla strike'? Do you find any difference between 'guerrilla strike' and 'lightning strike'?
7. Is there any difference between 'unofficial strike' and 'hunger strike'?
8. Do you think 'economic cause' is the only cause of strike? State the causes of strike in Indian industries.
9. What is Code of Discipline? Is there any necessity of Code of Discipline in industry?
10. Discuss three important tripartite bodies that contribute to promote peace and harmony in Indian Industries.
11. Explain the machinery that facilitate prevention and settlement of industrial disputes in India.
12. What is grievance procedure? Discuss the different steps for settlement of grievances under Model Grievance Procedure.

Case Study

Mr. P. K. R. Sundaram is the Chief Manager (HRM) of the Eastern Region of Universal Bank Limited. The Eastern Regional office of the bank is in Kolkata. Mr D. R. Putnis Dy General Manager is the Regional Head of the bank. The Administrative set-up of the Eastern Region is like this:

1. The bank has 70 branches (30 metropolitan, 25 Urban and 15 semi urban branches), 1350 employees (including officers, clerical staff and subordinate staff of all 70 branches and regional office) under Eastern Region
2. The bank has started operations in Eastern Region from 1975. However other regional offices, viz. Northern Regional office in New Delhi, Southern Regional office in Chennai and Mumbai Regional office have started functioning from 1965, 1970 and 1974 respectively. The bank's Head office is situated in New Delhi.
3. The union composition looks like this:
   - Three Unions namely Universal Bank Workers' Union , Universal Bank Employees' Union and Universal Bank Workers' Solidarity Union are having members in branches and regional office in Kolkata.
   - The Universal Bank Workers' Solidarity Union is majority union of Universal Bank Limited. The corporate management has recognised this union as a sole collective bargaining party, but this union is minority union in Eastern Region from the membership point of view.
   - The Universal Bank Employees' Union ranks third from the view point of union membership in the Universal Bank Ltd. as a whole, but in Eastern Region it has about 55% membership
   - The Universal Bank Workers' Union has 35% membership in the Eastern Region. The membership strength of this union (taking into account of membership strength of all regions and head office

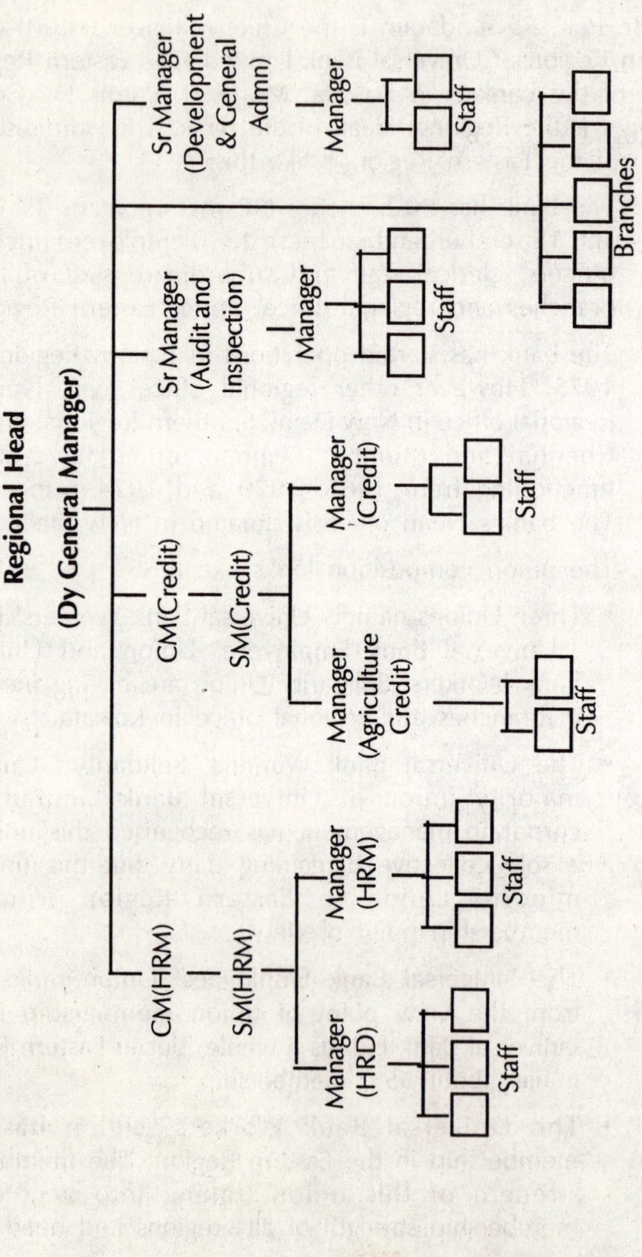
Regional Head
(Dy General Manager)
CM(HRM)
SM(HRM)
Manager (HRD)
Staff
Manager (HRM)
Staff
CM(Credit)
SM(Credit)
Manager (Agriculture Credit)
Staff
Manager (Credit)
Staff
Sr Manager (Audit and Inspection)
Manager
Staff
Sr Manager (Development & General Admn)
Manager
Staff
Branches

together) is next to the strength of Universal Bank Workers' Solidarity Union.

4. Some of the bank's salient activities overwhich union leaders launched agitational programmes against management are undermentioned.

   a. The bank's eastern regional authority in consultation with Head office made an agreement with Universal Bank Employees' Union (minority union in terms of all India union membership strength) in 1985 to provide canteen facilities to the employees at branches and administrative offices. Under this agreement the bank authority requires to appoint canteen boys (on permanent employee roll), provide utensils, furniture, room space, fuel at free of cost and arrange to serve the employees food, tea, snacks at subsidised rate (on 'no profit, no loss' basis). Mentionably, only the bank employees of eastern region are enjoying such benefits. The other unions started agitation to extend such benefit to all the bank employees in other regions. Looking into different perspectives top management in the corporate level agreed to provide a canteen allowance for all employees of the bank at different rates (Rs. 15 per day per officer, Rs. 10 per day per clerk and Rs. 5 per day per subordinate staff) linked to month's attendance of employees. The payment of such allowance came into effect from April, 1991. The Universal Bank Employees' Union was called by the management of eastern region in May 1992 for discussion on the 'canteen boy' issue in the context of introducing a similar benefit scheme for the employees of the bank. The management informed them about justification for discontinuance of 'canteen-boy engagement' system and told them that existing canteen-boys would be converted into peons. The management expressed their views that this practice of engaging/recruiting canteen boys would be stopped forthwith. The union leaders vehemently protested over the management's desire/intention to discontinue the system of appointing canteen boys in bank. They infromed management that if, such practice is discontinued they would cease work for indefinite period.

The practice of engaging canteen boy's in bank's branches/offices under Eastern Region continues and the employees are getting subsidised 'canteen facilities' and also canteen allowance.

b. In Universal Bank Ltd. non-officers (clerks and subordinate staff) were continuing with the same branch / office till their retirement, promotion or exit from the bank. No job rotation from one branch / office to other branch/office was in practice. In August 1986, the bank issued a circular in respect of job rotation scheme for clerks and substaff (i.e. for award staff members)of the bank for implementationfrom 1st September 1986. The scheme provided that in the first phase the staff members (including substaff) who had been working for 10 years and above would fall under job rotation and in the 2nd phase those staff members who had been working for 5 years and above in the same branch/office would be transferred under job rotation w.e.f 2nd February 1987. In normal situations union leaders of different unions did not have good understanding, relations amongst themselves. Inter union rivalry was a common cause to disturb industrial peace. After the issuance of management circular with regard to job rotation of staff, all the three unions joined together to launch agitational programme. They threatened management that they would face dire consequences if, job rotation scheme was implemented. The local management, in terms of circular, prepared a list of employees falling under job rotation scheme and gave one copy of the same to each union seven days before the date of effect, for information.

The unions gave deputation, demonstration, wore black badges, staged dharna in front of the chamber of Dy. General Manager and resorted to different forms of industrial disputes except strike. All these the unions did in the month of August 1986 when they came to know the management decision through circular.

On 31st August 1986, branch managers were advised to transfer the concerned staff members at the respective branches and confirm action of having complied with to HRM Department of eastern regional office. The concerned award staff members were issued transfer orders with the instructions to report to branches on 01.09.1986 as mentioned in the orders.

On 1st September, 1986, the staff members in eastern region, belonging to respective unions ceased work and declared for an indefinite period of strike if, transfer orders were not withdrawn by the management. The strike continued for some days and with the intervention of the State Government and the efforts put in by the top management the employees withdrew strike.

Additional information

(*i*) The Universal Bank Ltd. has introduced a system of holding discussion / negotiation on the issues raised by three unions separately in structured meetings twice a year in Regional Office and once a year in the Head Office.

(*ii*) The branches developed a practice to hold staff meeting on the personnel as well as non-personnel issues of the branches where free and open discussions are held to sort out differences / problems and promote understanding, faith amongst them.

(*iii*) For cleaning, sweeping the branch / office premises the bank has permanent sweepers at a different time rate (viz. 1/3 , ½, ¾, full rate of scale) depending, upon the floor space of the premises. The bank engages casual sweepers (from the enlisted panel of casuals) on a temporary basis when permanent incumbents go on leave.

You are required to form some groups with 5 to 6 members in each group, select group leader, discuss among the members the following issues / points, prepare group views to present before all the members by the leaders one by one. The rest members (other than leaders) also are required to present their views.

Q.1 (a) Do you think the agreement extending the canteen benefit to the employees of eastern region is a right step to promote industrial relations?

(b) What would happen if management would not have agreed to reach such an agreement meant for a section of employees of the bank?

(c) Is it violating norms of natural justice that deprives a majority of employees from getting canteen facilities simply because they are working in other parts of the country?

(d) What do you think could be specificity of such agreement?

Q.2 (a) What could be the reasons for expression of such attitudes of the union on the issue of discontinuance of appointment system of canteen boys?

(b) As IR Specialist of the bank how would you tackle this issue concerning appointment of canteen boys?

(c) Do you think management's proposal to stop engaging canteen boys is justified and proper particularly in the light of the agreement that still exists?

Q.3. (a) Do you think job rotation has any effect on improving quality of services of employees who are transferred under this scheme?

(b) How could you justify management action to implement job rotation scheme?

(c) Do you feel it is desirable to discuss with the unions on the matter of job rotation before such scheme is framed and implemented by the management?

(d) Can unions go for strike on such issue? What are the legal implications?

Q.4. (a) What do you think could be the roles of Regional HRM professionals before strike?

(b) Looking to the administrative set up of the eastern regional office, as CM (HRM) point out your plan of action during strike.

(i) to effectively utilize the services of officers of the regional office

(ii) to make a link with branch heads

(iii) to give the officers' community moral support

(iv) to render customers service

(v) to maintain industrial peace and harmony

(c) What should be your role as CM (HRM) immediate after strike is withdrawn'

Q.5. (a) Do you think structured meetings at regional and corporate level facilitate healthy industrial relations? Do you feel the necessity of such meeting?

(b) Do you think appointment of sweeper on permanentbasis at different time scales is justified in the context of obtaining competitive advantages as also social concept? What are other alternatives to appointment of permanent part time sweepers?

Q.6. As CM (HRM) of the bank what would be your suggestions to promote industrial relations in the Eastern Region?

Index